A Sound Word Almanac

A Sound Word Almanac

Edited by
Bernd Herzogenrath

BLOOMSBURY ACADEMIC
NEW YORK • LONDON • OXFORD • NEW DELHI • SYDNEY

BLOOMSBURY ACADEMIC
Bloomsbury Publishing Inc, 1385 Broadway, New York, NY 10018, USA
Bloomsbury Publishing Plc, 50 Bedford Square, London, WC1B 3DP, UK
Bloomsbury Publishing Ireland, 29 Earlsfort Terrace, Dublin 2, D02 AY28, Ireland

BLOOMSBURY, BLOOMSBURY ACADEMIC and the Diana logo
are trademarks of Bloomsbury Publishing Plc

First published in the United States of America 2024
This paperback edition published 2025

Copyright © Bernd Herzogenrath, 2024
Each entry copyright © by the contributor, 2024

Cover design by Louise Dugdale

All rights reserved. No part of this publication may be: i) reproduced or transmitted in any form, electronic or mechanical, including photocopying, recording or by means of any information storage or retrieval system without prior permission in writing from the publishers; or ii) used or reproduced in any way for the training, development or operation of artificial intelligence (AI) technologies, including generative AI technologies. The rights holders expressly reserve this publication from the text and data mining exception as per Article 4(3) of the Digital Single Market Directive (EU) 2019/790.

Bloomsbury Publishing Inc does not have any control over, or responsibility for, any third-party websites referred to or in this book. All internet addresses given in this book were correct at the time of going to press. The author and publisher regret any inconvenience caused if addresses have changed or sites have ceased to exist, but can accept no responsibility for any such changes.

Whilst every effort has been made to locate copyright holders the publishers would be grateful to hear from any person(s) not here acknowledged.

A catalog record for this book is available from the Library of Congress.

ISBN: HB: 979-8-7651-0905-2
PB: 979-8-7651-0909-0
ePDF: 979-8-7651-0907-6
eBook: 979-8-7651-0906-9

Typeset by Deanta Global Publishing Services, Chennai, India

For product safety related questions contact productsafety@bloomsbury.com.

To find out more about our authors and books visit www.bloomsbury.com and sign up for our newsletters.

Contributors

Selwa Abd is a multidisciplinary artist, musician and designer living in NYC (originally from Morocco). Under the guise of Bergsonist, she uses a variety of media to investigate social resonance through divergent conceptual aesthetics (minimalism and musique concrete to name a few). Selwa's extended creative practice uses intuition and fragment-based systems as legitimate and only modus operandi. Through her work, she explores notions of identity, memory, and social politics.

Mitchell Akiyama is a Toronto-based scholar, composer, and artist. His eclectic body of work includes writings about sound, metaphors, animals and media technologies; scores for film and dance; and objects and installations that trouble received ideas about history, perception and sensory experience. He holds a PhD in communications from McGill University (Montréal, Canada) and an MFA from Concordia University (Montréal, Canada) and is Assistant Professor of Visual Studies in the Daniels Faculty of Architecture, Landscape, and Design at the University of Toronto.

Ilgın Deniz Akseloğlu explores the plasticity of language both as constraint and auxiliary, with the aim of decoding the cultural to arrive at the natural. Since 2013, she has worked as a curator, writer, image editor, art book publisher and art-space director. Today, the concrete results of her collaborations vary from the design of a curriculum for a college art education program, to the exploration of sound as space through poetry and voice. Akseloğlu holds an MA in Art Praxis and Critical Theory in Dutch Art Institute (NL), and a BA in Philosophy in Galatasaray (TR) and Sorbonne (FR) universities.

Inês R. Amado was born in Leiria, Portugal. Her work spans several media: video, site-specific installation, sound and performance with a particular interest in interdisciplinary, collaboration and participatory projects through a process of dialogue, interaction and exchange. Her work is informed and immersed in Deep Listening® and she is an affiliate of D.L.® in the UK.

Her practice as an artist also involves curating and organizing. In 2014 she co-organized, co-curated and participated in **Bread**Matters IV ARtos Cultural Foundation, Nicosia, Cyprus.

BreadMatters is a research programme composed of exhibition and debate that questions and focuses on sociocultural, sustainable, ecological, political, historical and geographical issues around bread and the importance of bread in the history of humankind and which brings together artists, historians, writers, musicians, philosophers and the public in a programme of exhibition, collaboration/participation, debate and workshops.

In March 2020 coinciding with the pandemic, Inês started an online course Creative Attentive involving students, ex-students and others in a process of immersive creativity. This has now expanded into CREiA: Creative Attentive – an inclusive course based on Deep Listening and the 'Book/Home/Container', delivered in collaboration with a colleague.

Paul H. Amble is a Norwegian communications adviser, mainly interested in improving places. His latest commission of size was to lead the resurrection of the Natural Sciences exhibition at the University Museum in Bergen, in the oldest museum building in Norway. It has been voted Museum of the Year 2021.

Herbert Baioco is a multimedia artist who develops research related to the reconstitution of wiretaps, spaces and memory based on the creation of listening devices. This activity finds form in installations, kinetic sculptures, performances and collaborations with other artists. He is a master in the line of Studies of Artistic Processes by Universidade Federal Fluminense.

Johannes Binotto is a researcher in media studies and video essayist and teaches at the Lucerne School of Art and Design. In his video experiments he puts a particular focus on sound experiments and acoustical visualization. His experimental films 'Touching Sound' or 'Reproduction Interdite' have been shown at film festivals like the Videoex Zurich, the International Film Festival Rotterdam or Besides the Screen, Vitória.

Iva Bittová has for many years worked in a range of musical styles, including jazz, rock, folk, classical and opera. What truly inspires her is total silence and an absolutely positive atmosphere. Far from settled, everyday life, nature and silence are the most important conditions and surroundings in which her ideas spring to life, having a significant impact on her music. Being a part of musical culture, not only as a musician but also as a listener, nourishes her sense of being in tune with the Earth. Every moment is a new vibration, a new resonation, channelling new ideas and new messages from the universe

Despite all her educational experiences, it is the live, human-to-human, creative musical process that brings power to the planet. It is extremely important for new voices to emerge and resonate; nature is such a big source of inspiration for all of us.

Her performance of solo violin and voice is mostly improvisation; it is the liberated vibration of her present being.

Her approach to music is based on contact with nature. To access a natural, present musical moment within the group, I encourage students to centre themselves away from the noise and distraction of technology and stressful day-to-day activities. Her goal is to foster inspiration for everyone, and to this end, she will give as much energy as possible! Music makes us very happy! This is what we need!

Ingebjørg Loe Bjørnstad was born in 1978 and grew up in Surnadal in Norway. She has a Master's degree in improvised music from The Norwegian Academy of Music in Oslo. Her main instrument is vocals. She performs, composes, writes lyrics and works together with other artists such as musicians, composers, dancers and visual artists.

Dimitrios Bormpoudakis is a post-doctoral research associate at the School of Anthropology and Conservation, University of Kent. He likes to pursue various avenues of research, some of them fruitful, but most not. Research-wise, he has been combining various types of quantitative modelling with explorations of infrastructural futures, forays in anthropology, attempts at sound art, historical excavations of the Greek Civil War and planning with algorithms. Dimitrios has always been interested in sounds and drones, and the publication he is most proud of is an audio CD of frog recordings from Lake Kerkini in Greece called *Frogs of Lake Kerkini*. He has also recorded frogs in St Helena (the South Atlantic island). He lives between Canterbury, Southeast England, and Enschede, East Netherlands, and has two children.

Budhaditya Chattopadhyay is a media artist, researcher, curator, and writer; he holds a PhD in sound studies and artistic research from the Academy of Creative and Performing Arts, Leiden University. Chattopadhyay currently works as a visiting professor at the Critical Media Lab, IXDM, Basel. More information can be found on his website: https://budhaditya.org

Lucia D'Errico is an artist-researcher in the field of music with a specific focus on performance, experimental practices and transdisciplinarity. Her research interests include contemporary philosophy, psychoanalytic theory, semiotics and epistemology. She is a postdoc fellow at the Orpheus Institute (Ghent, Belgium), the co-editor of the recently launched book series *Artistic Research* at Rowman & Littlefield Int. and the coordinator of the doctoral program docARTES. Her publications include the monograph *Powers of Divergence. An Experimental Approach to Music Performance* (2018, Leuven University Press) and the co-edited volume *Artistic Research: Charting a Field in Expansion* (2019, London: Rowman & Littlefield Int.). She is active as a composer, sound artist, guitarist, video performer and graphic designer.

Friedemann Dupelius is a musician, journalist and sonic author. The interplay of sound and language is crucial to his thinking and practice. He writes radio features for *WDR3 Studio Elektronische Musik* and reports on electronic and experimental music for several magazines. The outcome of his artistic pseudonyms *Friday Dunard* and *Wednesday Dupont* ranges from club music to sonic research, from radio plays to poetry, and comes to form in live sets, records and airplays. He's co-running the music label *SPA* and co-curating Cologne's sound art festival *Brückenmusik*. He studied sound studies, musicology, media studies, media art and music informatics in Karlsruhe, Düsseldorf and Cologne.

Jimmy Eadie is Assistant Professor within the School of Engineering, Trinity College Dublin. He is Audio Engineer, Producer and Artist and his work covers recording, sound design and installation. His work uses a variety of sculptural and time-based media which are often presented through hybrid forms of installation and performance. His sound installation work has been exhibited in many Irish and international galleries and venues (National Concert Hall Dublin, Cork Opera House, Irish Museum of Modern Art, Edinburgh International Festival, Brooklyn Academy of Music, Lincoln Centre for Performing Arts, Barbican, London). He is a founding member of the Crash Ensemble (IRE).

Lawrence English is a composer, artist and curator based in Australia. Working across an eclectic array of aesthetic investigations, English's work prompts questions of field, perception and memory. He investigates the politics of perception, through live performance and installation, to create works that ponder subtle transformations of space and ask audiences to become aware of that which exists at the edge of perception.

Ingeborg Entrop is an artist-researcher based in the Netherlands. She holds a PhD in physics and a master's degree in fine arts and is fascinated by the mimetic quality of the narratives that are invented to grasp the world. Her interest lies in the nature of place and time and she predominantly uses her ears and sound-related tools for her explorations. Her work developed from onomatopoeic paintings to artistic scores, field recording compositions and (musical) performances. Currently, she focuses on sub-surface sounds, especially in 'liminal' grounds between land and water, such as wetlands, bogs and tidal mudflats.

Korhan Erel is a computer musician, improviser and sound designer based in Berlin. They treat the computer and electronics as instruments that can co-exist along with conventional instruments in free improvisation and other musical genres. Their music covers free improvisation, conceptual sound performances and structured pieces, the latter mainly performed at art spaces. They play solo, duo and group performances with other musicians and dancers. Korhan also does sound installations, sound design and music for theatre, video and dance. They have played in festivals, venues, museums and art spaces across Europe, Middle East, Southeast Asia and North America.

Jacob Eriksen is a researcher, lecturer and artist based in Berlin. With a background in sound studies, musicology and philosophy, he is currently undertaking his doctoral candidature in sound studies and sonic arts at Berlin University of the Arts focusing on posthuman theory within sonic arts practice. As a lecturer he has taught courses in musicology, cultural studies, sound studies, art theory and practice at Humboldt University of Berlin, University of Copenhagen, Rhythmic Music Conservatory, Copenhagen and at Berlin University of the Arts. As an artist he is working aesthetically and conceptually with sound in the form of performances and installations and has performed and exhibited internationally: transmediale (DE), Harmos Plural (PT), MIASTO:Wro (PL), SMK Thy (DK), STRØM (DK), Spektrum (DE), Petersburg Art Space (DE), Castrum Peregrini (NL), iMAL (BE), MMIFF (PT), Veilinggebouw De Zwaan (NL), Eavesdrop Festival (DE) and Akademie der Künste (DE).

Mark Fell is a multidisciplinary artist based in Rotherham (UK). His practice draws upon electronic music subcultures, experimental film, contemporary philosophy and radical politics. Over the past thirty years, Fell's output has grown into a significant body of work: from early electronic sound works and recorded pieces, to installation, critical texts, curatorial projects, educational systems and choreographic performances.

Alec Finlay (Scotland, 1966) is an internationally recognized artist and poet whose work crosses over a range of media and forms. Much of Finlay's work considers how we as a culture, or cultures, relate to landscape and ecology. Through permanent and temporary interventions, integrative web-based projects and publications, Finlay weaves together generous experiential works, often collaborative, sometimes mapped directly onto the landscape, embedded socially or accessed online. Recently Finlay's work has focused on place awareness and ecopoetics.

Reinhold Friedl is one of the most distinguished and radical musicians of his generation, more than hundred releases, numerous commissions as composers from international festivals. Friedl is also the director and founder of *zeitkratzer* and tours worldwide. Friedl holds a PhD from Goldsmiths University.

Maho Fujimoto is Assistant Curator of Fukuoka Prefectural Museum of Art. She curated exhibitions concerning Contemporary Art in Fukuoka.

Tania Giannouli is a pianist, composer, improviser and band leader from Athens, Greece. She is considered to be one of the most important new 'voices' of today's European music scene. Her albums, *Forest Stories, Transcendence, Rewa, In Fading Light, Solo* – all released by New Zealand's art-music label, Rattle – have received wide international acclaim. She has performed in the most prestigious venues and festivals in Europe. Her music for film and video has travelled at festivals, galleries, Biennales and museums throughout the world. Her music has global appeal. Variously described as complex, lyrical, intoxicating and highly original, she is inspired by many different traditions and influences, resulting in compositions and interdisciplinary projects that span an impressive range of styles.

As stated in the Korean magazine *Jazzspace*, 'This music invites the listener to dream of eternity'.

Jelena Glazova is an artist and poet from Riga, Latvia, working in experimental electronic music – creating ambient soundscapes, usually constructed from processed vocals. She performed at experimental music and sound art festivals Sound around Kaliningrad (Kaliningrad, Russia), Noise and Fury (Moscow, Russia), Poetronica (Moscow, Russia) and Vilnius Noise Week (Vilnius, Lithuania); music festival Skaņu Mežs (Riga, Latvia); electronic music festival Art's Birthday (Stockholm, Sweden); and so on. She was a guest composer at EMS Stockholm, WORM Rotterdam and so on.

Jelena is the author of four books of poetry. The first book *Transfers* (2013, in Russian and Latvian) was nominated for Latvian Annual Literary Award (LALIGABA), the second book *Plasma* (2014) was published in Estonia and in English, and the third book *Greed* was published in 2019 and was nominated for Latvian Poetry Days Award. Fourth book 'Naivete' was published in 2022. Jelena's poetry is translated into Latvian, English, Finnish, Polish, Estonian, Lithuanian Hungarian and Swedish languages.

As an artist and poet, she has participated in art projects and performed in Latvia, Estonia, Lithuania, Finland, Russia, Austria, Sweden, Netherlands, Germany, Turkey, Poland, Italy, Spain, the United States and other countries. More information at: www.jelena-glazova.com

Eyal Hareuveni is a researcher in the Israeli human rights NGO B'Tselem, freelance journalist and reviewer of free, improvised music for the Free Jazz Blog, the Scandinavian website Salt Peanuts and the Norwegian magazine *Jazznytt*.

Bernd Herzogenrath is trying to be a sound thinker. Apart from being a dabbler into field recording, he is a professor of American literature and culture at Goethe University of Frankfurt am Main, Germany. He is the author of *An Art of Desire: Reading Paul Auster; An American Body-Politic: A Deleuzian Approach* and editor of a.o. *The Farthest Place: The Music of John Luther Adams, Deleuze/Guattari & Ecology*, and *Media Matter: The Materiality of Media, Matter as Medium*. His latest publications include the collections *The Films of Bill Morrison. Aesthetics of the Archive* (2017), *Film as Philosophy* (2017), *sonic thinking* (2017), and *Practical Aesthetics* (2020). An art-projected he conceptualized and curated together with Lasse-Marc Riek during the COVID lockdowns, called *©ovid's metamorphoses*, will be released with the label Meakusma later this year (check their website)! It contains work by Lee 'scratch' Perry, Richard Reed Parry, Scanner, Lucrecia Dalt etc.

Ulf A. S. Holbrook works with sound in a variety of media, including composition, improvisation, electronics, sculpture, installation, text and research. His primary interest is in the representation of space and place through sound, using spatial audio, acoustics, sonification, field recording and custom software. He holds a PhD in music technology from the University of Oslo, which examines on the relationships between sound objects and spatial audio.

Kazuhiro Jo is a practitioner with a background in acoustics and interaction design. He has been presenting his practices at museums and festivals, as well as papers with his projects such as 'The SINE WAVE ORCHESTRA', 'phono/graph' and 'life in the groove'. Currently, he works as an associate professor in the Department of Acoustic Design at Kyushu University, Fukuoka, Japan, as well as an adviser (part time) at Yamaguchi Center for Arts and Media (YCAM).

Robert Jürjendal is an Estonian guitarist and composer who studied classical guitar and composition (Prof. Anti Marguste) at Tallinn Georg Ots Music School. In 1992-1997 he participated in Robert Fripp *Guitar Craft Courses*. He has written music for classical and contemporary guitar, harpsichord, mixed ensembles and choirs; documentaries, art exhibitions and theater.

He has recorded more than sixty albums and worked together with several artists: Weekend Guitar Trio, Fragile, UMA, David Rothenberg, Markus Reuter, Tim Bowness, Jan Bang, Colin Edwin, Miguel Noya, Paul Godwin, Sandor Szabo, Balazs Major, Jon Durant, Arve Henriksen, Five Seasons, Estonian Philharmonic Choir, Ellerhein Girls Choir and so on.

Jürjendal has released five solo albums: *Source Of Joy* (2013) *Balm Of Light* (2014) *Simple Past* (2016), *Water Finds A Way* (2021) and *Music For Long Nights* (2023).

Currently he works as a freelancer composer / artist / lecturer. He is a curator of the music program SOOLO at Tallinn Art Hall.
http://robertjyrjendal.com/
https://www.emic.ee/robert-jurjendal
http://www.newdogrecords.com/artists

Tomotaro Kaneko is an associate professor at Aichi University of the Arts. His field is aesthetics and aural culture. He has organized Japanese Art Sound Archive (https://japaneseartsoundarchive.com/en/) since 2017. His recent publications include 'Sounds in 1970s Japanese art' (in *Aida*, 2022), and 'Arrangements of sounds from daily life: Amateur sound-recording contests and audio culture in Japan in the 1960s and 1970s' (in *Asian Sound Cultures: Voice, Noice, Sound, Technology*, 2022).

Siegfried Kärcher is Artist Extraordinaire and known for his creative approaches to art and music. After passing the Test for the Highly Gifted, he studied free arts. He is an early member of the Computer Scene since Commodore Homecomputers appeared and infected with the Electronic Music Virus since his first dancing steps at Technoclub Dorian Gray Frankfurt Fame. Nowadays he hosts several underground events like Glitch it! Festival at Institute of New Media Frankfurt or the annual SK Art Days at a post-war Radardome in Hesse.

Peter Kiefer is a German composer and sound artist. He teaches as a professor at the Hochschule für Musik at the Johannes Gutenberg University, Mainz, Germany, as head of the Master's programme in Sound Art Composition. From 2001-2004 he was professor and head of the 'MusicDept'; at the Academy of Media Arts Cologne. As a sound artist he has exhibited at festivals in Germany and internationally. In 2004 he was artistic director of the festival 'Klangraum-Raumklang 2004', Cologne, and artistic director of GUSAC Gutenberg Sound Art Academy, Mainz, 2019. Since 2018, he is head of research project ARS art_research_sound. Editor: 'Klangräume der Kunst', 2010 Kehrer-Verlag and 'Exhibiting Sound Art' (with M. Zwenzner), 2022, Wolke Verlag. Kiefer works as a curator and adviser to museums throughout Europe. Member of the Academy of Sciences and Literature

Mainz and the German Artists' Association. ars.uni-mainz.de, www.peter-kiefer.de

Suk-Jun Kim is a Professor of Electroacoustic Music and Sound Art at the University of Aberdeen, UK. A composer and sound artist, Kim has received first prizes at Bourges Electroacoustic Music Competition, Metamorphoses in Belgium and CIMESP. He was a resident composer at the DAAD Artists-in-Berlin Programme in 2009. He is the author of *Humming (A Study of Sound)* and *Hasla* and published his solo CD *Humming* by Vox Regis.

Jan Kleefstra is a poet and has until now published nine collections of poems both in Dutch and in Frisian. His work has been published in numerous national and international magazines and websites. He also works together with painters and released recently a book with paintings and text around the loss of biodiversity. He and his brother Romke have performed for several years on Dutch poetry and music stages. In different collaborations they search constantly for the combination of poetry, music and sometimes video. With their way of performing and reciting, they create an atmosphere that compares to the space of the land and water in which human beings are only the disturbers. This has led, until now, in more than twenty-five music and film releases. For more see http://romkekleefstra.blogspot.nl/ or find me on LinkedIn under the name Jan Kleefstra, poet on music.

Malte Kobel has recently received a PhD in musicology from Kingston University, London, with the dissertation 'The Musicking Voice: Performance, Affect and Listening'. Prior to Kingston, Malte studied at the University of Vienna, Humboldt University of Berlin and Cardiff University. His work has been published in the *Journal for Cultural Research and Sound Studies*. Apart from academic work, he co-runs the record label Hyperdelia, curates radio programmes and is the initiator of the collective BLATT 3000.

Dalibor Kocián (Stroon) made his first mark in 2010 with his debut Ruine Noire. Since then he's been annually releasing EPs and LPs of different musical experiments. His latest piece is Meditations on Dichotomy, written for ensemble, electronica and soprano. In his music, he strives to achieve a fusion of experimentation, the emotional depth of film and stage music, the dynamic energy of club sounds and influence of classical music.

He often cooperates with artists across all media and apart from his solo production and performances, a large portion of his works consists of music for theatre, films, silent films, series, site-specific performances, events and even commercials. More information at www.stroon.bandcamp.com, **or social sites.**

Petri Kuljuntausta works as a freelance composer and sound artist. He is Adjunct Professor (Docent) of Sound Art and Electronic Music at Turku University, Finland. Kuljuntausta has performed music for an underwater audience, improvised with birds and made music from whale calls and the sounds of the northern lights. As an artist he works with environmental sounds and live electronics and creates sound installations for galleries/museums. Kuljuntausta has published three books on electronic music and sound art. He is a visiting lecturer at the University of the Arts Helsinki and Aalto University Espoo. Over 100 electroacoustic compositions and sound works by Kuljuntausta have been published by various record labels in Europe, Australia, India and the United States.

David Livingstone is an American citizen living and working in the Czech Republic for the past thirty years. He teaches English literature,

Czech culture and American folk music at Palacký University in the city of Olomouc. He has given papers and presentations connected with folk music in a number of places around the world. He also enjoys singing and playing on the banjo not only in class (currently via zoom) but also in the pub (currently only in the mind).

Andrey Logutov is Walter Benjamin Fellow at Goethe University in Frankfurt. Born in Moscow in 1980, he graduated in physics (1998) and literature (2005). His PhD on Emily Dickinson came in 2008 after he spent a year at SUNY (Buffalo) as a Fulbright researcher. Since 2009 he has taught courses in media studies, communication theory, song lyrics analysis and a graduate-level course in sound studies at Moscow State. His works include original research, reviews and translations on a variety of subjects including aurality in literature, sociology of music and media history. He has also taken part in multiple musical/sonic projects as a lyricist, sound engineer, organizer or just a random presence with no particular purpose.

Machinefabriek is the musical nom de plume of musician/sound artist and graphic designer **Rutger Zuydervelt** from the Netherlands. Machinefabriek's music combines elements of ambient, modern classical music, minimalism, drone, field recordings and lowercase. His pieces unfold as 'films without image', with a sharp ear for detail. After releasing a series of self-released CD-Rs, the official debut, 'Marijn', was issued by Lampse in 2006. Since then a solid stream of singles and albums was released on labels like Type, Home Normal, 12K, Spekk, Dekorder, Digitalis, Experimedia and Staalplaat.

Performing live has been an important expression for Machinefabriek. He took his gear to Russia, Israel, Japan, Canada, Switzerland, Spain, Czech Republic, Germany, Turkey and England. Rutger collaborated with many artists, including Ralph Steinbrüchel, Aaron Martin, Peter Broderick, Frans de Waard, Wouter van Veldhoven, Simon Nabatov, Xela, Simon Scott, Steve Roden, Gareth Davis and Tim Catlin. Rutger also works with visual artists. He scored music for dance pieces, films, video installations and sculptures. Zuydervelt resides in Rotterdam.

Tina Mariane Krogh Madsen is an artist and researcher who works in the intersection between performance art, sound, open technology and matter. Madsen is currently a doctoral candidate at Aalto University School of Arts, Design and Architecture (FI), researching in environmental, ethico-aesthetic performance art and affective relations in the context of climate change. Madsen has performed internationally in many formats and contexts and is the founder, organizer and curator of performance protocols, a nomadic platform for instruction-based art and collaborative processes. Madsen is further a certified facilitator of Deep Listening workshops from the Center for Deep Listening, Rensselaer Polytech Institute (US). More information at: http://tmkm.dk/

Soaham Mandal is pursuing his PhD at the Centre for English Studies, Jawaharlal Nehru University, New Delhi, working on the trajectory of rock 'n' roll music in India. He has been awarded MPhil from Jawaharlal Nehru University, New Delhi, for his dissertation titled, *The Pictures on the Walls: Understanding and Defining Street Art Narratives of Delhi*, 2015. He completed his Masters in English from the University of Hyderabad, 2013. He had been invited as a participant and contributor for the Summer Institute Cologne, [SIC!] 2017, for the Sound Studies programme. Additionally, an autodidact, he plays and performs on drums and percussion, since

2005. Though formally untrained, his major areas of interests include sound studies. He had been invited as a participant and contributor for the Winter School, Mapping the Aesthetics of Urban Life in Asia: A Dialogue with the Arts, which took place in Kyoto, 2016, jointly organized by The International Institute for Asian Studies (IIAS), Leiden, the Netherlands, and the Center for Southeast Asian Studies (CSEAS), Kyoto University, sponsored by the Japan Foundation. He is currently Assistant Professor of English (Substantive) at Dum Dum Motijheel College, Kolkata, under West Bengal State University, India.

Mpho Molikeng is a Lesotho-born multi-facet artist. He is a curator, actor, musician, poet, painter, storyteller and cultural activist. Molikeng plays a number of African instruments such as lesiba, mamokhorong, setolo-tolo, mbira and djembe. In 1995, he studied fine arts at Bloemfontein College. He also studied drama at Soyikwa Institute of African Theater in 1998. In 2016, Molikeng was the co-facilitator at the Music in Africa Instrument Building and Repair Workshop. As of 2017, he was a visiting lecturer at Wits University in Johannesburg, South Africa.

David Nadeau is an art historian, writer and musician and has lived in Québec City since 2007. He is particularly interested in the relationships between esotericism and artistic creation, from an anarchist perspective. He has published in *Ritual, Secrecy and Civil Society*. Since 2015, he has participated in more than 100 compilations, including the fourth edition of *60 Seconds Radio*, a project whose call for works has been launched on 13 February 2018, on UNESCO's World Radio Day. On 3 May 2018, his sound art piece 'Haunted Alphabet Toy' has been broadcast and discussed at the Composer/Computer Distance Conference (Sheffield, UK).

Mikel R. Nieto studied art in San Sebastián, Madrid and Barcelona. He is part of the sound map of the Basque Country and Mediateletipos platform. He coordinated The Listening Observatory in collaboration with José Luis Espejo and Xabier Erkizia during 2016. He has been working in collaboration with dancers and choreographers like Jone San Martin and Pascal Merighi in many contemporary dance projects, creating sound designs for dance pieces.

His first book, black on black, called *Dark Sound* was published, and it was described as the dark book of the soundscape. His second book in collaboration with Tim Ingold and Carmen Pardo, called *A Soft Hiss of This World*, was printed white on white and is focused on the loss of snow in the landscape because of the Antrophocene and how it affects to language and to the soundscape through the sound of snowflakes.

Lane Shi Otayonii is a Chinese-born interactive multimedia performer and sound artist residing in Brooklyn, New York. After graduating from Berklee College of Music in 2016 receiving Laurie Anderson Women in Technology Award and Best Vocalist Bronze Prize from Global Music Award, she had been on eight US tours with the experimental band Elizabeth Colour Wheel. Her self-directed music video Shaoxing Nomad was selected in numerous film festivals such as Rome Prisma Film Awards, Istanbul International Experimental Film Festivals, Independent Talent International Film Festivals and more. It is her calling to solve a puzzle with another puzzle that can't be seen, be touched, but to feel.

Torbjörn Ömalm is a guitarist, composer and minority language activist from Gällivare, Sweden. He is also currently a PhD student in artistic research (Musikalisk gestaltning) at Luleå University of Technology. In his thesis work, he explores how minority languages in Malmfälten (Northern Lapland), regional folklore and acoustic affordances of the cultural environment affect and shape a situated music practice, highlighting the transformations between thematic material – listening – creating. Ömalm has since the year 2010 released six music albums under his own name.

Pia Palme is a composer and artistic researcher from Vienna, Austria. Her works extend into interdisciplinary and spatial formats; she is also known as a performer with bass recorders. From 2019-2022 she headed the important research project 'On the Fragility of Sounds' at the University of Music and Performing Arts Graz, exploring terrains of music theatre and composition. Palme studied music, mathematics and geometry, and in 2017 finished her doctorate in composition at the University of Huddersfield, UK. Her awards include the George-Butterworth Prize (UK), Outstanding Artist Award of the Republic of Austria and scholarships from the City of Vienna, Siemens Foundation and The Banff Centre of the Arts.

Anat Pick is a creator in the field of sound poetry and sound installation. Since her European debut at The Vienna Festival 1997, she has performed in art, poetry and experimental music events around Israel, Europe and the US. Pick has recorded innovative renditions of *avant garde poetry featuring Dada, Futurist & concrete poetry* alongside her own compositions which are based on free play with fragments from eastern & western languages. Listen: http://www.ubu.com/sound/pick.html or visit Catalogue De La Bibliothèque Kandinsky, Center Pompidou.

Maja S. K. Ratkje is a composer and performer from Trondheim, Norway. Her music is performed worldwide by performers such as Ensemble Intercontemporain, Klangforum Wien, Oslo Sinfonietta, The Norwegian Radio Orchestra, Red Note Ensemble, Marianne Beate Kielland, POING and many more. Portrait concerts with her music have been heard in Toronto and Vienna; she has been a composer in residence at festivals like Other Minds in San Francisco, Trondheim Chamber Music Festival, Nordland Music Festival in Bodø, Avanti! Summer Festival in Finland, Båstad Chamber Music Festival and Huddersfield Contemporary Music Festival.

Ratkje has received awards such as the International Rostrum of Composers in Paris for composers below thirty years of age, the Norwegian Edvard Prize (work of the year) twice, Scottish Award for New Music for *Aeolian*, second prize at the Russolo Foundation and in 2001 she was the first composer ever to receive the Norwegian Arne Nordheim Prize. Her solo album *Voice* got a Distinction Award at Prix Ars Electronica in 2003. In 2013 she was nominated for the Nordic Council Music Prize for her vocal work. She was in 2017 accepted as a member of Akademie der Künste, Berlin. In 2020 she got the Liv Ullmann Prize in Norway.

Ratkje is active as a singer/voice user and electronics performer and engineer, as a soloist or in groups. Collaborations include SPUNK, Jaap Blonk, Joëlle Léandre, Ikue Mori, Zeena Parkins, Stephen O'Malley, Lasse Marhaug, Hilde Holsen, Stian Westerhus and many more. Ratkje has performed her own music for films, dance and theatre, installations and numerous other projects. Visual art or text material is often a part of her own work, in installations or staged works.

Her scores are found at Edition Wilhelm Hansen/Wise Music Classical and the National Library of Norway's publishing service, NB noter, and her records are released on Tzadik, Rune Grammofon, 2L, ECM, Important

Records and many other labels. Her homepage may be visited at www.ratkje.com.

Lasse-Marc Riek uses field recording as a means to capture and explore acoustic ecology, bioacoustics and soundscapes. Since 1997, he has operated internationally, staging exhibitions and concerts, releasing recordings and delivering lectures and workshops. Diverse venues have hosted his performances: galleries, art museums, churches and universities. His work has featured on public media, including public radio channels. He has received scholarships and participated in artist-in-residence programmes in Europe, the Middle East and Africa. He is the co-founder of the label Gruenrekorder, which, since 2001, has concentrated on soundscapes, field recordings and electroacoustic compositions and works in these contexts with artists and scientists on an international level. More information at: www.lasse-marc-riek.de

David Rothenberg has written and performed on the relationship between humanity and nature for many years. He is the author of *Why Birds Sing*, on making music with birds, also published in England, Italy, Spain, Taiwan, China, Korea and Germany. It was turned into a feature-length BBC TV documentary. His following book, *Thousand Mile Song*, is on making music with whales. It was turned into a film for French television.

As a composer and jazz clarinetist, Rothenberg has sixteen CDs out under his own name, including *On the Cliffs of the Heart*, named one of the top ten CDs by Jazziz Magazine in 1995 and a record on ECM with Marilyn Crispell, *One Dark Night I Left My Silent House*. Other releases include *Why Birds Sing* and *Whale Music*. He invited many musical colleagues to join him on Whale Music Remixed, with contributions from noted electronic artists such as Scanner, DJ Spooky, Lukas Ligeti, Mira Calix, Ben Neill and Robert Rich.

His book, recording and film *Nightingales in Berlin* was published in April 2019. In 2020 Rothenberg released a book he has been working on for more than two decades, *The Possibility of Reddish Green*.

His 2020 releases include *In the Wake of Memories*, with Wassim Mukdad and Volker Lankow, and *They Say Humans Exist*, with Jacob Young and Sidiki Camara, named the best jazz album of the year by Stereo+ Magazine in Norway.

Daniel Salontay is a founding member of the Slovak band Longital. Dano and Shina formed the band in 2001. Before that Salontay, with a degree in mathematics, was also an active musician with a background in jazz and blues, won an award of Slovak Jazz Society and, in 1997, also the Jazz studies scholarship at Tri-C College in Cleveland. After his return to Slovakia he continued with his previous jazz&blues collaborations and also co-founded the famous Slovak alternative band Neuropa.

The band's name Longital is an old name of the hill above the Danube River in Bratislava, Slovakia (currently known as Dlhé Diely), where the founding members Shina and Daniel reside and from where they have travelled all over the world. Since 2001 (for the first five years also under the name Dlhé Diely), Longital have been crossing borders both territorially and musically. Longital's path on the international scene is quite unique and relates to the creative process itself. The band achieves eclectic sound by strictly avoiding narrowly defined genres but still echoing them in band's own creative way. Aligned with the background of the band members, their inspiration ranges from classical, through jazz and experimental music to songwriting and poetry. All of this is tastefully mixed to serve the main goal: building and delivering the

songs and their message to listener's soul and body. The lyrics of love, freedom and nature are a piece of poetry written and sung exclusively in the Slovak language. This distinction has strongly influenced the rhythm and melody of Longital's music and paved the band's way to a number of international stages and festivals.
http://www.longital.com/en
https://www.slnkorecords.sk/en/daniel-salontay-dlhe-diely

Holger Schulze is full professor in musicology at the University of Copenhagen and principal investigator at the Sound Studies Lab. His research focus is the cultural history of the senses, sound in popular culture and the anthropology of media. Recent book publications include *Sonic Fiction* (2020), *The Bloomsbury Handbook of Sound Art* (2020, co-ed.), *The Sonic Persona* (2018) and *Sound as Popular Culture* (2016, co-ed.).

Halla Steinunn Stefánsdóttir is a violinist, composer, curator and artist-researcher. Born in Iceland she is currently based in Malmö, Sweden. She has been the artistic director of Nordic Affect since its inception in 2005 and made numerous appearances with the ensemble at festivals and concert venues in Europe and USA. Her compositional output and commissions have spanned everything from electroacoustic compositions to sound and media installations. Stefánsdóttir's playing and compositions are featured on albums by the Carrier Records, Brilliant Classics, Musmap, Bad Taste Records, Tally, and Sono Luminus labels. In 2023 she published her doctoral thesis from Lund University titled *HÉR! An Exploration of Artistic Agency*. More information: www.hallasteinunn.com

Daiva Steponavičienė is the founding member of the Lithuanian Folk Project Rugiaveidė. She is a folk singer, member of the creative-folk ensembles 'Sedula' and 'Dainaviai' and a reconstructor of archaeological costumes.

Nguyễn Thanh Thủy is a leading đàn tranh player/improviser in both traditional and experimental music. She was born into a theatre family and was raised with traditional Vietnamese music from an early age in Hà Nội. She has received many distinctions, including the First Prize and the Outstanding Traditional Music Performer Prize in the National Competition of Zither Talents in 1998. Nguyễn Thanh Thủy has recorded several CDs as soloist with orchestra and solo CDs, which were released by Phương Nam Film Vietnam; by dB Productions Sweden; by Setola di Maiale Italia and by Neuma Records & Publications, United States. She is currently engaged in Musical Transformations, a senior research project looking at musical change, in transcultural and intercultural settings.

Mark van Tongeren is a Dutch sound explorer and ethnomusicologist with an interest in the synergy of the arts, sciences and contemplative traditions. He has over twenty-five years of experience in theatre-, music- and dance productions and holds a PhD in artistic research from Leiden University's Academy of Creative and Performing Arts. His music studies encompass work in Siberia, Taiwan, Tibetan diaspora and Corsica/Sardinia with a special focus on timbre. His artistic output is a cross-over of experimental and traditional vocal techniques and performing arts. He is best known for his work in the field of overtone singing/throat singing. More information: www.fusica.nl.

Barbora Ungerová was born on 3 May 1981 in Liberec and since her childhood has been actively involved in music, dance, theatre and visual arts. Since 2012 she has been working as a self-employed artist.

Her theatre experience began in 2000 when she became one of the founding members of the DNO Theater, an independent theatre group founded by students and young artists in Hradec Králové.

Within the DNO theatre there were also music bands of which she was a member. In 2006 Jan Kratochvíl and she founded the musical duo *Dva*, which they have been doing since 2012 professionally. In the band Bara sings and plays the saxophone and the clarinet. The lyrics are written and performed in the fictional language Dva. The duo has performed regularly throughout Europe, touring the United States three times, and both Australia and New Zealand once. They have released three studio albums and have created many soundtracks for theatre performances, computer games (Amanita Design), movies, jingles and animations.

Bara also continuously works in the arts. In 2008 she founded her own brand Mœtïvï, in which she devotes herself to author-design articles of daily use (design of fabrics, articles of paper and porcelain). Under the nickname Janines Jansen, she has exhibited drawings of smaller formats and photographs of her land art realizations in nature. In their band *Dva* she creates the whole graphic identity (posters, album covers and merchandise).

Yashar Valakjie is a contemporary sound artist, cultural operator and independent researcher born in Tehran and based in France. In his works, he is interested in creating new modes for comprehending complex mechanisms through which the environment and time impact our perception of the world and our sense of identity.

His works consist mainly of the sonification of environmental data, field recordings and river listening. They are attempts to extend our sensory capabilities beyond the natural limits of auditory and tactile senses while examining time in ways we can't normally perceive. This is based on the idea that, through sonification and alternative modes of hearing, we could become aware of our impact on the planet over a larger timescale; and in ways that could not be possible otherwise. His recent artworks and research topics are on the effects of human and non-human cohabitation through biophony.

Esther Venrooij is Professor of Mixed Media, Performance and Sound Art. She considers her dual roles as artist and composer as occupying two different sensorial planes. She creates work in a variety of media, such as composed music, improvised combinations of electronica, video and site-specific installations. With a sharp focus, both in her studies and creative impulses on audio topography, Venrooij explores the way sound and movements inhabit space. Having collaborated live and in the studio with a variety of visual, sound and dance artists, Venrooij's biography reads like a mixed-media map of projects. She has performed and presented her works extensively for audiences in Europe, Asia and the United States. Most of the sound works are available on the British label Entr'acte.

J-T Vesikkala Wittmacher (Finnish: Juhani Vesikkala, *1990 Helsinki) is a doctoral student at HAMU, Prague, since 2018. Noisy acoustic sounds and their compositional functions are the subject of Vesikkala's upcoming dissertation. Vesikkala studied composition at the Sibelius Academy (Finland), Kunstuniversität Graz and the IEM Institute (Austria), among others. Vesikkala's earlier research has covered flageolets on the piano. Compositions by Vesikkala, spanning the acoustic, electronic and staged music genres and instrumentations from the orchestra to partly improvised works, have toured five continents. Some have been broadcast and a work for the ensemble was released as a studio recording in 2021. Recent victories include the 2019 DYCE competition. Vesikkala also works as a bass-baritone for the Helsinki Chamber Choir and as a freelancer, as a teacher and lecturer, curator of microtonal concerts and festivals, and an improviser. Vesikkala's creative flow has drawn influences from queer feminism and various spiritual-philosophical practices.

Stephen Vitiello is an electronic musician and media artist. CD releases have been published by New Albion, Sub Rosa, 12k, Room 40 and Farpoint Recordings. His sound installations and videos are in permanent collections including the Museum of Modern Art, the Whitney Museum and the Museum of Contemporary Art, Lyon. Originally from New York, Vitiello is now based in Richmond, Virginia, where he is a professor at Virginia Commonwealth University.

Salomé Voegelin is an artist, writer and researcher engaged in listening as a sociopolitical practice and as a methodology for a hybrid knowledge base. Her work and writing deal with sound, the world sound makes: its aesthetic, social and political realities that are hidden by the persuasiveness of a visual point of view. She writes essays and text-scores for performance and publication. Her latest book, *Uncurating Sound: Knowledge with Voice and Hands*, Bloomsbury (2023), moves curation through the double negative of not not to 'uncuration': untethering knowledge from the expectations of reference and a canonical frame, and reconsidering art as political not in its message or aim, but by the way it confronts the institution. Voegelin is Professor of Sound at the London College of Communication, University of the Arts London. More information: www.salomevoegelin.net.

Daniel R. Wilson is a writer, researcher, sound artist, composer and instrument-builder. He performs in the electroacoustic music quartet Oscillatorial Binnage and records solo as Meadow House and Radionics Radio. Oscillatorial Binnage's CD+monograph *Agitations: Post-Electronic Sounds* was released on Sub Rosa in 2020. Wilson is the author of *Dropping Out* (2006) and *The Magnetic Music of the Spiritual World: Electricity and Sound on the Victorian Stage* (2015), and art director for William English's *Perfect Binding* (2019). Wilson heads workshops and gives practitioner lectures at universities and writes variously for magazines and academic journals, including *Leonardo Music Journal*, *Organised Sound*, *Fortean Times*, *ArtReview*, *The Wire*, *The Brooklyn Rail*, *Nude Magazine* and so on. See www.miraculousagitations.com

Jana Winderen is an artist educated in fine art at Goldsmiths, University of London, with a background in mathematics, chemistry and fish ecology from the University of Oslo. Jana focuses her work around audio environments and ecosystems which are hard for humans to access, both physically and aurally. Among her activities are immersive multichannel sound installations and concerts, which have been performed internationally in major institutions and public spaces in America, Europe and Asia. Winderen lives and works in Oslo.

In 2011 she won the Golden Nica, Ars Electronica, for Digital Musics & Sound Art.

'Listening with Carp' (2019) was part of the exhibition 'Now Is the Time', Wuzhen International Art Exhibition, China. Recent works include 'Through the Bones' for the Thailand International Art Biennale in Krabi (2018–19) and the multichannel audio installation 'bára', a commission by TBA21 Academy, shown at the exhibition OCEANS. Imagining a Tidalectic Worldview, Dubrovnik Museum of Modern Art (2018), at Le Fresnoy, France (2018), and in Tidalectics at Augarten in Vienna (2017). Other recent works include 'Raft of Ice', a permanent temperature interactive sound installation for the United Sates Embassy in Oslo (2018), 'Spring Bloom in the Marginal Ice Zone: From the Barents Sea to Lake Ontario', The work of WIND AIR LAND SEA in Toronto (2018), 'Rats – secret soundscapes of the city', commissioned by the Munch Museum on the move/NyMusikk in Oslo (2017), 'Transmission' commissioned by the V-A-C foundation for Geometry of Now, Moscow (2017), 'Spring Bloom in the Marginal Ice Zone' for the Sonic Acts festival, Amsterdam (2017). Earlier works include the large multichannel installation 'DIVE' in Park Avenue Tunnel, for New York Department of Transportation, 'Ultrafield' for MoMA in New York and 'Watersignal' for Guggenheim Museum/Unsound festival.

Her upcoming exhibitions include 'Rising Tide' solo show at Kunstnernes Hus in Oslo, 'I Hear Your Dream' at OCAT, Shanghai, 'Greenlight District', Grenland Kunsthall, Porsgrunn. Jana releases her audio-visual works on Touch. Her latest release includes 'Spring Bloom in the Marginal Ice Zone' on Touch in November 2018.

A short note on the way...

As Roland Barthes once said – 'nothing is more reassuring than a dictionary' (*Eiffel Tower*, 116).

This little book is not a 'dictionary' in the accepted sense of the word – although it is nonetheless reassuring, mind you!

It is an almanac. An almanac (from the Arabic المنحة *al-minḥa* oder المنح *al manḥ*, meaning 'gift' or 'present') was some kind of early calendar, a collection of texts and hints at the positions of planets, sunrise and sundown, and so on.

Our almanac is such a gift, and it's also 'astronomical' in such a way, that it presents a very personal and playful astronomy. It gives a collection of 'sound words' that have figured as the individual guiding stars for the participating sound artists and scholars, guiding stars perceived from various positions and locations on this planet.

John Cage's wish for mankind was 'Happy New Ears'. Maybe this almanac can inspire us to listen differently.

A playlist with examples for most of the sound words can be found here:
https://www.youtube.com/playlist?list=PL7WIBueKmjKhMD-_N9znKzwqhvHnLqlL5

Works cited

Roland Barthes. 'Literature according to Minou Drouet', *Eiffel Tower and Other Mythologies*, trans. Richard Howard, Berkeley: University of California Press, 1997, 111–18.

Mission Statement

Alec Finlay

Homage to Velimir Khlebnikov

```
        S   S
    P   O   E   M
        U   N
        N   S
        D   E
```

Ääni (Finnish)

Petri Kuljuntausta

The writing introduces three Finnish words, ääni, äänittää and äännännän, all related to sound and the same root word 'ääni'. I wanted to stay on the same root word as then the reader can realize how Finnish language work. Instead of prepositions and articles, we modify the end of the root word, and the end of the word is changed differently in different situations. For this reason, the Finnish language can be difficult for some. After the word comes the phonetic version of the word, according to the International Phonetic Alphabet (IPA) standard.

1. 'Ääni'

IPA: ['æːni]
Noun

'Ääni' means sound, voice, note, tone, audio, noise and vote. 'Ääni' in these example sentences: Do you hear that sound? There is a strange sound in the machine. This is my (speech) voice. You have a beautiful singing voice. In the election, I will vote for the candidate.

'Ääni' is a very common Finnish word. I use the word almost daily as 'ääni' is a central concept in my work as a sound artist, composer and researcher. The word is soft and poetic, and easy to pronounce. The word forms in the muscles of the mouth with very little energy and glides airily out of the body. Sound Art in Finnish is Äänitaide.

In Finnish language, the 'ääni' is ambiguous. It is all that can be sensed by hearing. In colloquial language, the use of the 'ääni' is flexible. It can be said simply: you have a beautiful 'ääni' (Engl. voice), when referring to a singing voice. But one might say as well: you have a beautiful 'lauluääni' (singing voice), which refers directly to voice.

But when, for example, a singer or a vocal soloist is mentioned on a record cover, it is not written that her/his instrument is ääni (sound). Instead, it is expressed: 'laulu' (Engl. sing or singing) or 'laulaja' (singer or vocals) derived from the word 'laulaa' (to sing or singing). Of course, one can play with the concepts and write/say the singer makes noise or sound; this is more common in underground and avant-garde circles.

If 'ääni' is mentioned as the musician's instrument, it usually means that the musician produces noises and/or other non-conventional musical sounds. In the case of mouth-produced voices and speech (e.g. text-sound pieces), 'ääni' or 'teksti-ääni' can also be said ('teksti-ääni' is a straight translation of text-sound).

In an election, people give a vote ('ääni') to a candidate. They don't say it out loud but write on paper or press a button on a voting machine. Historically, it's about giving your own voice for something you want to support.

For a very long time, I have thought that Finnish is a consonant-winning language, but it is only in recent years that I have begun to understand that there are also many beautiful and soft vocal words in the language. For a recent book project about recording history, I listened hundreds and hundreds of old shellac recordings (78 rpm) and noticed that traditional Finnish tango music is actually a very unique phenomenon, as the words end by vowels, and this is a very special character in that kind of lyrical expression and allows a singer to make very effective endings in their vocal phrases.

2. 'Äänittää'

IPA: ['æːnitːæː]
Verb

'Äänittää' means to record sounds. When someone captures sounds on a recording machine, this work or procedure is 'äänittää' in Finnish. As in this example sentence: Today I am going to record a bird song on my portable sound recorder. Although the root form of the word is 'ääni' (sound), the verb 'äänittää' is also used for the operation when recording video, which is illogical but in common use. The word 'äänittää' has been understood in this sense, as making a recording, for decades. But historically, until the 1920s, it had a different meaning.

A very specific and not very common knowledge is the meaning of the term 'äänittää' in the building of a church organ. 'Äänittää' in this context of church organ building means fine-tuning the organ pipes to produce the desired sound. In fact, it means giving sound to the instrument. In this special fine-tuning ('äänitys') technique, the core plate of the flue pipes, the core and lips, is bent to obtain the desired attack and sound colour. The sound of the organ is handcrafted during the construction phase to suit the space in which the instrument is installed. The professional who fine-tunes ('äänittää') the sounds of the organ gives the organ its soul. From lifeless organ pipes, the organ builder creates a personal instrument with a characteristic sound and volume adapted to the surrounding space. In addition to this, the organ is a whole and when sounds are played at the same time, their sound colour must also fit well with each other. At the same time, the pitch of each pipe is checked when the organ is constructed and the organ is tuned, but tuning the instrument is actually separated from the fine-tuning process, which is called 'äänitys'.

The 'äänittää' appeared in the current sense on the pages of newspapers with the invention of sound film at the turn of the 1930s. The word referred to the recording of sound on film. From now on, 'äänittää' meant recording sounds on a disc or reel tape or other media.

3. 'Äännännän'
IPA: [ˈæːnːænːæn]
Noun
'Äännännän' means pronunciation, enunciation, articulate and sound. A very rare version of 'ääntää' (Engl. 'pronounce'), the noun is derived from the word 'ääni' (sound). The word is a specialty and strange. It may not have been an orthodox form of the word at the time, but it can be well understood. I was particularly interested in the word because there are nine letters in the word but only two different ones, 'ä' and 'n'. Probably another word of this length, with only two different letters, does not exist in Finnish.

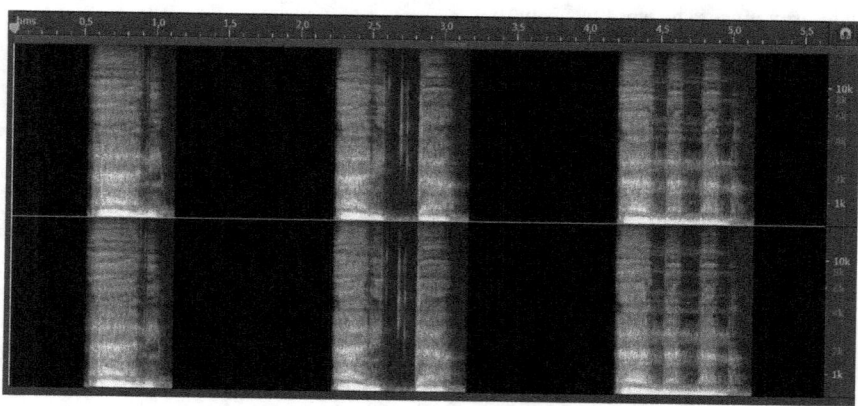

Figure 0 Ääni, Äänittää, Äännännän © Petri Kuljuntausta.

아득한 [adeukan] *(Korean), adjective*

I found this word by chance a few years ago in an old newspaper article about the new recordable phonograph technology and its advantages. In 1937, the Arma sound studio opened its doors in Helsinki and anyone could go to the studio to make a direct-to-disc recording on lacquer or lathe disc. One magazine wrote about the studio and in this text I saw the word 'äännännän' for the first time. The writing informs: 'It depends on the playback device (gramophone), what the human voice sounds like when played again. Hearing your own voice from a disc is not only a whimsical thing for the experimenter, it is also very useful for proper pronunciation.' The end of the sentence, after comma, in the original text is: '. . . se on myöskin oikean äännännän kannalta erittäin hyödyllinen'.

From the database of the Finnish National Library I found only five cases when this noun has been used in the history of digitized Finnish newspapers, three from 1937, one from 1945 and one from 1968. 'Äännännän' is a very odd version of 'ääntää'; it is something that no one used later in the twentieth century. I am sure most of the Finns will understand what it means, but it is a word no one uses today. A word that is extinct.

아득한 *[adeukan]* **(Korean), adjective**
Suk-Jun Kim

Of the distance
An *adeukan* sound, that which is distant, far away, farther than I can project, farther than my dreams and their echoes, at a distance that is beyond my reach, not necessarily because of the space that separates me from it but because its being distant is of a time, not of a space – an *adeukan* sound shares no space with me; an *adeukan* sound, that which continues to fade away from me, and as it does, it fades away even from itself, that is to say, even from the point of its origin, birthplace, the point where it may have emerged, the point that I can somehow remember, and as it emerges and as I can remember it, it keeps recalling itself as if it were to make futile effort to renew itself, and what is this renewing of the *adeukan* sound if it is not of its decaying, collapsing, imploding quietly, and thus, the listening to it becoming the being present, still from a distance, at the emerging of the *adeukan* sound that has no beginning and no end, only the airy body at a distance; an *adeukan* sound, that which scatters away at an unfathomable, quivering speed, that is to say, at a speed slower than the pulse of my breathing, in and out, in, and a wait, and out, in, and a wait, and a wait, and out, as I try to follow its speed, I feel out of breath, losing breath, my breath, as if, like a siren, the *adeukan* sound were to be taking it from me, and the distance between me and the *adeukan* sound is the time it takes for me to reach it, 'impossible', as I catch my breath, 'or I will die, suffocated', as the listening of an *adeukan* sound is that of me in the status of withering away; an *adeukan* sound, that which I know, *I know*, had once been close to me, so close to see no difference between me and it, so close that hearing of it would have meant being at the peril of my eardrums being burst out, as it was my call, my cry, it was I who made the *adeukan* sound, which I have now lost, and thus, the distance that I am experiencing, as I listen to it, is the depth of regret that I had made the cry, the depth of yearning that pulls me to the listening to it, empty wishes, to bring it back, to hear it close, to see it close, to touch it close, to have it close, as if there were no distance between us.

Of the time
An *adeukan* sound, that which, unlike all the other sounds that I can see (and some say you can't see sounds, but it's not true; just close your eyes, and sounds are everywhere), I can only assume, conjure up, imagine only as an image, but this image is, as you find out, the copies of the image, each of which is rendered null by

what follows it, the effect of the nulling leaving a void between me and the *adeukan* sound, a void that is of a time, not of a space, a void that leaves a dusty trail of wave, pulling me through and through, wavering, undulating, the pitch black dusty wave, a void where the time is ordered by each copy of the image of the *adeukan* sound, and by each of the copies of me who pitches an ear out for that each copy of the image of the sound, who, while throwing an ear out to the void, leaves the traces of each of the copies of me hearing out, wishing, wanting, sobbing and listening; an *adeukan* sound, that which never stays or dwells as it knows no place, but only direction, the only plausible designation of it is to say *from where*, but never *to where*, and thus, and only in this regard, it exists only as a pure virtuality, as a becoming on the one hand because it is a potential to become anything, and as a having-become on the other because it is a residue, a trace, a reverberation, what's been done, an after-the-fact, say, 'well, it's done with me', and as such, it has forgotten that which was real, and as such, it forces me to lose touch with that which is real, and as such, it makes me dwell on the things that had passed, and as such, it shores up that which people say, *time passes*, and as such, it winds me up, even from afar, and drags me down the pit of guilt, the guilt that I had committed it, the *adeukan* sound, and as such, it connects me up to a web of whispers, hushed convictions, long-forgotten promises, the sticky love and hate of the mother; an *adeukan* sound, that which binds me to a time which will bring me nowhere, a time that which will come to pass.

Of the memory
An *adeukan* sound, that which calls me, used to be me, to know me, as it is a memory that has become *adeukan*, that is no longer of me, with me, for me, whose shape, touch, gaze I have long forgotten, as it causes me to ache, to stutter, to become mute – because what else can I say about that which is about nothing, towards nothing, all it wishes is to become nothing, but not yet nothing; an *adeukan* sound, a singular, lone impulse, a trajectory of which is a thin, faint line that shoots up and away; an *adeukan* sound, that which emerges, as if I as a self would emerge only through its improbable relations – the distances, the gaps, the holes, the voids – to the other, that which my ear can barely catch, as if an atom would have almost no chance of hitting another atom in space, that which I would barely understand, as if the perpetual cycle of remembering and forgetting would be the natural process of how I lose light, sound and touch of the real; listen, *listen* to the *adeukan* sound, if it is a sound at all, as its aim, its impulse is to lose all relations to itself, and as such, if a sound is relational, an *adeukan* sound, you could say, is relational only so far as it is memories of having been in relation, to what I would not know by now; an *adeukan* sound, that which soars and flutters, whirls and swirls, with its smooth and dim face towards me, whose gaze I cannot bare, but I long to hear it again and again as it sounds and resounds so that I could remember, for nothing is left for me, of me, other than flakes of desire, a makeshift shell that has long been hollowed, stained with ashes of wishes, but a shell ready to ring, to rattle, to break apart, to be spirited away, like an *adeukan* call.

'ALAAF!' (German)
Peter Kiefer
A personal reflection on the word/term/interjection/sound

The exclamation 'ALAAF!' is used in Germany during the Rhenish Carnival. The word itself does not signify or refer to anything. It does not denote any specific object or action, and its etymology is not straightforward.

When I was a boy, there were a few particularly important events in the year: Christmas, which we looked forward to excitedly long before December; birthdays, which were great celebrations, and not just because of the presents. And then there was the Aachener Bend – a people's event with a funfair and Ferris wheel. Later there were bumper cars. And of course Carnival. As a child, Carnival was carefree – everyone dressed up and you could be an Indian (in very itchy costumes made by our mothers, sewn out of coarse sackcloth and with your face painted blue), a cowboy, a clown or many other things. The horror figures inspired by Halloween didn't exist at the time; Darth Vader and Star Wars were as yet unknown.

The Carnival session begins every year on November 11 at 11:11 a.m.: we would briefly hoot out loud in our classrooms, quickly drowned out by the teacher's stern look, and so we returned to our lessons. Outside school, however, it went on; on November 11 the town hall was 'stormed' by Carnival revellers, and the regency of Carnivalists and fools kicked off. That's a custom that all mayors of towns and cities celebrating Carnival abide by even today. In actual fact, the particular local prince of Carnival has a sceptre as a sign of his fool's regency. In the cold season after November 11, Carnival is celebrated almost exclusively at many so-called 'sessions' in halls, hosted by the scores of Carnival societies. Depending on the Carnival society, these are attended by greater or lesser VIPs – and of course, they're a networking opportunity for local businesses. In Aachen, for instance, there's the Bakers' Ball, which it's a great honour to be invited to.

Street Carnival is what we call the actual Carnival days, which precede Lent. That's where the term 'carne vale' ('meat, farewell!') comes from.

The 'mad days' begin on Fat Thursday with the so-called 'Weiberfastnacht' or Women's Carnival Day, and the main holidays are Carnival Sunday, Rose Monday (Carnival Monday) and Shrove Tuesday (in German: Violets Tuesday). They are followed by Ash Wednesday, on which practising Catholics (and that was practically everyone in my youth) go to church to get an ash cross painted on their foreheads. In fact, Monday is customarily an official day off in the Carnival strongholds, and many people take time off for the entire period.

Sunday and Monday are the days of the street parades: colourfully decorated floats with dressed-up Carnival revellers, marching bands, dance groups, costumed groups and individuals wind their way through the town in a long line. On Carnival Sunday in Aachen, there's the children's parade, with its own Carnival prince and, in the past, children's parties in the Kurhaus. The children's parade was shorter, but nevertheless we as children were delighted because candies and caramel sweets were thrown to the crowd of people standing at the roadside. We children tried to catch them or pick them up off the ground. Usually they were simple sugary candies, but sometimes there was a small bag of gummy bears, and that was hitting the jackpot. The Rose Monday procession was more opulent and sometimes lasted for more than five hours. Here too, the float with the grown-up Carnival prince wrapped up the parade, and the candy-throwing activities were much more extensive. Here they would sometimes serve themselves booze on the floats, and the gaiety was also accompanied by the grown-ups' moderate consumption of alcohol. And at all the parades, there resounded from the floats over the loudspeakers a 'three times thundering Oche – ALAAF!' Later, as a musician and conductor of a youth orchestra I was on stage many times and had a chance to gain insights into the not always just light-hearted structures of the Carnival, as is probably the case in any club. From those relatively carefree teenage years (to the extent that my memory hasn't romanticized them), the exclamation 'ALAAF!' was practically inscribed in my blood, as possessed of the cheerful character typical for the Rhineland.

In the following, I would like to approach 'ALAAF!' by other means and reflect on what distinguishes the word. Several specific features occurred to me:

'ALAAF!' is regional, spatial, temporal, contextual and ritual. It has a positive agitational character; it is apolitical, possibly gender-compliant, creating community and nevertheless actually devoid of meaning.

Time of year – 'ALAAF!' is used solely in the context of Carnival. In the Rhineland, Carnival is even called the 'fifth season', which makes it possible to draw conclusions about its fixed place in local culture. You won't hear it outside Carnival season; you'll occasionally hear it at Carnival in the halls starting on November 11; it's ubiquitous at Street Carnival. But it's not street terminology, and no one would use Alaaf instead of okay, tutto bene, awesome or got it.

Regional – there are several aspects here: 'ALAAF!' is not in general use during German Carnival, but rather is used primarily in Cologne and surroundings as well as in the region of Aachen, Düren, Würselen and so on. In Cologne's perpetual rival, the state capital of Düsseldorf, you call out Helau, just as they do in Mainz and more southern Carnival sites. Throughout Germany there are different fools' shouts, whereby 'HELAU' and 'ALAAF' are the best known. They are of course distrustfully dismissed by cities that hardly celebrate Carnival, such as Hanover and Berlin.

The German Wikipedia entry for 'Narrenruf' – or fools' shouts – is of great length: there you can find an extensive list of additional shout-outs, including also 'Ahoy!' and 'Aloha!'

This Alaaf map can, however, be further differentiated locally. That's because the shout is almost always associated with a specific place: in Cologne you shout 'Kölle ALAAF!', in Aachen 'Oche ALAAF!', in Würselen 'Wöschele ALAAF!' and so on and so forth for progressively smaller units or neighbourhoods. You're celebrating yourselves as a community from this special region, this very specific residential neighbourhood – you could almost say tribal site.

The shout also serves as a recognition of certain people or groups. If, for example, a speaker named Jupp at the lectern (the 'Bütt' because it has the shape of a barrel) has held a particularly good (usually rhymed and witty) speech, he may be rewarded with a 'Jupp ALAAF!' thundering out three times. Or if a dance group was particularly good, then they may say: 'To the Aachener Prinzengarde dance group, three times a thundering . . .'

So there is almost always a very referential **context** in which 'ALAAF' is shouted out.

The shout itself is usually **agitated**, meaning it is called out with sudden force, not just shouted into the group any old way. Usually there's a speaker at the microphone who eggs the people in the hall and on the street on – that means he calls out: 'And to that, a three times a thundering Oche . . . ' and the whole crowd then answers 'ALAAF!' followed by 'Oche' – 'ALAAF!', 'Oche' – 'ALAAF!'. And as there can easily be several thousand people in the hall, it really thunders loud in the seats. There can be tens of thousands of people at the big street parades. (In Cologne in normal times, up to 1.5 million people celebrate Carnival Monday (Rose Monday)). But it also works at a smaller scale, when, for example, in the Veedelszug (the parades on Sunday in individual city districts) one of the revellers in the parade calls out 'Würselen' and just the ten to fifteen people standing close by shout back 'ALAAF!'

At the same time, the action is like a **ritual**: not just an expression of sound, but also linked with a gesture. When you shout ALAAF, you throw your right hand loosely up from your midriff; your fingers are raised as if you're throwing something into the sky. It's almost like a reverse military salute, where you briskly move your hand to the cap of your uniform.

This leads me to my hypothesis that the shout-out is intrinsically **apolitical**. At the Rhenish Carnival there is nevertheless a strong military

Figure 1 ALAAF https://commons.wikimedia.org/wiki/File:Rosenmontagsempfang_der_Oberb%C3%BCrgermeisterin_von_K%C3%B6ln,_2016-6920.jpg, © Raimond Speking/ CC BY-SA 4.0 (via Wikimedia Commons) per requirement on Wiki Commons.

look-and-feel, which originated during the French occupation of the Rhineland. Many of the former citizen's militias had been banned, as had political statements. But at Carnival you were able to dress up in a military way, and the uniforms in Cologne and Aachen (the Blaue and Rote Funken, which could be translated as the Blue and Red Sparks) are parodies of the Napoleonic army's uniforms. These sometimes quite old Carnival societies also carry wooden guns with posies of flowers in their barrels. And the food is handed out from a goulash 'cannon', and sutlers accompany the Carnival soldiers; there are also confetti cannons. One anecdote tells how Napoléon (early in the nineteenth century) wanted to be celebrated in a parade through Aachen. The people, who had unwillingly become Frenchmen and -women, were obligated to stand on the street and shout 'Vive l'empereur' (all hail to the emperor). Aachen's residents, who were not very enthusiastic about doing so, shouted out 'Fies Lamperöhr' instead, which roughly translates as 'filthy stovepipe', but in Napoléon's ears sounded like a somewhat poorly pronounced, but still French paean of tribute.

The tradition of mocking the authorities can still be found today in the slogan-bearing floats that caricature a political topic by placing groups of figures larger than life on floats, leading in turn to discussions in the press and public sphere.

Nevertheless, despite these borrowings from politics and war, I think the cry 'ALAAF!' itself is apolitical. For instance, never in my life have I heard someone shout-out 'Germany ALAAF!'. And if one day someone shouts 'NRW ALAAF! NRW = the State Northrhine-Westfalia', then it'll no doubt be a politician, wanting to act in a folksy way.

It seems to me that the cry itself is strongly rooted in the regional and almost refers to a kind of tribal culture where **belonging to a group** and mutual understanding are paramount. In this form, it also creates community. In this context you can quite proudly observe these days that, to this very day, the Rhineland is considered a tolerant place for all nationalities, skin colours and sexual orientations. To what extent gender equality is implemented during Carnival, I won't dare to discuss here – but many of the performers are celebrated female stars.

And Altweiber-Donnerstag – Women's Carnival Thursday – is clearly the day allotted to women – if, as a man, you walk through the streets of Aachen or Cologne wearing a necktie, you shouldn't be surprised if all of a sudden a horde of ladies stand around you and, without further ado, cut-off your sign of male dominance using scissors. Rhenish men thus start the morning wearing an old tie, but guests from abroad, for instance from England, are truly terrified when the women dressed up as *Möhne* (old maids) come up to them carrying scissors. In general, Carnival is considered a relatively permissive celebration where, for just a few days and without any other obligations, you can go a bit overboard, with the comforting knowledge that everything really is over on Ash Wednesday.

And where does the word Alaaf actually come from, and what is it supposed to mean? You can find various explanations. The toast 'all af' ('everything gone') is supposed to have been recorded in writing in 1635 as a forebear – it could signify something like 'over everything' or 'away from everything else' – or away from all cares? In the cry 'Kölle ALAAF!' shouted three times, it would mean something like 'Cologne above everything' or 'All praise to Cologne'. And since the 'modern Carnival', starting in 1823, 'ALAAF!' is a regular cry of revellers in the Rhineland. You can also find, however, other, different etymological interpretations.

Possibly its exact provenance is not even so important here, because the person shouting it out probably does not know it himself: for him or her it's a spontaneous expression of joy, of belonging and of communal experience. So, to all you readers exploring sound words: "three times a thundering: . . . .!"

(translation Nancy Chapple, Berlin)

Bim Bam (Czech)
Iva Bittová

            Bim | | Bam | |
            Bim | | Bam | |
            Bim | | Bam | |
            Bim | | Bam | |
Ťuk   Pšš   Ťuk   Ťuky   Ťuk
Ťuk   Pss   Ťuk   Taky   Ťuk
Ťuk   Pšš   Ťuk   Ťuky   Ťuk
Ťuk   Pss   Ťuk   Taky   Ťuk
Cink   Cink   Bum   Trr   Tydlidum
Cink   Cink   Bum   Trr   Tydlidum
Cink   Cink   Bum   Trr   Tydlidum
Cink   Cink   Bum   Trr   Tydlidum
Trr   Tydli   Tydli   Bum   Cililink
Trr   Tydli   Tydli   Bum   Cililink
Trr   Tydli   Tydli   Bum   Cililink
Trr   Tydli   Tydli   Bum   Cililink
            Bim | | Bam | |
            Bim | | Bam | |
            Bim | | Bam | |
            Bim | | Bam | |
Cuk   Kšš   Cuk   Cuky   Cuk
Cuk   Kšš   Cuk   Cuky   Cuk
Cuk   Kšš   Cuk   Cuky   Cuk
Cuk   Kšš   Cuk   Cuky   Cuk
Klink   Klank   Klonk   Trr   Tydli   Dom
Klink   Klank   Klonk   Trr   Tydli   Dom
Klink   Klank   Klonk   Trr   Tydli   Dom
Klink   Klank   Klonk   Trr   Tydli   Dom
Klink   Klank   Klink   Bum   Cililink
Klink   Klank   Klink   Bum   Cililink
Klink   Klank   Klink   Bum   Cililink
Klink   Klank   Klink   Bum   Cililink
            Bim | | Bam | |
            Bim | | Bam | |
            Bim | | Bam | |
            Bim | | Bam | |

Bim Bam evokes the sounds of the bell,
. . .
Ťuk in the Czech language means pit-a-pat or knock knock on the door
Pšššš shush pssssst be quiet
Kššš shoo, go away, . . . shout down to the chicken in the backyard:)
Psss evokes the sounds of snake or a balloon losing air
Trrrr could be also the mechanic sound of an alarm o'clock or clatter; there is a special big wooden clock in traditional Easter time celebration,
. . .
Klink klank these are percussive sounds of glasses

Cililink is the old fashion bell on a bicycle
Cuk Cuky twitching, jerk, tangle of yarn, thread
Trrr Tydli if you put in one word, it sounds like TRDLO – The Goof
Tydli (šmidli) also could be an expression for fiddling, playing the violin

This text I created for my programme with the girls' choir in Lelekovice (Moravia, CZ). It was recorded and released on the CD *Kolednice*.

All sounds are percussive, and that rhythmical little composition is still alive, performed around Christmas time with different groups of children choir.

Bla (Spanish)
Mikel R. Nieto

bla bla bla bla bla bla bla bla bla bla bla bla bla bla bla bla bla bla bla bla bla bla bla bla bla bla bla bla
bla bla bla bla bla bla bla bla bla bla bla bla bla bla bla bla bla bla bla bla bla bla bla bla bla bla bla bla
bla bla bla bla bla bla bla bla bla bla bla bla bla bla bla bla bla bla bla bla bla bla bla bla bla bla bla bla
bla bla bla bla bla bla bla bla bla bla bla bla bla bla bla bla bla bla bla bla bla bla bla bla bla bla bla bla
bla bla bla bla bla bla bla bla bla bla bla bla bla bla bla bla bla bla bla bla bla bla bla bla bla bla bla bla
bla bla bla bla bla bla bla bla bla bla bla bla bla bla bla bla bla bla bla bla bla bla bla bla bla bla bla bla
bla bla bla bla bla bla bla bla bla bla bla bla bla bla bla bla bla bla bla bla bla bla bla bla bla bla bla bla
bla bla bla bla bla bla bla bla bla bla bla bla bla bla bla bla bla bla bla bla bla bla bla bla bla bla bla bla
bla bla bla bla bla bla bla bla bla bla bla bla bla bla bla bla bla bla bla bla bla bla bla bla bla bla bla bla
bla bla bla bla bla bla bla bla bla bla bla bla bla bla bla bla bla bla bla bla bla bla bla bla bla bla bla bla
bla bla bla bla bla bla bla bla bla bla bla bla bla bla bla bla bla bla bla bla bla bla bla bla bla bla bla bla
bla bla bla bla bla bla bla bla bla bla bla bla bla bla bla bla bla bla bla bla bla bla bla bla bla bla bla bla
bla bla bla bla bla bla bla bla bla bla bla bla bla bla bla bla bla bla bla bla bla bla bla bla bla bla bla bla
bla bla bla bla bla bla bla bla bla bla bla bla bla bla bla bla bla bla bla bla bla bla bla bla bla bla bla bla
bla bla bla bla bla bla bla bla bla bla bla bla bla bla bla bla bla bla bla bla bla bla bla bla bla bla bla bla
bla bla bla bla bla bla bla bla bla bla bla bla bla bla bla bla bla bla bla bla bla bla bla bla bla bla bla bla
bla bla bla bla bla bla bla bla bla bla bla bla bla bla bla bla bla bla bla bla bla bla bla bla bla bla bla bla
bla bla bla bla bla bla bla bla bla bla bla bla bla bla bla bla bla bla bla bla bla bla bla bla bla bla bla bla
bla bla bla bla bla bla bla bla bla bla bla bla bla bla bla bla bla bla bla bla bla bla bla bla bla bla bla bla
bla bla bla bla bla bla bla bla bla bla bla bla bla bla bla bla bla bla bla bla bla bla bla bla bla bla bla bla
bla bla bla bla bla bla bla bla bla bla bla bla bla bla bla bla bla bla bla bla bla bla bla bla bla bla bla bla
bla bla bla bla bla bla bla bla bla bla bla bla bla bla bla bla bla bla bla bla bla bla bla bla bla bla bla bla
bla bla bla bla bla bla bla bla bla bla bla bla bla bla bla bla bla bla bla bla bla bla bla bla bla bla bla bla
bla bla bla bla bla bla bla bla bla bla bla bla bla bla bla bla bla bla bla bla bla bla bla bla bla bla bla bla
bla bla bla bla bla bla bla bla bla bla bla bla bla bla bla bla bla bla bla bla bla bla bla bla bla bla bla bla
bla bla bla bla bla bla bla bla bla bla bla bla bla bla bla bla bla bla bla bla bla bla bla bla bla bla bla bla
bla bla bla bla bla bla bla bla bla bla bla bla bla bla bla bla bla bla bla bla bla bla bla bla bla bla bla bla
bla bla bla bla bla bla bla bla bla bla bla bla bla bla bla bla bla bla bla bla bla bla bla bla bla bla bla bla
bla bla bla bla bla bla bla bla bla bla bla bla bla bla bla bla bla bla bla bla bla bla bla bla bla bla bla bla
bla bla bla bla bla bla bla bla bla bla bla bla bla bla bla bla bla bla bla bla bla bla bla bla bla bla bla bla
bla bla bla bla bla bla bla bla bla bla bla bla bla bla bla bla bla bla bla bla bla bla bla bla bla bla bla bla
bla bla bla bla bla bla bla bla bla bla bla bla bla bla bla bla bla bla bla bla bla bla bla bla bla bla bla bla
bla bla bla bla bla bla bla bla bla bla bla bla bla bla bla bla bla bla bla bla bla bla bla bla bla bla bla bla
bla bla bla bla bla bla bla bla bla bla bla bla bla bla bla bla bla bla bla bla bla bla bla bla bla bla bla bla

bla bla bla bla bla bla bla bla bla bla bla bla bla bla bla bla bla bla bla bla
bla bla bla bla bla bla bla bla bla bla bla bla bla bla bla bla bla bla bla bla
bla bla bla bla bla bla bla bla bla bla bla bla bla bla bla bla bla bla bla bla
bla bla bla bla bla bla bla bla bla bla bla bla bla bla bla bla bla bla bla bla
bla bla bla bla bla bla bla bla bla bla bla bla bla bla bla bla bla bla bla bla
bla bla bla bla bla bla bla bla bla bla bla bla bla bla bla bla bla bla bla bla
bla bla bla bla bla bla bla bla bla bla bla bla bla bla bla bla bla bla bla bla
bla bla bla bla bla bla bla bla bla bla bla bla bla bla bla bla bla bla bla bla
bla bla bla bla bla bla bla bla bla bla bla bla bla bla bla bla bla bla bla bla
bla bla bla bla bla bla bla bla bla bla bla bla bla bla bla bla bla bla bla bla
bla bla bla bla bla bla bla bla bla bla bla bla bla bla bla bla bla bla bla bla
bla bla bla bla bla bla bla bla bla bla bla bla bla bla bla bla bla bla bla bla
bla bla bla bla bla bla bla bla bla bla bla bla bla bla bla bla bla bla bla bla
bla bla bla bla bla bla bla bla bla bla bla bla bla bla bla bla bla bla bla bla
bla bla bla bla bla bla bla bla bla

Figure 2 bla © Mikel R. Nieto.

Boori (nightingales)

David Rothenberg

The sexiest syllable sung by male nightingales in the midst of their 200-note song, a raspy, bluesy, funky hook of a bird song easy enough to hear at midnight in Europe in spring.

Nightingale scientist Silke Kipper is intrigued by the occasional penchant of the male nightingale to insert a strange 'buzz sound' into his clarion whistles, clicks and ratchets. She admits she finds this buzz unpleasant – not that her opinion matters, as the female nightingales find it especially pleasant. I had noticed this sound as well, and that the nightingales would sing it only occasionally, like an ornament, a grace note or even a blue note – that cool, unclassifiable sound human music is known to offer up in many forms, a hip tone, a most excellent riff that only makes sense if used sparingly.

Electronic musician Korhan Erel named this 'the *boori* sound' because it's neither buzzy nor bluesy, neither ugly nor human. Decide for yourself whether it is music or noise.

Through various playback experiments, Kipper and her collaborators established that the female nightingales like this *boori* sound far more than any other note the males can belt out.[1] 'Then why', Kipper wonders, 'don't the males just sing this "sexy" sound over and over again? Do they not know how well it works?'

I had to laugh a bit when I first heard the sound. It's like a bluesy riff, an out-of-tune quip, a wah-wah pedal tone. These effects are cool, to be sure, but any guitarist knows one shouldn't play them all the time. You've got to hold in your best licks, only letting them out when your audience least expects it.

Music is an exercise in contrast between the expected and the unexpected, the beat and the stop, the patterned and the patternless.

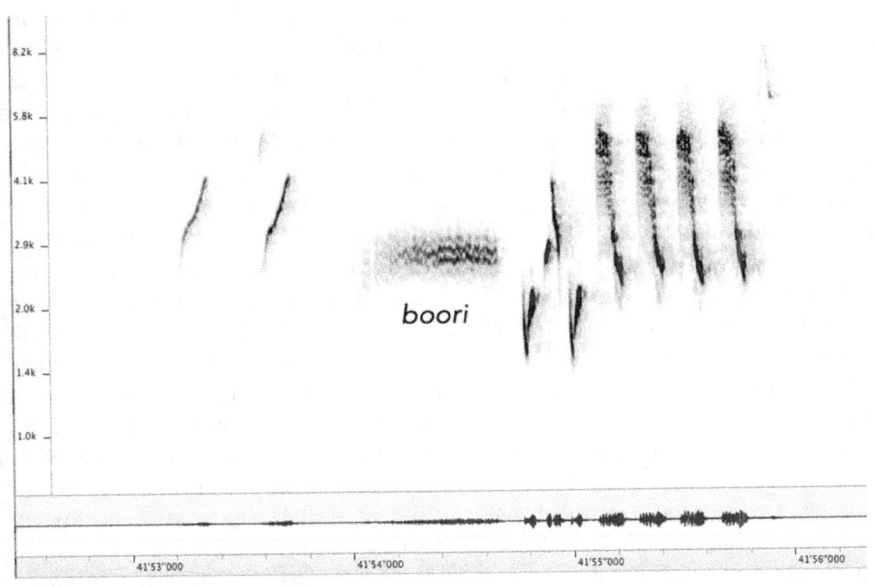

Figure 3 Boori © David Rothenberg.

Brummkreisel (German)
Siegfried Kärcher
Engl. Humming Top
In 1913 the Lorenz Bolz company in Zirndorf invented the humming top.

The humming top is a nostalgic tin toy that produces a humming sound when it rotates around its own axis. The company Lorenz Bolz in Zirndorf, which had existed since 1880, patented the drill rod in 1913. With this invention, the classic string top was replaced.

A metal rod with a wooden handle (now mostly made of plastic), around which helical grooves wind ike a screw, is pressed into the top. The gripper engages in the recesses in the rotor head. The thread turns the gyroscope, which continues to turn even when the screw spindle is raised again, as a free wheel is formed in the process.

By pumping again the top is accelerated, and the faster it turns, the louder it 'sings'. This is made possible by small incisions that are made where the sheet metal body of the gyroscope is largest. As soon as the top rotates, air is periodically interrupted by these blowing edges like a flute and the vibrating air is directed into the resonance chamber inside. The small metal tongues attached to these holes also vibrate through the air flow and make the top hum.

(Wikipedia Germany, translated by Google)

The typical sounds of a humming top emerge when I sit down and try to write about it. First, you charge the humming top strongly. Then you let it go and the humming starts with a full spinning motion. After a while it gets slower and the sound vanishes. It slows down until it stands still or even falls.

This kind of combination of sound and movement attracted me since I was a little kid. There is the charging, where I put energy in this system and the humming top immediately responds. It starts to move while the charging process is ongoing. I can decide how much energy I will put in. The more energy it gets, the more movement and the more sound are provided.

But the end is unavoidable. When the energy vanishes all comes to an end.

This can only be restarted by putting more energy in it and let the spinning and humming begin once more.

The Brummkreisel Sound is very special and driven by movement. It sounds very organic and interesting due to its speed modulation. Together with the movement it creates an audiovisual sensation with a hypnotic effect. I get fascinated by this easy trigger up to today. When the colours of the Brummkreisel start to meld due to speed and the sound appears I enjoy the play and I kind of feel sorry when it stops. When I become a teenager and started clubbing in the 1980s I discovered a bass rhythm which triggered similar feelings. When I entered The German Techno Club at Dorian Gray Frankfurt Airport I got addicted to the power of the emerging Techno Movement. At the early times a lot of Music by Front 242, Nitzer Ebb, A Split Second, The Klinik and Deutsch Amerikanische Freundschaft was played loud and it had this typical basslines. These basslines were created by synthesizers and never of too many notes. The repetition of the maybe five notes draw me in completely and I started to dance. I could not resist the easy hypnotic effect this electronic body music had on me. I was hooked like I was as a child with the Brummkreisel. And I loved every minute of it! Dancing, moving with the repeating bassline, brought so much joy to me. Later the 4/4 bass drum was invented and the whole Techno Movement got even more hypnotic.

And all reminds me on the Brummkreisel-Experience I made as a child.

Even nowadays the principles still apply. And I smile while a DJ drops the beat again, withdraws it and so on.

A drop or beat drop in music, made popular by electronic dance music (EDM) styles, is a point in a music track where a sudden change of rhythm or bass line occurs, which is preceded by a build-up section and break.

Originating from disco and 1970s rock, drops are found in genres such as EDM, trap, hip-hop, K-pop and country. With the aid of music production applications, drops can vary in instrumentation and sound. Electronic instruments and tools for making drops include oscillating synthesizers, vocal samples, a drum beat, and basslines.

Certain drops can include a 'beat-up' (so-named because it is a point where the volume of the foundational kick drum beat is increased, after it has been faded down during a break or build-up) and 'climax' (a single, striking drop done late in the track). There are also types of drops which deviate from the standard, such as 'anti-drops' (songs in which the chorus is more minimal than the build-up) and consecutive 'superseding-drops'. (Wikipedia on Drop)

On my journey as an artist I was going to be and still am a VJ and when the beat gets faster and it peaks I often mix my visuals in a movement which reminds me of the melting colours of the pacing Brummkreisel.

VJing (pronounced: VEE-JAY-ing) is a broad designation for real-time visual performance. Characteristics of VJing are the creation or manipulation of imagery in real-time through technological mediation and for an audience, in synchronization to music. VJing often takes place at events such as concerts, nightclubs, music festivals and sometimes in combination with other performative arts. This results in a live multimedia performance that can include music, actors and dancers. The term VJing became popular in its association with MTV's Video Jockey but its origins date back to the New York club scene of the 70s. In both situations VJing is the manipulation or selection of visuals, the same way DJing is a selection and manipulation of audio.

One of the key elements in the practice of VJing is the real-time mix of content from a 'library of media', on storage media such as VHS tapes or DVDs, video and still image files on computer hard drives, live camera input, or from computer generated visuals. In addition to the selection of media, VJing mostly implies real-time processing of the visual material. The term is also used to describe the performative use of generative software, although the word 'becomes dubious (. . .) since no video is being mixed'. (Wikipedia on VJ'ing)

The dwelling and repeating of the Drone musical style comes also to my mind when I think about Brummkreisel.

Drone music, drone-based music, or simply drone, is a minimalist genre that emphasizes the use of sustained sounds, notes, or tone clusters – called drones. It is typically characterized by lengthy audio programs with relatively slight harmonic variations throughout each piece. La Monte Young, one of its 1960s originators, defined it in 2000 as 'the sustained tone branch of minimalism'.

Music which contains drones and is rhythmically still or very slow, called 'drone music', can be found in many parts of the world, including bagpipe traditions, among them Scottish pibroch piping; didgeridoo music in Australia, South Indian classical Carnatic music and Hindustani classical music (both of which are accompanied almost invariably by the Tanpura, a plucked, four-string instrument which is only capable of playing a drone); the sustained tones found in the Japanese gagaku classical tradition; possibly (disputed) in pre-polyphonic organum vocal music of late medieval Europe; and the Byzantine chant's ison (or drone-singing, attested after the fifteenth century). Repetition of tones, supposed to be in imitation of bagpipes, is found in a wide variety of genres and musical forms. (Wikipedia on Drones)

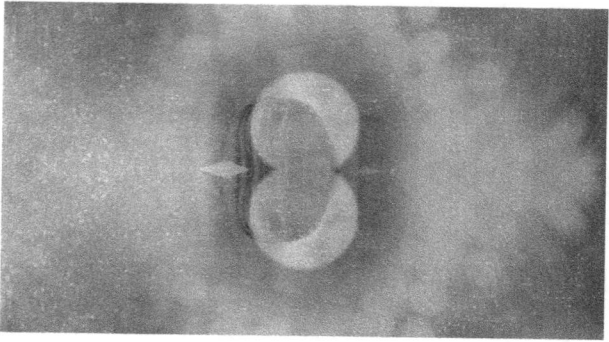

Figure 4 Brummkreise-Träume (Videostill 1), 2021 © Siegfried Kärcher.

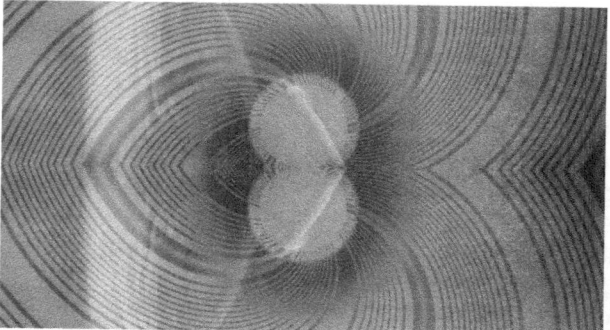

Figure 5 Brummkreise-Träume (Videostill 2), 2021 © Siegfried Kärcher.

The Brummkreisel-Experience is very easy but also very deep and it might be anchored in myself forever in a warm and welcoming place full of Sound and Visuals. Beginning in my earliest childhood, up to today it influences my thinking as an artist. It still has a kind of Mystic or Magic to me because it transforms a dead object into something soundful and colourful in movement.

The Brummkreisel Motif often shows in my works, even if it is more in an abstract form and contains Sound and Visuals. Drones, minimalistic repeating figures and moving colourful images are the main ingredients of my work 'Brummkreisel-Träume'. This work is meant to be projected on a large scale in a music-club setting where people are able to stand in the installation and dance to the hypnotic sound.

Everything is in movement and changing. Forms evolve and vanish, and tones appear and disappear. The Recipient of Brummkreisel-Träume even might get into the visual motion that he loses orientation and gets dizzy from the ever-changing, moving and spinning.

Brummkreisel-Träume gets exhibited at the Siegfried Kärcher Kunsttage, which takes place every Year at The Radom auf der Wasserkuppe near Fulda. The Radom is an old post-war Radar-Dome with one-of-a-kind acoustics. The dome generates thirteen times folded echoes.

Siegfried Kärcher Art Days, every Year at Radom auf der Wasserkuppe, Fulda

In this special environment, the Brummkreisel-Träume can unfold its whole potential and guide the recipient into a very immersive art experience.

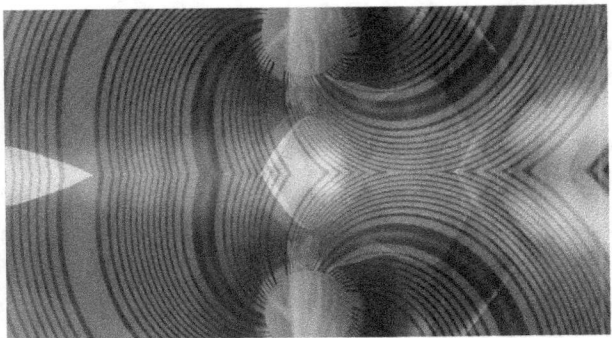

Figure 6 Brummkreise-Träume (Videostill 3), 2021 © Siegfried Kärcher.

Figure 7 Siegfried Kärcher Art Days, every Year at Radom auf der Wasserkuppe, Fulda © Siegfried Kärcher.

BWO (Slovak)

Dalibor Kocián

Each decade has its own music style expressions. Whether it's the 1980s synth pop, psychedelia of 1960s, 1990s (mostly) decadent euro dance or not so decadent, but still dirty, grunge, hip-hop of the 2000s (2010s, and 2020s as well? We'll see), each decennium is musically remembered for something. We can arrange these significant musical genres even vertically, from mainstream to underground. With the exponential development of things (tech, information spreading, etc.), the pace of music styles coming and going has rapidly increased. Some of them are relevant for half a decade and some only for a year.

One of those genres that made a dent in music history but their dominance didn't last as much as a decade was, I believe, dubstep. The so-called early one. There might be many different reasons why this, originally underground, style from South London still makes people writhe in craze on the dance floors (not in 2020 much though). Although, in this case, people dance more inwardly rather than on the outside, as, according to some hard-core dancers, the tempo of dubstep is slowish. A way how to solve this is to perceive

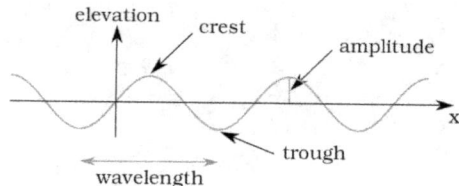

Figure 8 Sine Wave https://commons.wikimedia.org/wiki/File:Sine_wave_amplitude.svg.

the precise rhythmic values (quarter notes rather than half notes) and dance accordingly. One of the significant elements of dubstep that contributed to the style becoming huge in half a decade is its signature sub-bass sound. Electronic music styles are well known for their bass sound that makes the walls and windows (if there are any) of clubs resonate. But dubstep's bass is somehow different and one reason is because it goes even lower and reaches as far as 40 Hz or even 30 Hz. Although this is perhaps common in nowadays dance music styles such as trap, it wasn't that frequent in the wake of the century.

The sonic power of dubstep's bass lies not only in its depth and low but in the subtle movement within the low-frequency spectrum. 'LFO (low frequency oscillation) is an electronic frequency which is usually below 20 Hz and creates a rhythmic pulse or sweep. This pulse or sweep is used to modulate musical equipment such as synthesizers to create audio effects such as vibrato, tremolo and phasing[2]'. For techno-(musico)logically less-skilled readers, imagine a swing-like movement within each individual bass tone. Sometimes audible but sometimes not at all. The LFO is often not perceived as an audible sound message, but more often as a movement within one sound in frequency of, for example, ten oscillations per second. This movement is carried out by a sound parameter such as a high-pass filter, low-pass filter, frequency cut-off and so on. When it comes to using LFO in dubstep bass, imagine you make a constant 'aaah' sound coming out of your mouth at the lowest tone possible, covering and opening it with your palm at the frequency of about 5–10 per second, or let's say per beat. More specifically at the tempo of 140 beats per minute, as this is dubstep's most common BPM. You can vary this rhythmically within the beat or within the 4/4 measures. You can also use eighth notes, triplets, irregular movements and so on.

As we are speaking of sounds in the lower spectrum of audibility, it is quite unsurprising that such sounds were 'never heard before'-like for the club-goers of the 2000s. Yes, there were techno, house, jungle and drum 'n' bass of the 1980s and 1990s, but they had their bass riffs not yet enriched with the sub-frequencies that only later sound systems were capable of playing. This is rather an empirical supposition of an Eastern Europe teenage club-goer and the explanation might be simpler; a lack of music styles that would utilize on the possibilities of sub-bass frequencies. But as a partier mostly active during the first decade of the twentieth century I had a chance to dive into a phenomenon typical of dubstep genre. The sound element BWO [bwuo].

In order to embrace the sound of BWO, it is vital to be exposed to its sound coming from a sufficient sound system. Most likely this won't be headphones or laptop speakers but a proper club system. A religionless term initiation was once used by a friend of mine in connection to experiencing sub-bass BWO sound from a club sound system for the first time. 'When did you have your initiation?', he asked me once. 'At a BWO party', in about 2007 listening to Japanese producer Goth-Trad's heavy-weight tunes rolling out from the speakers and entering my head, chest and abdomen, making my heart tingle with joy of hearing something I hadn't heard before.

According to musician/YouTuber Adam Neely's video, Why pop music sounds bad, to you . . ., the strongest musical experiences one can go through very often occur at about the age of fourteen. It is when changes in the human's hormonal system create a sort of bond with the music a subject listens to at this age. Any time you come back to the songs of youth, you can get a huge dopamine hit. I experienced my adolescence 'dopamine for life' moment with music in the later 1990s listening to a lot of metal/hard-core music of that time. Although I don't listen to it nowadays, the then music of Machine Head, Sepultura, Biohazard and others has still the same emotional effect on my psyche and goosebumps as back then. And the explanation is very simple – the sound of distorted guitar. But fortunately such bonds of life periods and music aren't always unique and one can have more 'dopamine for life' sounds. Recalling the initiation moment with dubstep and listening to the late noughties and

Figure 9 BWO © Biomat.

early 2010s dubstep playlist while writing this essay triggers the same emotional reactions coming from the recesses of my mind. That is how strong an impact the very little musical element on one's psyche can have.

The sonic effect of sub-bass is not a culture-specific phenomenon and the physical experience of these low frequencies and the low oscillation knows no borders; therefore, it is not a language-bound concept. However, I think the common term wobble sound, or wobbly bass, does not describe the heaviness, intensity, depth and captivation of this sound phenomenon the way I imagine it could. Wobbly seems too funky, too jolly and light-hearted. BWO, on the other hand, is more solemn, darker and deeper, as the sound of early dubstep was when the term was coined by Peter Meluš of BWO collective at around 2005. However I openly admit this of course might be my language bias and you should pronounce both wobble and BWO words together with listening to the sound examples and choose the one that fits you more. One can ponder whether it is cock-a-doodle-doo or kikiriki for roosters or woof-woof or

Figure 10 BWO © Biomat.

haf-haf for a dog and discuss which is more descriptive, but let's assume it is subjective or language-specific similar to the phenomenon called 'multilingual onomatopoeia'[3]. Different language has a different onomatopoeia for an LFO in bass frequencies.

What differs BWO from wobble is, however, the fact that BWO is also a collective responsible for promoting the sound at many wonderful events in the years 2008–13. Although the venues varied from a military storage bunker (legendary U-Club/Subclub) or an old string factory with a limited capacity of fifty people to more common club venues, the emotional charge of the events was the same throughout the years. Whether it was a guest from afar (Headhunter, Ramadanman, Jamie Vex'd) or a local support (Biomat, Detlef Dakar) giving the sound system hard time, the crowd was leaving the venue delighted, uplifted and blissfully exhausted by the heavy bass sounds. It seems almost like a dream from today's Covid pandemic perspective and absence of club events, but in the old days a party's night name was very often synonymous to hours spent enriching one's musical taste; with a drink or two.

What about BWO today? As for the BWO collective, the guys became active in different realms than promoting events, although from time to time they host a streaming event of music-listening journey for club music enthusiasts. As for the sound element BWO, its heyday was over in the early 2010s when it was replaced by a more sharp, piercing and ear-splitting bass of brostep. A genre that very quickly became the new 'dubstep' in mp3 shops, charts and music reviews. Some prominent producers even gave up on the genre of dubstep and steered their activities to different music directions. From that perspective, the original sound moved back to little clubs, warehouses and out-of-spotlight venues. To its original place of birth.

I think it is important to observe, analyse and give names to different progressive musical phenomena. It's questionable how frequent new occurrences of such elements emerge. Perhaps it was more common in the previous times when classical music was the main object of music theorists' magnifying glasses. Today, trap-style hi-hats, EDM metal bass and Flume-like synths do appear now and then, and I believe it's pleasant to enjoy them in their fresh and true form and useful to label them and thus enhance our musical vocabulary.

LFO picture source: https://sites.google.com/site/synthaquarium/lfo---low-frequency-oscillator

clang clang (Tintinese)
Bernd Herzogenrath

Hergé – a pun on his real name George Remi (his initials backwards: RG) – was a master of the Belgian Comics (or, *bande dessinée*, as they are called in French). Without a doubt, his most famous series is *Les aventures de Tintin* – a series about Tintin, a Belgian reporter, who has to survive many adventures.

Change of location and context – cut to Kermode and narratology.

In Frank Kermode's *The Sense of an Ending*, we read the following:

> Let us take a very simple example, the ticking of a clock. We ask what it *says*: and we agree that it says *tick-tock*. By this fiction we humanize it, make it talk our language. Of course, it is we who provide the fictional difference between the two sounds; *tick* is our word for a physical beginning, *tock* our word for an end. We say they differ.... The interval between the two sounds, between *tick* and *tock* is now charged with significant duration. The clock's *tick-tock* I take to be a model of what we call a plot, an organization that humanizes time by giving it form; and the interval between *tock* and *tick* represents purely successive, disorganized time of the sort

that we need to humanize. . . . *Tick* is a humble genesis, *tock* a feeble apocalypse. (Kermode 44–5)

What it boils down to is that repetition – but repetition with a difference! *tick-tock!* – creates newness, a newness with beginning, middle and end. On the other hand – as with the case of *tock-tick* – this 'organization of time' we might call narrative is based on noise – *tick-tock* makes sense, *tock-tick* doesn't.

Now, if meaningful sound and noise here basically differ not in their mode of organization (tock-tick is as organized as tick-tock), then what is their significant difference? I am not sure this entry will give an answer, but I'm looking forward to the way how to get there.

According to poststructuralist thinkers, a sound receives meaning once it's repeated (or – at least – once it can be repeated) . . . tragic is, that this doubling also creates redundancy or noise.

Cut back to the location we started in.

Hergé's stories are full of *doublets*, *doppelgänger*, repetitions – his detectives Dupond & Dupont (in the English version: Thomson and Thompson) are just a prime example . . . it is as if Derrida's *différance* had been their godfather! More so – the whole series is based on a character whose name sounds like a stutter, a stumble, redundant repetition personified: Tintin (in the German translation, he is simply called Tim – we no-frills-efficient Germans scrapped the superfluous double, and 'tick-tock'-icized the remainder into a name we could make sense of . . .). And if this were not enough, Hergé's comics are full of sound words that always come in doubles . . . drrrring drrring . . . boom boom . . . and so on . . . lots of noise here!

Now this is funny, because Hergé was close friends with Michel Serres, the noisiest philosopher on the planet (one might say, if it weren't for the fact that although still noisy, Serres is not on this planet anymore). Serres had even written two essays about the concept of noise in Hergé's work. In his reading of Hergé's comic book Les *Bijoux De La Castafiore* (English: *The Castafiore Emerald*, 1961), Serres shows that the medium of the comic – itself an *inter*medium, in which images and text combine to create more than the sum of their parts – does not (have to) follow and imitate traditional media such as literature, music, painting or film. In fact, Hergé's comic book is revealed by Serres as being an essay about communication channels (another version of what 'media' stands for) gone wrong and wild: Serres' reading of Hergé shows the scrambling of media in all its guises – so much so, that through Serres' eyes (and ears), we may read Hergé's comic as his version of *Beaucoup de bruit pour rien* – Much Ado (noise) about Nothing.

Serres is particularly interested in how, in Marlinspike Hall, all acts of communication are drowned out by noise, and the noise increasingly pushes itself to the fore to such an extent that the message and the meaning of the communication are lost. This interpretation should actually have been a bitter pill for Hergé. His fame, after all, is largely associated with being the 'Ur-Father' of that style of comics known as *ligne claire*, clear line, a style that was devoted to utmost clarity, up to being obsessed about it. In the world of ligne claire, however, there is no noise, no transitions and no blurring. Every object is delineated from its surroundings by a neat contour. Everything, and with it every meaningful signifier, is meticulously separated from everything else. Noise is not intended in this world and is actually not possible. Without too much exaggeration, it can be said that Hergé's career is based on not allowing any noise whatsoever.

However, as we know from his modus operandi, Hergé did not set out from or start with the clear line: he rather found it. From the various sketches with many open, scraggy and unfinished strokes, he distilled, as it were, in several stages of copying and tracing, the clearest and most ideal lines. Abstraction is thus suspended in the working process itself, but remains perceptible behind this seemingly simple contouring as an invisible, because highly condensed process: the birth of the *ligne claire* from the foam of noise.

Thus – paradoxical situation!

Cut to Hergé's *Tintin: L'Affaire Tournesol* (English: *The Calculus Affair*, 1956). Although published five years before *The Castafiore Emerald*, these stories are related by their opening scene: both comics start with Tintin and Archibald Haddock walking through the estate of Marlinspike Hall. In both stories, Haddock's impression of purity is disturbed: in *The Calculus Affair*, his impression of quietness is interrupted by the noise of an approaching storm . . . brrrom, in *The Castafiore Emerald*, Haddock's enjoyment of clean air is belied by the stink of a garbage dump.

The Calculus Affair is a story replete with sound words – *Bang, Bong* and *Rrrrring* – my favourite being the word pair '*clang clang*' (152–5). When Haddock follow the traits of the intruders who broke into Prof Calculus laboratory, they find themselves in a house where they hope to find the professor. There, they hear the sound (or noise?) 'clang clang'. For Haddock, this double entendre 'sounds like something bumping against a pipe' (154) – I heard it through the pipeline . . . and indeed,

it is another Professor, Topolino, who had been assaulted and thrown into the cellar.

Once more a doubling, a doubling which might make sense at its second appearance only, but maybe even a sense engaged in a repetitive difference. Even more – clang clang here appears to be posed between being a meaningful sign, and simply an item of noise . . . and maybe this is what 'Klang' (sound) – or clang clang – is all about . . . .???[4]

Reference

Kermode, Frank. *The Sense of an Ending: Studies in the Theory of Fiction (with a New Epilogue)*. New York: Oxford University Press, 2000, 44–5.

'dåm' (Norwegian)

Maja S. K. Ratkje

Music is a shared experience, a magical moment where everyone in the room, and the room itself, tunes in on the same wavelength, a deeper understanding, a deeper listening and a perfect, irreplaceable moment of shared musical time. Everyone knows it, when the experience is just magical. The expression 'to have "dåm" in the performance' is used by the folk instrument: the Hardanger fiddle. The

Figure 11 Bjarne Herrefoss (1961) © photographer unknown, photo.Source: Sigmund Krøvel/Hallingdølen.

Figure 12 Benedicte Maurseth © Elisabeth Emmerhoff.

special tunings, and the extra set of resonating strings that this fiddle has, encourage a hypnotizing, altered sound free from the classical waves of crescendos, ritardandos and pauses. To have 'dåm' in your play suggests that the musician is in contact with otherwordly powers. I can't think of a better word for what happens in music when you can't put the finger on what makes it so magical.

Ḍhyāṁ kuṛā kuṛ (Bengali/ বাংলা/Bānglā)
Soaham Mandal

The Bengali language, or endonymously বাংলা/Bānglā, is considered as one of the most mellifluous languages by the general Bengali populace, along with many non-native enthusiasts across the world. Comically rumoured to be ranked at the top of the mellifluity chart by UNESCO, this popular, controversial hoax is a matter of another debate. But the reason for citing this unofficial, anecdotal and almost parodic observation is to illuminate that Bangla, like most other Indic languages, has a peculiar abundance of 'dvirukti/দ্বিরুক্তি' or 'double utterances' where a pair of alliterative words are used to emphasize and/or exaggerate, reduce and/or understate and explicitly express sounds. As onomatopoeia or sonic expressions, they are legitimized by a lexical subdivision of 'ধ্বন্যাত্মক দ্বিরুক্তি/Dhvañātmak dvirukti', which roughly translates as 'phonetic/sonic doubling or double utterance' under the grammatical category of 'ধ্বন্যাত্মক শব্দ/Dhvañātmak śabda', which translates as 'phonetic/sonic words'. The recurring particle 'ধ্বনি/dhvani' essentially means 'sound'.

Among many expressions, I am attempting to describe three instances in particular, owing to my love for drums and percussion:

1. **Ḍhyāṁ kuṛā kuṛ/ঢ্যাম্ কুড়া কুড় or Ḍhyāṁ kuṛ kuṛ/ঢ্যাম্ কুড় কুড়**

This is a quintessential Bengali drum beat representing the drum strokes of Dhāk, a large barrel-shaped drum that is played on one side with thin drumsticks made of shaved bamboo, accompanied by Kāṁsar/কাঁসর (a type of gong), in and as an integral part of the Ḍurga Puja, that is, festival of worship of the Goddess Ḍurga in the dominant Hindu religious traditions of Bengal. This particular sound is exclusive and cannot be attributed to any other instrument or premise. It has musical, religious and cultural connotations. Ḍurga Puja is celebrated by Bengalis everywhere all across the world, but especially in the city of Kolkata, the annual festival, takes a form of a sort of Carnival, happens approximately over a period of a week with five days of worship. The diasporic population driven by nostalgia try to visit their ancestral homes to celebrate and be with family. This particular sound and its linguistic representation have a deep sense of belonging and nostalgia. The drum beat accompanies the celebration at every step of the festival: starting with the initiation of the ceremony, through every step, to, finally, the immersion of the idol. So in a way, the expression is almost a metaphor for the entire festival.

2. **Tāk dum/টাক ডুম or Ṭāk ḍum/তাক দুম**

This is a generic expression of a drum beat with each syllabic particle representing two styles of drum strokes. These beats can be imagined on many indigenous drums found in the Indian subcontinent, except, for instance, Tabla and Mridangam, which have their own individual vocabulary of sounds just like the Dhāk. While not being specific to any particular instrument, the sound, however, is popularly associated with a barrel drum called 'Dhōl/ঢোল', a variant of the instruments of same or similar names (e.g. Dhōlak) existing in different languages and cultures across the peninsula. The Dhōl is smaller than Dhāk and is played on both sides, either by hands or with angularly shaped drumsticks made out of cane. This stroke sound is an expression of celebration and mirth, devoid of religious connotations. There is a popular eponymous Bengali song composed by Sachin Dev Burman that starts with this sound and its lyrics depicting that the singer is ecstatic to be playing those strokes on the Dhōl of Bangladesh and remembering joyously the lap of their Bengali motherland. Since then, the expression has been loosely particularized with the specific instrument, but that merely has popularized the expression rather than attributing a fixed analogy. For example, sometimes in the most generic way, it also depicts a chaotic way of playing the Tabla.

3. **Runujhunu/রুনুঝুনু**

Even though, by definition, not only exactly alliterative but also rhyming, this onomatopoeic sonic expression falls under the category of 'ধ্বন্যাত্মক দ্বিরুক্তি/Dhvañātmak dvirukti' or 'phonetic/sonic doubling or double utterance'. Typically, this expression is associated with the sonorous trill of a brass, bronze or silver anklet called নূপুর/Nūpur in Bangla, worn as ornaments by women as part of traditional attires or by dancers/performers, irrespective of gender, as part of a costume for a formal dance/musical performance. The sound is quite self-explanatory in the sense that when a person walks around or takes choreographed steps after wearing the anklets, they will create this sound. Not only is this expression mimetic of the sound source but it is also an aesthetic representation that is widely used in Bangla poetry, prose and lyrics. It is a semi-formal expression that appears more in written form than in everyday parlance.

Flokje (Norwegian)
Ingebjørg Loe Bjørnstad

Flokje means tangled, like my hair could be tangled and needs to be combed.
Or a knitting thread.
It could also mean that something is complicated, chaotic and messy.
Like life. Or love.

I like the sound of this word, and how it feels in my mouth when I say it. My tongue moves very rapidly and hits my palate first and then land next to my lower front teeth before it curls up in the back on the kj/ç-sound.

f ɾ u ç ə = pronunciation of flokje, written in the International Phonetic Alphabet.

Geroezemoes (Dutch)
Rutger Zuydervelt
'Geroezemoes' (pronounced 'guh-rooh-zuh-moos', with the typical Dutch hard 'g') is the Dutch word for 'hubbub'.

Although the term can just as easily describe friendly chit-chat in a nice coffee bar, as well as a room of annoyingly chatty concert-goers ruining your evening, the word itself sounds beautiful, like a little dance of the voice.

It sounds soft and gentle, sympathetic and just plain funny. I can imagine a room of people pronouncing the word 'geroezemoes' to create a nice bed of sound (doing the same with pronouncing 'hubbub' would actually result in something really absurd).

If 'geroezemoes' would be a person, it would be easy to become friends with.

- **Goception**
Daniel R. Wilson

Goception is a word invented by British chemist John Carrington Sellars, appearing in his oratorical poem *Chemistianity* published in 1873.[5] The word combines the old English 'go' with a Latin root 'praecipio', i.e. 'to command' – an unusual hybrid of languages. Goception signifies a form of chemical reaction, and while not intended as a term to describe sound, it was originally conceived purely on the basis of it sounding satisfactory to Sellars' ears in the poetic flow of his verses. According to Sellars, after contacting a language professor to enquire about the rules of verse, he received the reply: 'it is more a matter of ear than of law'; therefore, Sellars wrote his verses 'from sound' with 'lines measured according to sound', affording him the liberty to create such a new word.[6] With the Victorian musical/acoustical climate in mind (viz. Helmholtz), in the 2019 essay 'Goception in the Mess: Byways in the History of Noise's Ongoing Transmutation into Music' sound artist and theorist Daniel Wilson argued that the word 'goception' is symbolic of the ever-present osmosis of noise into music, drawing attention to Sellars' own poetic[7] illustrations of widening musical vocabularies, noises being formalized into music and futuristic means of soundmaking.

고요 *[goyo]* **(Korean), noun**
Suk-Jun Kim

Size

A literal translation of this Korean word would be silence or calmness. However, what seems to be missing from that direct translation would be the *size* of that silence or calmness. How can a word of a silence or a sense of calmness convey its immensity?

In and in

Goyo brings to the listener the scene of the silence and calmness and connects her to the soundscape. That connection is not of the observer and the observed. *Goyo* directs her to the heart of the silence, and she is in it; when she hears *goyo*, she is always, already, part of that calmness. That she being part of *goyo* is never the part–whole relation, either. What it means to listen to *goyo* is the very sense that she has the full and complete awareness that she, too, makes this silence, this calmness. This awareness, in turn, puts her in a spell under which she cannot say a word, make any move, even the slight of which would cause it to tremble. For *goyo* is a thick and heavy stillness, and uttering a word, making a sound in it, requires her whole self. It is an act of moving mountains. And the instant she does, though, *goyo* becomes airy and flies away. (See *adeukan* for more information about what becomes of *goyo* when it becomes airy and flies away).

Heã (Yanomami)
Stephen Vitiello

Heã is a Yanomami word for an announcing sound. A Yanomami shaman, named Lorival taught us this word when I visited a remote Yanomami community in 2003.

I was invited by the Cartier Foundation, Paris, to travel to the Brazilian Amazon to do sound recordings and create a sound installation that related to exposure to shamanism. The curatorial team at Cartier had learned of my work through Paul Virilio's interest in my World Trade Center Recordings. To date, I'd done little field recordings, at least not in the sense of going out into nature. In the WTC, I'd used contact microphones and a hand-built photocell device to listen to frequencies of light. I knew little of field mics, wind protection and portable power options. I also really hadn't tuned my hearing to the natural world yet.

After two days of commercial flights, I landed in an outpost town in Venezuela and boarded a tiny Cessna plane with anthropologist, Bruce Albert, and a powerful Yanomami shaman, Davi Kopenawa. We landed at a tiny airstrip, a day's walk from any other humans, greeted by the members of the community. The village is at the base of what translates to 'the windy mountain'. It took a day or so to start hearing all that was around me. Step by step, I started to listen with more care as I shed my own self-consciousness and became better attuned to hearing with and without the assistance of microphones.

On the first morning I slept in the village, the eldest shaman in the village, Lorival, came over to my hammock and said it was too bad I'd slept late as animals had come down from the mountain to be 'captured' by my things – which I took to mean that they had come to me to be recorded. When I asked him if there were sounds that I should particularly pay attention to, Lorival started to speak of *heã*. I could sense surprise in Bruce's face as he translated Lorival's words. Bruce had visited the village countless times, dating back to the 1970s and knew a lot about the culture but had likely never asked about sound. Lorival spoke of specific sounds and their meaning. He told me stories related to these sounds. Bruce translated a good deal of what was said.

Bruce later wrote about this word, citing examples of *heã* such as, 'two low notes followed by the full-throated call of the screaming piha are considered to be the *heã* of thunderstorms,

while the blue-crowned motmot's gloomy, repetitive morning song presages the "time of the fat monkeys" (the peak of the rainy season, from June to August). ("*Yaro pë heã*: Voices of the Forest Animals").' I remember hearing that the sound of a woodpecker in the late afternoon signified a woman in the village would become pregnant with her second child.

The breakthrough in research was to learn about *heã*. For me, the lasting impact was how this trip opened my ears to a world of beauty of listening to the natural world and ways of starting to hear with a greater depth, alert to layers and textures that my then-New York-attuned senses were more aware of the density and texture of city sound, industrial rhythms, the sound of a creaking building but not yet the sound of a creaking tree. Here, there were no machines. What at first seemed to be the sound of something electric would turn out to be the buzz of cicadas, what might be the thunderous sound of a distant plane could be howler monkeys, a buzz behind me, heard in my headphones turned out to be a flash of light and sound from a passing hummingbird. Even what I thought might be a malfunction of my microphone, a clicking, bumping sound was from bats flying dangerously close to my mic, seemingly smacking it with their wings in passing.

Each sound, each moment was a revelation but so was becoming aware of the changes, the transitions as one cycle of birds, insects and animal sounds ended and another began.

A scatter of memories, aided by a hard drive full of transferred tapes – a tape labelled 'Outside Village @ stream 6am; Crown 0-20:00; Royer 20:00-24:00; People coming to wash. 1st distortion is bat(s) hitting the mic'. *The clicks are intense and seem an error. Off to the left is a gorgeous call of a higher-pitched bird. To the right is a soft pulse, a combination of insects, birds and maybe wind through the leaves.* I was with Bruce and a young man who brought a bow and arrow to keep us safe. *A new calling of buzzing off to the right and a steady rhythm,*

Figure 13 © Stephen Vitiello.

Figure 14 Stephen Vitiello with Yanomami children, 2003. Photo by Bruce Albert.

only occasionally speeding up and returning to its base. The waveform verifies a stereo recording with very different voices on the left compared to the right. After a time, *the snapping of branches and a moment of voice or maybe howler monkey.* Actually, I think it's the latter. *More footsteps around 6' and human voices calling out too as people go to bathe in the morning light. There's a lovely lower-pitched whistling off in the distance on the left. As the sun continues to rise and light cuts through the trees, the sound gets louder and brighter. A deep helicopter-like sound buzzes the mic and flies start to appear too. Now, a man singing sounds like Lorival speaking – just a moment but so present – footsteps receding and then more clicks.*

Another tape, 'walking through water', recorded with a quasi-binarual setup, mics clipped to my glasses. *I can hear my own*

Figure 15 Commission of the Fondation Cartier pour l'art contemporain for the exhibition: Yanomami: Spirit of the Forest (14 May to 12 October 2003), © Stephen Vitiello.

breathing as I struggle to keep up and wish I could move more silently. To the right, I hear Bruce speaking to someone in the Yanomami language. The binaural recordings are magical in placing one in a three-dimensional space. As I move through the timeline, *I can sense that the water was deeper and heavier.*

A tape labelled 'girls, chorus'. In return for permission to bring me into the village, the women asked for glass beads which Bruce collected and brought on the trip. I remember Bruce saying that as a return thank you, we could come out and listen to the girls singing. *You sense the presence of the women, some with babies strapped to their sides. Footsteps and pauses, one sings and then the rest respond. There's a kind of repetition and variation that goes on beautifully. The file I have up is nineteen-minutes long but it is one of many. Perhaps the event went on for an hour.* The next night the boys did their own version of the same, but it was a mess of laughing and goofing around (at least my interpretation) compared to the more orchestrated performance by the women and girls. *There's a schoolyard feeling to listening only.* The memory, helped by some photos that I took, reveals figures in a dusty area, in the centre of the village – a round structure, covered in banana leaves, open to the sky in the middle. The flash of the camera captures reflections in eyes. My circa 2003 digital camera seems to be inhaling the dust and leaving spots and shadows all over the image. Still, the pictures can't come close to the hyper presence of the voices and listening with eyes closed. Towards the end, *what feels like a longer chant by one voice before the others respond, a child laughs beautifully* and then they're nearly done.

The last recording is with Lorival, as he speaks to me via Bruce's translation. Lorival tells a story and even without understanding the language, it's clear he is voicing sound effects to enhance the narrative. Bruce later confirms the onomatopoeic approach by Lorival to give me a sense of not just experience but the sounds of that experience, the sound of a bow, the arrow moving through air and the sound of a particular bird. In the next file, I hear Bruce tell me, 'he told of a myth where he spoke about the origin of the painting and the voice of the animals. In the end where says "[the animals] are discussing and choosing their call, and then they become such and such animals." But when

Figure 16 Path to Demini, © Stephen Vitiello.

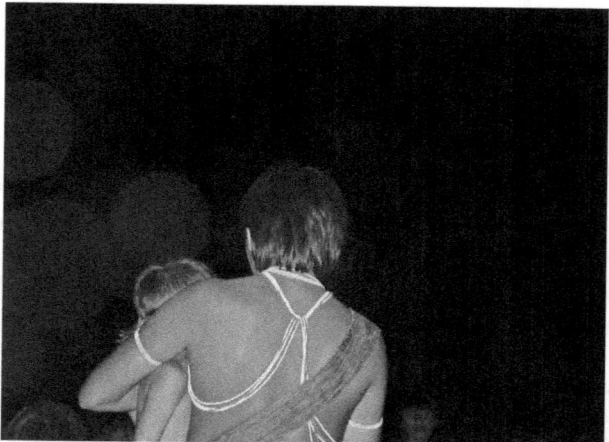

Figure 17 Women's Chorus Back, © Stephen Vitiello.

he imitates animals, the animals are discussing to choose their voice. . . . The original of the myth and the call of the animals'.

In some ways, I regret not having a more detailed document of the various calls and their significance. Thankfully, I was allowed into a world where I was an absolute outsider but privileged to listen and to learn and to bring back recordings to speak within and to share.

inaudível e inaudito (Portuguese)
Herbert Baioco

I chose these two words – inaudível e inaudito – because of the similarity between the written words themselves and also because they are neighbours in a Portuguese dictionary (HOUAISS, 2001). I guess that two words work together to create a knowledge about listening and imagination, the boundaries of what we hear.

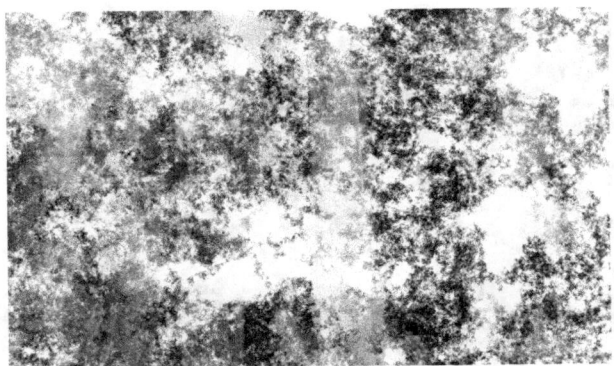

Figure 18 Inaudível, © Herbert Baioco.

Inaudito (inawdʒ'itu) – possible translation – unknown or unprecedented

The Portuguese dictionary entry for this word refers to something that has never been heard to sound or that has simply never been heard. In addition, something that no memory found and not an example. This word brings a possibility of reflection on the unknown of auditory practice, on what we hear and which remains beyond the sound and which together build the listening. A flash of old paint on the wall, an unbalanced motorcycle engine and some street vendor passing by on the street.

Inaudível (inawdʒ'ivɛw) – possible translation – inaudible

The dictionary entry about that word tells us what is impossible to hear, something that is not audible. I think this word brings an inventive way to expand the possibility of what we hear, the inaudible is not limited to just opposing what is audible, but, for example, it can be imagined.

Klang (Norwegian)
Ulf A. S. Holbrook

In Norwegian, the word *klang* really has a beautiful ring to it. *Klang* is used to explain and describe a wide range of sonic experiences, from the *klangfarge* of an instrument to the klang of a bell, the klang of a room or even a name can have a good klang. For the financially inclined, *klingende mynt*, the ringing sound of coins, describes the hard cash in your hand, the sound of the coins in your pocket or the sound of coins in your cash register – *klingende mynt i kassa*, as one would say. *Klinge*, from the Norse *klingja*, 'to ring with a bell', is related to the word klang, derived from the same in German. *Å klinge* means to give klang, to give sound to something, to sound or to ring. But importantly, it gives sound to something. Most things have, or can have, a *klang*. Indeed, you can *krysse klinge*, cross swords with someone and hear the clanging of blades, but rather it is the infinitive to how we perceive the sound of something.

Hermann von Helmholtz introduced the term *klangfarbe* to describe sound quality or tone colour. In English we usually refer to this as *timbre*, a term which is horribly inaccurate and is founded upon what it is not. It describes how sounds of the same pitch and loudness can be told apart, but only for sounds that are pitched, and thus ignoring the wealth of all possible sound and musical experiences. Indeed, *klangfarbe* can in many ways be a more accurate description of experience as it relates to the 'colour', or quality of sound, and how this is typically divorced from pitch and loudness.

The sound of an instrument is in its *klang*, and *romklang* is the reverb experienced in a

Figure 19 Klang https://en.wikipedia.org/wiki/Bell#/media/File:St_Bees_bells_in_up_position.jpg

room and tells us how the different frequencies spread, reflect and decay – this is how a room 'rings' – or *klinger*. This is also described in many other ways, for example, as *ekko, etterklang, gjenlyd, atterljom*, to name just a few. Many instruments sounding together in a room, they *klinger sammen*, they sound together and resonates with one another. When Alvin Lucier in 1969 recorded his famous 'I am sitting in a room different from the one you are in now. I am recording the sound of my speaking voice and I am going to play it back into the room again and again until the resonant frequencies of the room reinforce themselves so that any semblance of my speech with perhaps the exception of rhythm, is destroyed', he specified in the score to choose a room that has musical qualities you wish to evoke. By your voice you can evoke the *klang* of any space. Your voice can ring out into a space but the space can also ring of itself, with its different resonant qualities.

Klang describes so much more than simply an acoustic instrument, its timbre, the way it might be played or even perceived. Timbre is usually reserved for describing conventional playing on conventional instruments, but how then, as Michel Chion asked, does a trombone sound when struck? That would be its *klang*. Regardless of how one feels about analogue or digital sound, everything has its own *klangfarbe*, sound quality or 'klang'. What distinguishes different drum machines from one another?

We can talk for a long time about different qualities of instruments, analogue and digital, and about different rooms and what these instruments sound like in many different rooms and how the room has its own sound and how the instrument can transform the room and how the sound of the instrument can be distorted by a room. Simply the limited and rather formal qualities of *klang* or *klangfarbe* or sound quality. But what if there is more to *klang*?

Take, for example, Jonathan Harvey's 1980 composition *Mortuous Plangos, Vivos Vocos* for eight-channel tape. Here he used a recording of the tenor bell at Winchester Cathedral and cross-synthesized it with the singing voice of his son. This locates the piece within the physical and conceptual confines of the cathedral and draws upon the sound, effect and memories of the bell, the boy soprano, and extends the composition far outside of the confines of the cathedral. The bell, or rather, the *klang* of the bell becomes a *soundmark*, the auditory counterpart of a landmark, which R. Murray Schafer called a sound that has a specific meaning to the local community. The soundmark is unique to that place, which means that it is the character of this sound that makes the place unique. So to speak, the *klang* of the sound, how the sound resonates with the place and with the people, the *klang* of the place.

With place, we no longer are confined to think only in terms of an instrument's sound quality or the reverberant characteristics of a room. Rather we connect to a broader sense of belonging among other peoples and spaces. The sound of the bells of Winchester Cathedral has special meaning to the local community, this sound, with its ringing overtones and decaying partials, now connects all who hear Harvey's famous composition to the place where this sound exists. Voices, bird calls, rivers, foghorns, church bells and so many other sounds root a place into a cultural and acoustic geography where one can walk, listen and resonate. *Klang* is all of this; it tells us how sounds resonate around us, how sounds resonate within us and how beautiful it all sounds.

Tor Halmrast in memoriam

Knurr (Norwegian)
Jana Winderen

The first word I can think of is 'Knurr'. In Norwegian it is a word that describes a sound of an angry dog, but it is also a name of a fish, which makes the sound 'knurr'. It is curious to me that the idea of there being no sound under water at all settled in the last century, when this fish and also many others have sound-related names and have had for many years . . . and still now people are surprised when I talk about fish sound communication.

Kropsresonans (Danish, body-resonance)
Tina Mariane Krogh Madsen

A body is a mass of matter, a material form. It can be human and non-human. In this account of a resonating body, a body-resonance, it has a capacity to be affected by other bodies and relate and vibrate with them. A body is also a tool, which I as a performance and sound artist over the years have used to activate layers of sensation. It is sometimes a broken tool, it hesitates, it activates and it engages. It can be fluid and function by means of intensities, where I have worked with it as an interface (Madsen 2016; 2019), a body without organs, and a critical listening device (Madsen 2020/2021; 2021). It began in 2015 in the rough landscape of Iceland and continued in 2016, when spatial resonance experiments were created as a part of the performance installation Body Interfaces, A Performative Scripting at Grüntaler9 in Berlin (DE). This was taken further in 2017 with the sound installation Body Resonance at the art space Liebig12, also in Berlin. The latter was based on the sound of my body hitting walls and floor of an echoing space recorded two years earlier and now installed to facilitate an affective resonance with the visitors. These experiments have expanded to include other bodies as well but always with a focus on the environmental, where two further examples will be explored in this essay.

I am advocating for a relational and affective resonance, which to a higher extent move across bodies. I name this body-resonance, a combined word, which in Danish language is 'kropsresonans' – with the 's' in the middle as the conjunctive force that in its English version becomes a hyphen to emphasize this connectivity.

Resonance occurs when two or more entities are sounding together, and in music it 'refers to an oscillating system's enhanced response to a driving force at or near any of its natural frequencies' (Hopkins, 1996/2007, p. 30). In body-resonance the sounding is extended with a relating, which goes beyond the modes of audible sound. It becomes a collective body where the intensity of the encounter replaces that of volume. In creating concepts, resonance already becomes an important word, and according to the philosophers Gilles Deleuze and Félix Guattari, '[c]oncepts are centers of vibrations, each in itself and every one in relation to all the others. This is why they all resonate rather than cohere or correspond with each other' (Deleuze and Guattari, 1991/1994, p. 23). Resonance is, then, at the core of the meaning made by a concept, which, in this essay directly and indirectly, activates ideas related to resonating bodies, engaging what is happening here and now in the performative encounter.

Resonance activates the body(ies) that it is surrounded with. It is anchored in sensation – and to return to the words of Deleuze and Guattari: 'Sensation itself vibrates because it contracts vibrations. It preserves itself because it preserves vibrations: it is Monument. It resonates because it makes its harmonics resonate' (Deleuze and Guattari, 1991/1994, p. 211). This is further anchored in the ideas of sonic materialism and agency of the invisible and marginal (see also Voegelin, 2019). In body-resonance, a special encounter happens, it enters into relation with something else. It is not just a human body which sounds and relates, but multiple types of bodies, human and non-human ones. They trigger responses to movements.

- **Example 1: I resonate with those stones and the stones resonate with me**

A human body moving and sliding over geological bodies. The surfaces interact, and they encounter each other. A sound appears. An echo. The other gives in to the movement of the other. They resonate. The human body responds to the edges of the geological bodies. The stones additionally give sound together with the body of the floor, metal sheets, electronics and the spatial acoustics of the room which they vibrate with. Each variation in the movements generates a new tone, a new impulse and a gesture feeding into the next motion. This continues as long as the encounter takes place. Minor differences and variables are important in the sensuous landscape, which is body-resonance, 'kropsresonans'.

Essential is a method of tapping into these various modalities and thus be embracing ways to compose with other agents and entities. Who – and what – generates the next flow and which dynamic gesture manifests the next movement. The body-resonance of the stones becomes their voice too and a means of forwarding energy and impulses to me as a human collaborator and to the rest of the space; they also affect the audience in their different tonalities, strengths and delicacies.

- **Example 2: I resonate with that staircase and that staircase resonates with me**

A metal structure, a staircase, twirling up in the air. It is attached to other metal structures, at the same time being both organically shaped and strictly defined by its metal frame. Each step appears light since it is made as a grid structure. The fact that its skeleton is so freely available already speaks for a potential evident sound and resonance present.

When my body enters the frame of the staircase, they start to sound together: each step and movement vibrate. The shape of the staircase makes the sound flow over the edges of the sonic. It enters the soles of my feet, moves along the legs and up through the rest of my body. It pulsates back a flow into the metal and the solid yet light structure of the staircase. It multiplies. It is at the same time many bodies as one; bounces off the structure of a defined form.

The further I move upwards, the more the staircase vibrates; also body weight plays a crucial part here. Each property of me as a human body and the staircase as a metal body generate a unique resonating encounter

Figure 20 Tina Mariane Krogh Madsen, The Voices Of Stones, performance at Kiasma Museum of Contemporary Art (FI), 2020 © Elina Vainio.

and event. The wind is strong too since this staircase is located at the harbour side and when it catches between the grids and steel plates of the stairs, a third body is joining in.

- **Words resonating beyond**

My native tongue is Danish and when using body-resonance as 'kropsresonans', it additionally changes its structure through the resonance of the word itself. This is applicable to affective relations as a whole, and resonance is a way of knowing and being, with other agents and the traces of those encounters as remembering. These bodies sounding together facilitate a collective entity of resonance, tuning in and out, moving to and from, but always together. The resonance also lies in the composition of the words, of the sound and of the bodies constituting them, wherever they are originating from. Different voices in a multiplicity of new variations.

By working with concepts as resonance and combining words in new constellations and vibrations, meanings are facilitated and explored. These might challenge the traditional perception of certain expressions but give way to a collaborative mode of meaning-making across disciplines. Here sounding is expanded to include the loud and the silent as well as the minor resonances happening as a consequence of different relations and bodies joining each other, in composition.

References

Deleuze, Gilles, and Félix Guattari. *What is Philosophy?* Translated by H. Tomlinson and G. Burchell. New York: Columbia University Press, 1991/1994.

Hopkins, Bart. *Music Instrument Design, Practical Information for Instrument Making*. Arizona: See Sharp Press, 1996/2007.

Madsen, Tina Mariane Krogh. "A Distributed Body: Non-binary Becoming Through Sound". Paper presented at the 13th Deleuze & Guattari Studies Conference 2021 (not published).

Madsen, Tina Mariane Krogh. "A Liminal Body of Performative Becoming". In: *Taboo-Transgression-Transcendence in Art & Science 2020*, edited by Dalila Honorato, Ingeborg Reichle, González Valerio, María Antonia, and Andreas Giannakoulopoulos, 278–87. Corfu: Ionian University, 2023.

Madsen, Tina Mariane Krogh. "Body Interfaces – Becoming-Environment". In *Women Eco Artist Dialog, Issue 10: HER<e>TECH*, edited by P. Pilar, 2019. https://directory.weadartists.org/body-interfaces.

Madsen, Tina Mariane Krogh. "Body Interfaces – Contesting Agency". In *Interface Politics*, edited by T. Martínez and J. L. Marzo, 341–58. Barcelona: Gredits/BAU, Centre Universitari de Disseny, 2016.

Voegelin, Salomé. *The Political Possibility of Sound, Fragments of Listening*. New York and London: Bloomsbury Academic, 2019.

Loď (Slovak)
Dalibor Kocián

In music and art, the debate on simplicity is paradoxically often complex and difficult. Although there are some borders which are imaginarily defined by musicologists, fans and reviewers, there are many unprecedented realms of simplicity and types of simplicity. And simplicity in some cases equals kitsch. We often know kitsch when we hear it, but we also often miss it even though our ears are trained. Because kitsch can have many facets and there are many nexuses of kitsch and simplicity. One of them is loď.

Loď means ship in English, but for this purpose a more precise translation would be boat. The pronunciation is [logy], where ď sounds as [gy] in Magyar. Not because of the meaning, but because of the sound, its phonetics. It has uncompromising weight of sound in both words boat and loď. An impact that can be caused only by a load of unbearable heaviness of hearing or heaviness of missing. Missing musical information that would transform the otherwise simple and uncomplex piece of musical information into something more complex. Here it is not only about the meaning of the word itself but rather about the sound of it. I learned the term in one of the few lessons with our jazz harmony teacher at the conservatory school. He played a decent jazz chord progression, all chords being enriched by sevenths or fourths and sixths, and then he finally resolved the progression into a tonic chord that was too plain and simple; only a mere triad (a chord containing the first, third and fifth tone). 'Ale toto je loď, vážení!', 'But this is loď, dear friends!' He said with a bit of pain in his gesture, as if he suffered by hearing the chord and playing it. Being a top jazz musician in Slovakia it must have hurt him badly. Since then I have come across the word in many informal conversations. I emphasize the word informal because I have never seen the word written in a musicological text.

The above-mentioned triad (e.g. c–e–g) is a simple musical element, but it is not a loď per se. Whether it is loď or not depends on the context of its use. Loď emerges from the context, musical progression, comparison and subjective/objective preferences. When a simple chord is played at the beginning of a musical phrase it is different from the chord played at the end of a progression. A standard triad is a common musical element for making of, what is called in Czech, trampské písne – campfire songs or kettle songs. But using complicated seventh chord in a campfire music might result in being expelled from the camp. Of course we might debate how relevant such expulsion is from an artistic point of view and how relevant campfire music is and whether the whole genre is not loď.

A simple beat in dance music, a 4/4 house beat is not loď itself either. However, it can become such when mediocre drum sounds are used to create the beat. Or when it doesn't have the necessary groove or feeling in otherwise groovy track, because it is snapped to the rhythm grid too much. But even when a 4/4 house beat or track is groovy enough it can still seem as loď. For instance, when a DJ drops such a track in the midst of a tracklist full of complex post-club bangers. I can imagine the dancers gazing in awe and asking themselves 'why?'. Teleporting to a house party a week later, all 4/4 beat tracks are just fine and they fit well. Loď would be something rather more complex, perhaps a post-club music track.

During my studies at the conservatory I noticed that students of composition were warned, and I bet they still are, against using parallel/consecutive fifths – an interval of a perfect fifth followed by a different perfect fifth between the same two musical parts.[8] Despite this fact, one of my vibraphone compositions from the studies era does contain consecutive fifths. When my classmate heard me playing such an interval progression, she implied that such a progression is somewhat cheesy. The fact that the song was in, not too cheesy, 7/8 rhythm didn't help. Previously to my conservatory studies I played metal and 90 per cent of my tracks were based on using parallel fifths – movements of power chords. Nobody complained. But there was one element in metal music, which I knew wasn't completely loďless. Released low E power chord used as a transition to another riff called puštačky (releases) and that one I used a lot. Still, nobody 'complained'. As the metal music has progressed a lot since then, would some argue today? Definitely.

There is something I would call bearability of simplicity in music and art in general. And it is often difficult to assess the level of bearability of simplicity. How much simplicity one can bear or stand? How simple is simple enough and how much is too simple? Simple sounds, simple forms, simple chords and simple compositions can be pleasure-bringing but also annoying, hurtful to our ears or even painful to some. What does this depend on? Is the inability to perceive simple moments in music a result of honed taste and ear, or is it our snobbishness for which our senses are deprived of certain music forms and styles. The former reason, I personally think, is rather a noble one. Honed musical taste that takes years of crafting is a virtuous and admirable pursuit, which we music lovers and fans, envy in those who have it or have been able to develop. The Wire's or the Quietus' staff and John Peels of local radio stations are the ones we look upon. However, the latter reason, the snobbishness of music connoisseurs, often accompanies the evolution of one's music-listening skills. Therefore, what our local radio curator or music magazine editors might find to be a clear example of loď, I might perceive as . . . a complex symphony-like composition. Because what ordinary music lovers, the mass majority and the contraries of connoisseurs often look for in music is not complexity, it is often simplicity, simplicity of musical emotion, a simple emotion.

Sometimes it is even excruciating to learn that some music close to our hearts is (almost) loď. As a huge fan of compositions by Steve Reich and some by Philip Glass I felt really devastated to learn that some might consider these musical works too simple. I knew that person would have used the word loď if he knew it. Being in a group of contemporary music composers for a moment, I caught a trace of disdain for New Simplicity of Arvo Pärt and Henryk Gorecki. Although the word disdain might be an exaggeration on my side, looking down on simple styles is not a new thing for composers using complex structures, avant-guard expressions and tonal complexities rather than modal simplicities and rhythmic modesty. And I can't blame them for that. But to learn it is rather aching, especially when one feels a strong attachment to our favourite music. Of course, it doesn't mean too much and one needs to get over it.

On the other hand, many composers/producers strive for simplicity, plainness and unsophistication, they strive for it, when in fact, strife for something simple is in itself dichotomy, isn't it? We shouldn't strive for simplicity; it should only be achieved. Just by mere doing, mere creative activity. But how to find the balance between simplicity and lod? Where is that (thin) line cutting those two.

As very often, balance is the key. To be aware that lod' means too far, it's a boat that sailed too far into the ocean of simplicity. To be on guard that if something has attributes of this level of simplicity subjectively, when composing or producing one's music, it is time to 'thicken' the chords with more tones, to make the rhythm more complex or to perfect the sound of individual instruments. But we should be aware that if making musical elements more complex means departing from our aesthetic path or is even against our creative spirit, we can sail the lod' of simplicity and we can cut ourselves some slack.

In the end a composer or a producer needs to make a decision. Decision on what chord to use (seventh or non-seventh, sus or plain), whether to change the monotonous rhythm into something more Euclidean-like or to embellish the melodic line with some new tones. In order to make the 'right' decision it's good to follow some sort of inner compass. Compass of musical taste and endeavour that can be enriched, musical skills that can be enhanced, new realms of creativity that can be roamed and new limitations that are supposed to be torn down. It's up to our own decision to decide how we will know our way around, but I assume using lod' as a musical concept might come in handy. Specifically, when we feel that the simplicity level of our creation is painful to the ears.

MA'TOSH (מָטוּשׁ Hebrew)
Anat Pick

MA'TOSH (מָטוּשׁ Hebrew) means 'Swab'.
The object was much in use during recent pandemic.

Note: When I examine the sound impact of a verbal object I usually relate to it as raw acoustic material. Sometimes the immediate content of such an object calls for a different approach. Apparently this is the case.

Let's look at the sound particles of **MA'TOSH**.

MA (like 'Marvellous') is a sound unit much common in the Hebrew language.

Fx: **MA** מָה-CV Heb.) means 'What' (between other meanings). It's a word easy and soft to pronounce though it's up to the speaker the amount of stress or urgency she puts behind the question mark. In our case, the **MA** is like a handle to an instrument which is easy to hold without. When people speak fast, they tend to suppress it and rather hum the **M** with closed lips. The result would sound – *mmm*'**TOsh**.

Figure 21 MA'TOSH, © Anat Pick.

A different case is when **MA** ends a word loaded with meaning like mother – ('**IMA**אִמָּא Heb.). Here, also, we tend (in casual speech) to suppress the opening and quasi hum the '**I**, in preparation for the **M** to come – '**Imm** (like 'Inn', Eng.). It's an undertone produced just before you open your mouth like a hungry chick for her to respond. In contrary to the swab case, here the **MA** is what we are aiming at – *imm*'**MA**.

Let's proceed to **MA**'**TOSH** balancing point – the **TO** (like 'Tore', Eng.), which is a poignant issue with a poignant edge. One can pronounce the T with tongue pressed against the upper palate like a slingshot in hold on. When you set free the curved, highly stretched tongue and fling the sound projectile – which is the great **T** – you get a knocking sound with a touch of bass resonance due to the **O**.

To conclude there's a **SH** tail, which you can marvel upon as much as needed to make your point. As we experience a great deficiency in the matter of swabs, people usually spit the word like I've described above and fail to use the many possibilities of such a nice **SH** tail.

Here's what happens when we apply in the plural form (**MTO'SHIM** – מְטוֹשִׁים):

'. . . we need urgently more *mmm*TO'SHI*mmm*!'

Regarding the longish-narrowish form of the object in question and the nature of the test performed (shoving it up the patient's nose to take sampling), no wonder the **MA** sound, with all its sweetness and consoling connotations, is much neglected.

Minn (Scottish)
Alec Finlay

(minn)

munnr
mūða
mouth
mouther
mother

mooth

minn
mynni

mer
mere
minsmere

minnmouth
mouthminn
mouthing
murmurashen

Minni, mynni, Old Norse, *mijin*, Shetlandic, mouth of a stream, inlet; *munnr*, the mouth, from PIE **ment-*. *Minn, mijn*, Scots; *minni*, Shetlandic, the mouth, a child's word. *Mynnye*, Old Scots, *moy*, Yorkshire, mother, a child's instinctive utterance; also bay or inlet, sound or strait.

3.

(flood)

floe
flouer

floo
flod

felot
fleet

flœðrin
floodin
flodder
fluther

floodin

4.
(isle)

a
ey
ay
oy
eá
eið

in various forms these poems exist in Alec Finlay, minn*mouth* (2017).

Mololi (Sesotho)
Mpho Molikeng

In Sesotho and a few other languages in the sub-Saharan Africa, a place that boasts a big vocabulary of amazing phrases, poetry/praises, music and generally a beautiful language. There are a number of sound words that are versatile and over the years have been employed by institutions, corporations and entrepreneurs as well as students in their projects. One such word is MOLOLI/MOLODI. It loosely translates to a whistle (n) (s) or whistling (v) and Meloli/Melodi (p).

Mololi/Molodi is a very versatile sound word that encompasses an array of communicable expressions, feelings, gestures and so on. It has, over the years, changed forms, styles and uses by and from the convey or and those with whom he/she communicates and, in some instances, to communicate with animals. An early Mosotho man even came up with a saying that goes something like 'Bana ba Khoale ba bitsana ka meloli', which is and equivalent of 'Birds of the same feather flock together' even though the interpretation of the two idioms are parallel.

Mololi/whistle or whistling is an act of creating a sound up through your oesophagus and out through your pressed lips to stimulate senses that trigger certain emotions to respond accordingly. It is one of the earliest sounds a child recognizes either coming from an orifice of a loved one, or a toy from a shop blown onto, or shaken to help pacify a restless baby if not in distress. It is one sound that demands attention from both the dispenser and the receiver even when one is merely whistling for personal amusement. It is also one of many sounds or sound words that human beings easily get accustomed to from many sources of, and can easily distinguish any mololi as well as evoke a certain emotion attached to it, but not subjected to.

Birds chirp away to communicate with the world; their unique sounds that serve as their identity are also known as mololi/molodi(s) (meloli/melodi) (p). Basotho herdboys have spent countless hours mimicking the sounds of birds to communicate with their stock in the fields, and that has proven fluent as it's a practice that's been going on for many generations now. There are many parts of the world where a similar interpretation of birds' chirps as mololi/molodi exists, just as it does with the Basotho.

A direct translation of 'melody' of a song in Sesotho is mololi/molodi. It is also in many cases for Mosotho; a melody of a song and its harmonies are also defined as mololi/molodi.

A soulful taste in one's mouth is known as mololi/molodi; this is an expression synonymous with boys' chat around the fire with peers as an emphasis to help them understand the feeling.

The word in some cases is a name (first or family name, brand, street). The below-mentioned points serve only as an example. I have a friend of Xhosa descent (a South African language) whose surname is Somfiyana, which means the one who whistles. I believe in Sesotho would be Ramololi/Ramolodi or Rameloli/Ramelodi, and I have asked how did they become Somfiyanas? I heard that their grandfather was known to whistle at all times and the whole village ended up nicknaming him Somfiyana, a name that stuck with him to his death, some of his children dropped their official family name and opted for the Somfiyana one to keep his legacy alive.

(1) Mololi/Molodi Molikeng or Meloli/Melodi Molikeng. – First name
(2) Mpho Mololi/Molodi or Mpho Meloli/Melodi – Family name
(3) Mololi/Molodi Pens – Brand name or an establishment
(4) Mololi/Molodi Street or Meloli/Melodi Street – Street name

In music, Basotho use Mololi/Molodi to enthuse both the musician/dancer and the audience to signal a need to uplift the performance; either the performer wants a particular entrance or a breather in between verses or choreography, and it can also serve as a remark for an end to a performance in which nowadays a whistle is used as a substitute.

It also serves as a colloquial term for a beautiful sound (emitted by machinery) or music (blasting from the radio or live) and more often you will hear people substituting the actual lyrics of a song with mololi/molodi or add mololi/molodi as a percussion to complement an existing musical arrangement of a song.

There are at least six different types of Molodi/Mololi or Meloli/Melodi and all of which are sounded by mouth and are all age and gender appropriate among Basotho communities. They are personal as well as territorial as much as they are ceremonial.

- Serobele-se-setona – This is a sparrow sound by herd boys that cows heed. This one is a more bass/macho sound.
- Serobele-se-sets'ehali – This one, unlike the aforementioned one, is more soprano/feminine-like and still a whistle that cows can easily relate to.
- Serobele-sa-lipuli/linku – This one is a sparrow not airborne like the first two, and it's more relaxed, and herd boys mimic the sound that sheep and goat can easily hear.
- Lekolilo – This is a kind of whistle that young boys use for personal amusement with the help of hands serving as a resonator.
- Mololi – This is a common whistle that is common with men of all ages.
- Molilietsane – Ululate by women is a different kind of whistle.

Mololi: Basotho – Lesotho

Molodi: Basotho, Batswana, Bapedi – South Africa

Molodi: Batswana – Botswana

mpfft [mpft] (onomatopoeic)
Ingeborg Entrop

Mpfft emerged in 2010 in my studio. It appeared in paint applied on a stretched canvas with a paint roller. Templates of letters were used in three subsequent layers in either blue or magenta in such a way that different hues of mixed colours made the word become visible. The typeface partly refers to musical symbols and divides the word into three fragments: *mp*, *ff* and t. The reference to music greatly confuses the pronunciation of the series of characters. Are *mp* and *ff* supposed to be part of the word? Or is it only about the [t] and are *mp* and *ff* meant to be the (very contradictory) indications for its vocalization? And what are possible interpretations of the painting, its image and its sonification? All of these questions made me decide to follow the painted onomatopoeia to the places and situations it would materialize after its birth in my studio. That trajectory eventually grew into a project entitled *Framing the Bigger Picture*, which is still running, up to this very moment of you reading this text.

A short hesitating hum.

Soon after its first appearance mpfft travelled from the studio to a music conservatory. It hung for a while in a corridor, on a wall between rooms used by students for practising their etudes. Muffled sounds from behind doors seeped into the hallway and carefully married with the written characters on the wall. The painting made one aware of the soft polyphony of sounds that unceasingly filled the entire space. At the opening of the exhibition which mpfft was part of, a student played on a chest organ, which transformed the whispering air into a great variety of pitches and timbres. Mpfft liked that performance a lot, presumably

Figure 22 mpfft, © Ingeborg Entrop.

because it identified itself with the noises coming from the inner mechanics of the organ. That festive moment seemed to be the anacrusis of a joyful future.

The following year the painting had the opportunity to hang on a wall in a bank building. The natural habitat for big colourful paintings, one would think, however less so at the time. That period was still marked by the financial crisis that started with the bankruptcy of the Lehman Brothers investment bank in 2008. That event caused the financial system nearly to collapse on a global scale, and in many countries, governments were forced to support all the banks that were 'too big to fail'. Costs for these rescue operations were, at least in the Netherlands, largely withdrawn from budgets dedicated to public affairs. The cultural domain, and in particular the arts, had to face huge budget cuts that practically clearcutted the field. Considering these circumstances, what would it mean when a painting as a representative of the cultural domain is allowed to comment on events on a stage that persisted to exist due to the systematic suffocation of that very domain? Mpfft indeed.

What doesn't kill you makes you stronger, is how the saying goes. True or not, the fact is that shortly after the painting recovered from its manifestation in the financial realm, it raised its voice loud and clear through an essayistic contribution in a newspaper about autonomy, published by the Autonomy Project in collaboration with Onomatopee in Eindhoven, the Netherlands. In that story mpfft tells about its emergence and subsequent manifestations up to that point. Being an empty shell at birth, it has desperately looked ever since for a context to give meaning for its existence. In a music conservatory it associated itself with unwanted noises that appear when students practise on their winds, with the sound of failure even. In a bank building it had been struggling against commodification and its letters were interpreted as a sign of contempt and restrained anger. The story ends with a conversation between the painting and the artist, who apologizes that she had to take part in an exhibition involving a financial institute. The painting encouraged the artist to look for other ways to disclose its being, its mode of existence and its autonomy. Showing solidarity with her painting, the artist tried to do so by publishing its biography in a magazine on the agency of non-human objects. Mpfft, thus being heard, shifted from failure and anger into a sigh of relief.

Can a painting ever be more than a pretty face on a wall? Not long after the publication of mpfft's biography, the artist joined an international conference on language and social psychology. She was invited to present her view on onomatopoeia from an artistic perspective. Of course mpfft was part of the gathering, both physically on the wall and digitally included in the artist's slide show. The presentation of the artist turned the painting into a serious object of research. Nevertheless, its manifestation on the wall in the conference room did not succeed in being more than some superficial colours and shapes. Perhaps it is its construction –paint on canvas– that is continuously smothering its voice?

Slightly tired of the efforts to make itself heard beyond its surface, the image took its temporary refuge to a place it wanted to avoid so badly all along: on a wall above a couch. That couch was, however, not situated in someone's living room –more often than not the last resting place of many a painting– but in a small exhibition space where an updated version of the painting's biography was displayed in different installations that mimicked the various contexts the painting had visited up to that moment. During the opening hours of the exhibition, pictures were taken from visitors who were seated on the couch below the painting. Despite the fact that mpfft echoed throughout the exhibition in various forms, its most memorable manifestation remained that despicable place above the couch.

Semiquaver rest.

In the years that followed mpfft seemed to be stilled for good. Had its couch surfing experience been just one step too far, the final blow before its eternal silence? Bubble wrap seemed to hide not only its bright colours but also its supposed agency. There had been movements, though. Through the years the enwrapped painting had been carried from one studio to another, mostly without much care or consideration. It must have felt quite neglected at the time. Things changed completely, when another occasion to be appreciated by the public arose. The painting had submitted its face to an online painting of the year (of 2016, to be precise). Suddenly, mpfft was displayed between hundreds of other paintings, so the chance to make itself heard was rather limited. Besides, since the first selection was made on the basis of the online submitted material only, the bubble wrap cloak had de facto been replaced by a concealing monitor screen. Mpfft nevertheless believed in its qualities but, unfortunately, the painting was not selected as one of the few to be exhibited in a museum as part of the final selection procedure. Its ranking came not even close: number 1151 among 1552 submissions. Mpfft could not have been more associated with the sound of deception.

If the couch surfing experience did not bring mpfft close to surrender to its fate, the catastrophic contest adventure surely did. Again the painting hid itself in layers of bubble wrap and again the painting was carelessly moved in that state to yet another studio. Moments for a fruitful encounter with the public remained scarce. It took quite some years before another opportunity came along. That opportunity is in fact this publication, this sound word almanac, which offers mpfft again the chance to be the protagonist in a piece of writing. Being older and slightly stiff around its corners compared to its previous performance in the publishing domain, the painting encouraged the artist to write the piece by herself this time.

> *Then, a sudden escape of air, releasing accumulated tension.*

This text is the result of that undertaking. I tried to include all the manifestations of mpfft in the past ten or so years. Painting, image, sound word and sound mingled and merged more than once in the course of that task, reflecting the very elusiveness of mpfft. The physical painting is still covered in bubble wrap, but its image, a mpfft in various hues of blue and magenta, seems to continuously escape and vaporize from the canvas surface into the realm of volatile actuality. Not so long ago, for example, mpfft arose in as many variations as there were people wearing face masks to protect themselves and others from infection with a virus. It exemplifies the many contexts an index such as mpfft is able to adapt to. Failure, anger, relief, ambition, anxiety, deception and mutual fear are just a few connotations that have been pinpointed so far in that vast pool of possibilities. Perhaps I should add admiration to that list as well. It is after all that versatility that I appreciate so much in mpfft.

Musicistica (Italian)
Lucia D'Errico

> '*Music* and *the spirit of music* are obviously two different things. This is not to say that the specific "*musicistico*" may not sometimes be musical. It can be, as can the image, the gesture, sound, etc. *Music* is not always *musical*'.
>
> (Carmelo Bene [1995: 1013], translation mine)

The word *musicistica* does not officially belong to the Italian dictionary. Invented by actor and theatre director Carmelo Bene (1937–2002), its construction as a neologism follows a conventional linguistic process according to which the suffix *–istica* in its feminine form is employed 'in the formation of names of disciplines, techniques, methodologies, or activities' (Treccani, 2012: n.p., translation mine), usually implying 'a derogatory connotation [. . .] or a more technical and scientific undertone' (ibid.). Both implications are contained in Bene's usage of this word: excessive technicity and scientificity in a given discipline, to the point where it becomes grotesquely pedantic or bureaucratic. An English counterpart would then be a neologism along the lines of 'musicianistics', indicating the science, ideological current or activity (or all the three together) relating to professional musicians.

While Bene does not care to define this word as a concept and uses it scarcely and incidentally, the conceptualization of such a term and the analysis of its construction in this almanac can help us identify a specific artistic posture and a modality of music-making that is distinguished from what Bene, somehow enigmatically but nonetheless convincingly, calls *musica* (music) (or, in the wake of Nietzsche, 'the spirit of music'). In Bene's theatrical practice, music is not regarded as a discipline regulated by conventions and technologies (such as notation or musical instruments); rather, music is the force of a pure orality and vocality able to saturate the theatrical written text, a phonic flux in friction with words and situated beyond meaning and communication. In this sense, Bene defines himself as a musician, even without being one strictly speaking; conversely, *la musicistica contemporanea* ('contemporary musicianistics' [Di Giammarco,1998: n.p.]) is for him in a deep crisis, because it finds itself in a self-ghettoized state, and deprived of the driving force of real musicality.

Importantly, Bene uses the words *musica* and *musicistica* in the context of an anti-

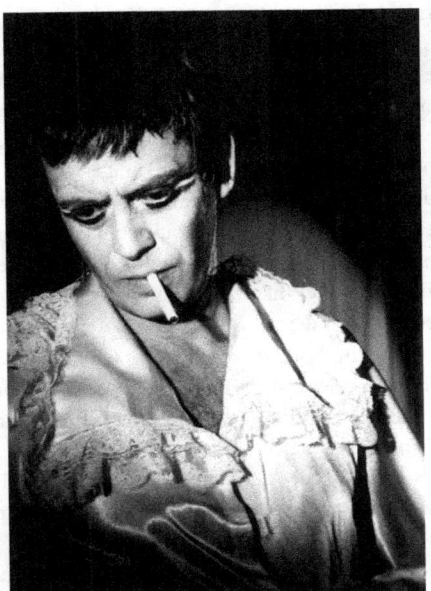

Figure 23 Carmelo Bene (Wiki Commons).

disciplinary practice directed towards his own starting artistic territory – prose theatre – and towards what he experiences as its unbearable vices, namely implementing diction, enunciation and action in order to convey a meaning and, ultimately, to 'represent' a theatrical text. Music becomes for Bene an 'outside-of-theatre' that allows him to provide a counterpoint to the theatrical text understood as the bearer of meaning and original matrix that demands to be infinitely replicated on stage. Bene upholds the supposed superiority of the musical score (see ibid.; Gilles Deleuze too, commenting on Bene's theatre, echoes the same point [1997: 246]); but the risk in creating such an opposition would be a caricaturization of both music and theatre, where the one would be 'better' than the other. In this respect, Bene's construction of a discrimination within musical practice itself (between *musica* and *musicistica*) helps in circumventing such risk. Bene recognizes that such duplicity of levels does not simply juxtapose musical practice and theatrical practice, as if the first was free from meaning, text and a particular form of diction and enunciation. Actually, positing music as an absolute 'outside of text' would have the detrimental effect of rehearsing the idealism according to which sound can arguably be conceived as a non-linguistic (or pre-linguistic) category. In Bene's view, music as sonic flux does not lie 'before' categorization and specification, to be later captured by the specialistic apparatuses of *musicistica*: rather, it is what emerges in the process of dissolution of a text, as the *product* of its combustion. *Music is, therefore, both in fight with a given text and unthinkable without it.*

Western music itself is characterized by a strongly textual dimension: the score (even if both Bene and Deleuze use this word, somehow simplistically, to contrast it with the primacy of text in theatrical plays). Written music[9] is embedded in the 'linguistic' categories of notation, which provide a segmentation of the audible continuum. Such segmentation is not only symbolic, philosophical and abstract: linguistic categories have a concrete effect on the artistic posture of musicians. In a seminal text on music semiology (or rather, on its impossibility and paradoxicality), 'Rasch' (1985), Roland Barthes relates to this problem proposing the articulation of musical linguistics in terms of 'figures of the body', or what he calls 'beats'. It is in the body (both the body of the listener and, fundamentally, the body of the musical interpreter) that musical writing gets inscribed; and different bodily reactions correspond also to different levels of textual-bodily inscription. Barthes' description of the professional musician's body resonates with Bene's aversion towards *musicistica*: 'a mediocre body, trained, streamlined [*gommé*] by years of Conservatory or career [. . .] he plays the beats like a simple rhetorical mark; what the virtuoso then displays is the platitude of his own body, incapable of "beating"' (303). Barthes also provides concrete examples, citing Rubinstein as a typical case of such professional banality, while Nat and Horowitz would have 'glimpsed' 'here and there' the necessity of a beating body. 'It is not a question of strength, but of rage: the body must pound – not the pianist' (ibid.): Barthes seems to come to a conclusion similar to Bene's, distinguishing a musical level that affects an anonymous and not necessarily trained body (Bene's *musica*) from another that remains indifferent, unaffected by the musical beats (Bene's *musicistica*: Barthes' pianist is too professional and therefore too mediocre).

On the one hand, then, *musicistica* seems to imply that a musician coincides too much with a text. Too preoccupied with the analytic textuality of music, the musician forgets his/her own body (Barthes uses terms such as 'bypass' or 'annul', ibid. 307). Would it then mean that in order to forestall *musicistica* one has to redirect one's practice towards one's own body as a locus of subjectivity able to contrast the capture of external objectivity? Let us take another example. In the short video 'Carmelo Bene in musica' (1980), Bene discusses with Sandro Bolchi the lieder singing of Dietrich Fischer-Dieskau. Bene describes it as 'mellifluous, caramel-coated, round', and 'the summa of what a singer should not do' (translation mine). In contrast to such a sentimental way of moulding phrases through extensive use of vibrato and 'filatura', Bene proposes Heinrich Schlusnus' technique, where 'the plane is still; still still still' (ibid.). In the examples proposed (Schubert's Lieder An die Musik), we can hear Fischer-Dieskau shaping musical phrases through the infinite nuances of his subjective expressivity, making them swell or wane along the profile of passions. By contrast, Schlusnus' voice occupies a single plane: a wall of sound, as if restrained, compressed. But it is precisely this stillness that seems to allow Schlusnus to operate an exploration in place of a single vocal band, producing an incredible amount of variation and nuance in a very restricted sonic range. Fischer-Dieskau's singing seems to be too concerned with the exterior 'meaning' he is trying to convey. Subjectivity, passion and emotion are still too meaningful and therefore still devoted to the representative aspects of the musical text.

Bene's conception of *musica* as opposed to *musicistica* has then nothing to do with displacing the interpreter's focus away from sterile, 'streamlined' objectivity and towards warm, passionate subjectivity. Both object and subject positions are the business of meaning; they are, so to speak, 'too textual'. As Barthes also argues, the body per se does not stand in idealistic opposition to writing: training, habit and discipline (both in the sense of a code of behaviour and in the sense of a branch of knowledge) are performative forces able to inscribe the body as textuality. Bene's *musica* is, therefore, an attempt to define an artistic posture beyond both subject and object, which are actually two sides of the same coin: they are each other's product and cannot but engender an infinite rebound in their mutual mirroring and identification.

References

Barthes, Roland. 'Rasch'. In Barthes 1985c, 299–312. First published 1975 as "Rasch," in *Langue, discours, société: Pour Émile Benveniste*, edited by Julia Kristeva, Jean-Claude Milner, and Nicolas Ruwet. Paris: Seuil, 1985.

Bene, Carmelo. *Opere. Con l'autografia d'un ritratto*. Milan: Bompiani, 1995.

Bolchi, Sandro. 'Carmelo Bene in Musica'. *Variety*, 8 May 1980.

Deleuze, Gilles. 'One Less Manifesto'. Translated by Eliane dal Molin and Timothy Murray. In *Mimesis, Masochism, and Mime: The Politics of Theatricality in Contemporary French Thought*, edited by Timothy Murray, 239–58. Ann Arbor: University of Michigan Press, 1997. First published 1979 as "Un manifeste de moins" in *Superpositions* by Carmelo Bene and Gilles Deleuze (Paris: Minuit), 85–131.

Di Giammarco, Rodolfo. 'Carmelo Bene: Nella vertigine di Leopardi'. *La Repubblica*, 1 June 1998. Accessed 14 July 2021. https://ricerca.repubblica.it/repubblica/archivio/repubblica/1998/06/01/carmelo-bene-nella-vertigine-di-leopardi.html.

Treccani Encyclopedia. (2012). '-ista e – istico'. In *La grammatica italiana*. Accessed 14 July 2021. https://www.treccani.it/enciclopedia/ista-e-istico_%28La-grammatica-italiana%29/.

Figure 24 Thalassa, © Tania Giannouli.

summer house in Peloponnese. When mistral is blowing, you can feel, hear and smell the wind, yet, due to the special local geography there are no big waves. The sea moves, feels like the sea itself is travelling. It's a warm wind that takes you away with it. Swimming in the sea, when mistral is blowing, is for me a liberating experience. It reminds me of past summers, when there were no worries of the adult life, happy innocent vacation and the feeling that the summer will last forever. Feelings of freedom, connection with nature, hope and reassurance that all will be well. This word is, for me, connected with happiness.

Μαΐστρος (Greek)
Tania Giannouli

Μαΐστρος (Mistral) or maestro (in Latin languages) is a north-west wind. It blows during most of the summer and has soft to moderate intensity.

This is my favourite wind, since I have connected it to summer vacation at my family's

Namaroku (Japanese)
Tomotaro Kaneko

In the 1970s in Japan, an activity called Namaroku, where people enjoyed recording various sounds, became popular. Audiophiles carried portable recorders and recorded not only music played at concerts but also conversations, birdsong, steam locomotives and festivals. The term 'Namaroku' is an abbreviation of Nama-Rokuon (live recording), which means the recording of live sounds rather than prerecorded sounds such as music from radio and disc records. It seems to be similar to sound hunting (chasseurs de sons), which appeared in Europe and the United States from the 1950s to the 1960s and has connections to present field recording practices. However, it was unique because of its deep connection with the Japanese youth culture, audio culture, music and broadcasting of the same period.

Namaroku could be included in field recording in the broadest sense, but it is different from field recording in that it included the recording of live music performance in a studio and concert hall and that of electronic music. Moreover, the extensive practice by amateur recordists of the time came to be called Namaroku, and the meaning of the term became vague. It is certain that Namaroku was a culture that became popular for a short period of time in a local area, mainly among those who were interested in audio. Some might see it as a strange mini-column inserted into the cultural history of sound technology in Japan. Otherwise, it might provide valuable knowledge for thinking about the relationship among the human being, technology and sound, especially in terms of creativity. This article will first provide a historical background of Namaroku, and then it will outline how it became popular, and finally, it will reconsider the significance of this culture.

At the height of the boom of Namaroku, articles featuring the activity could be found not only in audio, music and broadcasting magazines but also in general and juvenile magazines. However, it seemed to be the audio culture that started and centred the movement. Thus, take a look at the development of the audio culture in post-war Japan. Through the rapid economic growth that began in the mid-1950s, audio devices became recognized as luxurious home appliances. In the early 1960s, there were stereos that became big hits. To appeal to a wide range of consumers, one advertised that it would 'never release a new model'. In the latter half of the 1960s, the component stereo, which sought even higher sound quality and stereo effects, became popular and increased the number of audio enthusiasts in Japan.

One of the factors that led to the widespread use of tape recorders, which are indispensable for Namaroku, was the full-fledged development of FM radio in the late 1960s. Tape recorders were mainly used for private copying of music broadcast on the radio, called 'air check' in Japan. The emergence of the cassette tape recorder, which went on sale in 1965, made the practice of outdoor recording more accessible to many people. The following introduction of the high-fidelity portable cassette tape recorder in the early 1970s was a major catalyst for the popularity of Namaroku.

The background of the history of audio described above shows the transition of the post-war Japanese society from the rapid economic growth to its end. Television, which spread in the households with the 1964 Tokyo Olympics and other national events, has greatly changed the media environment in Japan. Stereos, once items of luxury, gradually became associated with an alternative youth culture to the mainstream culture represented by television. The manufacturers of consumer electronics also regarded stereos as the next leading product after television. The 1970s also witnessed the development of an industrial society from mass-produced reproductions to cultural services. With these backgrounds, Namaroku was accepted by young people as a way to enjoy recording live sounds rather than reproducing radio broadcasts and records.

The following two movements in the 1960s could be considered as prior practices of the boom of Namaroku. In the early 1960s, a recording contest without any restriction on the recording subject was held by a technology magazine dealing with electronic engineering. This contest was organized in reference to an existing amateur film contest and was supported by a group of amateur builders of tape recorders. In the latter half of the 1960s, as interest in stereo technology grew, audio manufacturers began to hold 'recording sessions', where participants gathered at live concerts with recording equipment. Even today, the term Namaroku is sometimes used to refer to such recording sessions. This movement could have led to the spread of interest in live sound recording among audio enthusiasts.

The Records of the Audio Union Recording Contest, which began in 1971, showed that audiophiles were discovering a variety of recording subjects in the early 1970s. However, what probably led to the major expansion of Namaroku was the hi-fi portable cassette tape recorder introduced in the early 1970s, as mentioned earlier, and its sales promotion activities by audio manufacturers. Sony, for example, not only published articles on Namaroku in audio magazines but also used field recordings made in Africa for radio commercials and organized Namaroku tours. In addition, a series of introductory books on recording and the appearance of the rajikase (radio cassette player), which was a combination of a radio receiver and a cassette tape recorder, also contributed to the early spread of Namaroku.

The popularity of Namaroku was also linked to the domestic travel and steam locomotive boom at the same period. The 'Discover Japan' campaign of the Japanese National Railways, which started in 1970, brought about a boom in domestic travel among young people. This campaign emphasized individual experience in unfamiliar places rather than family

Figure 25 'Outdoor special: 21st century special machine', *Rokuhan (Recording Hunting)*, no.12, Tokyo: Ongaku No Tomo Sha Corp, 1977, p.6., scan taken from an old out-of-print magazine, no photographer credited.

Figure 26 'Seikatsu no oto: Namaroku nyumon (The sounds of life: Introduction to Namaroku)', *FM Recopal*, vol. 1, no. 2, Tokyo: Shogaku-kan, 1974, p.42, scan taken from an old out-of-print magazine, no illustrator credited.

sightseeing of famous places. Namaroku, which, as previously mentioned, represents the activity of live recording rather than dealing with prerecorded content, was in line with the aims of this campaign. The steam locomotive was also 'discovered' by many young people as it was about to be discontinued in 1976, and the fascinating sound attracted many recording fans.

The heyday of Namaroku was in the late 1970s, when radio programmes and magazines specializing in the culture appeared and the Sony All Japan Namaroku Contest was held on a large scale. In 1976, the All Japan Amateur Recording Association was founded, and it joined the International Federation of Soundhunters. However, by this time, various recording practices were called Namaroku, and the term's meaning became blurred. The prize-winning works in the Audio Union Recording Contest included the following: a hi-fi Namaroku work, electronic music and progressive rock by youth, sophisticated drama by a university broadcasting club, comedy using vocal mimicry, snapshot of everyday scenes, improvised music on a musical instrument by beginners and audio play by kids.

In 1979, the radio shows, magazines and several contests all came to an end. If we limit ourselves to technology as a factor towards the end of the boom of Namaroku, we can point to the advent of the CD, mini-component audio, synthesizer, MTR, home video cameras and the Walkman. Further research is needed to understand how the emergence of these technologies is connected to the changes in the Japanese music and society in the period.

What is the significance of looking back at the short-lived minor audio culture? Of course, it is an important case study in the history of soundscape and field recording. It seems difficult to find the names of famous musicians among the winners of the Namaroku contests: some of the winners went on to become music directors, engineers and designers. However, if musicologists attempt to do research not on famous musicians or popular styles, but on the hard-to-document, trial-and-error nature of amateur musical practice, Namaroku could provide valuable examples.

In the cultural history of post-war Japan, the records of Namaroku are a remarkable documentation of creative consumption by ordinary people on the threshold of postmodernism and consumer society. Audio equipment was one of the most coveted consumer electronics by young people in Japan in the 1970s, in addition to being an important corporate export. Namaroku could be regarded as one of the strategies by the manufacturers of electronics to market audio equipment as consumer-generated media in a postindustrial society. In addition, there seems to be a continuity in the creation of amateur content using 8-mm film cameras, sound recording and video. Therefore, by taking Namaroku into consideration, we can envision a cultural history of creation by amateurs using reproduction technology that goes beyond the distinctions between media platforms and that between the aural and the visual.

Namaroku was the first opportunity for many young people in the 1970s to hear real sounds through recording devices and to create original content with sound equipment. Therefore, this culture could be a useful sample for thinking about the relationship between human beings, technology and art. How did the practitioners perceive the difference between their ears and the microphones, and how did they reconstruct the world they heard through the tape recorder? Also how did they connect the new media with the existing cultures around them to create unique hybridity? In the pursuit of these questions, we might glimpse clues to sound works that we have not yet heard of.

References

Smith, Martyn David. 'Sound Hunting in Postwar Japan: Recording Technology, Aurality, Mobility, and Consumerism'. *Sound Studies* 7 (2020): 64–82.

Kaneko, Tomotaro. 'Namaroku Culture in 1970s Japan: The Techniques and Joy of Sound Recording'. *Aesthetics (Japanese Society for Aesthetics)* 23–24 (2021): 60–75.

napevalka 'напевалка' (Russian)
Jelena Glazova

I often work with: вылка – 'vylka' – long vocal sound recorded in order to be transformed with the help of filters into a drone recording; шипелка – 'shypelka' – long hissing sound recorded in order to be transformed with a help of filters into a drone recording; напевалка – 'napevalka' – vocal sound with an element of melody, recorded in order to be transformed with a help of filters into a drone recording (this is the most common of the three, so I chose that as the heading for my entry). The sounds are recorded via a recorder or directly in a PC programme via a microphone. I try to improvise each time I record these vocal sounds, so all pieces sound like a sound poem, sometimes more aggressive, sometimes tender. For me those long vocal pieces (usually phonemes), hissing sounds and humming sounds represent the unpronounced speech; they are in a way substitute of a poetic speech. The sound recording then is transformed with the heavy layers of filters into something unrecognizable, but I nevertheless always try to leave a warm feeling to the sound, so that it doesn't sound too 'synthesized' or mechanical; there is always an undertaste of human voice in its essence. Hence for me these drone ambient sounds are a continuation of sound poetry practice and interpretation of musique concrete experience, seen through the lens of digital technologies. I want the impulse sound for my recordings to reverberate with emotion and post-processing to make it 'calmer' and structured, allowing me to perform intellectual manipulations. The word 'выть' in Russian means to produce sounds in grief (to howl, to wail), so this word refers to very negatively hued emotion; the word 'шипеть' in Russian means to produce sounds while trying to negatively attract someone's attention (to hiss), so this word refers to very negatively hued emotion; 'напевать' in Russian means to make a low, steady continuous sound, like singing to yourself (to hum), for me it refers to a positive emotion (like singing to yourself in a good mood). But in all three cases I try to use this type of sonic utterance as something neuter, allowing PC programme post-production to manipulate the sound and to interweave the sounds into a soundscape that wouldn't suggest an immediate emotional reading. I'd like it to reflect what Eliane Radigue stated about her own compositions: 'music as a reflection, where you see your own emotions'.

I am interested in the perception and possibility of different readings of the same work, I search for perceptive switch possibilities that could arise from the juxtaposition of media, such as text, image and sound. I am also preoccupied with the issue of physicality and individual's physical identification in private/public space, that's why I often use myself as a source of material for work. As a conceptual sound artist I am primarily using my voice as a generator, heavily altering it and manipulating with the help of digital processing. I consider that type of vocal elements deconstruction as a form of expressing unpronounced speech – connecting it with my practice as a poet. As a visual artist I am often dealing with physicality, which is also a basis of my work as a sound artist.

Conceptual justification for my artistic practice: sound art approach – experimental/drone/noise/ambient as an art form, with occasional use of poetic texts. As a conceptual artist I am primarily working with filtered recordings – usually my own voice (as a generator) or other conceptually justified material (voice as a material is justified due to practice as a poet), heavily altering it and manipulating it with the help of digital processing. Considering voice processing to be a kind of deconstruction of vocal elements – a form of expressing unpronounced speech (as a metaphor for individual's unconsciousness) – connecting it with practice as a poet and the issue of physicality (preoccupied with my practice as an artist, physicality also serves

Figure 27 Jelena Glazova Sound Around Kaliningrad fest 2013, © Alexander Lyubin.

Figure 28 Jelena Glazova Process Festival Riga March 2017, © Aivars Ivbulis.

Figure 29 NU performance fest 13 11 20 Tallinn © Madis Kurss.

as a main basis for my sound art practice). Formally, technique is inspired by the sound poetry tradition of using the human voice, having roots in Dadaism and Futurism. Drone/noise (drone as an archaic form, ancient Near East, etc.) form is a metaphor for an eternally flowing development of 'primary' matter versus human body development (at the macrocosmic/microcosmic levels). Combining interest in postmodernism with its collage aesthetics and deconstruction practices and interest in Eastern philosophy with the concepts of nothingness and eternal development; for example – deconstruction/fragmentation practice (methodologically – granular synthesis as a digital processing) as one of the metaphors reflecting the concept of unsustainability of elements, as a non-existence of individual as an indivisible substance, but a chain of perceptive phenomena (David Hume – Buddhism connection).I have chosen experimental and drone/noise forms of expression after disappointment with tonal music, as I did not find it creative enough as a form of expression. (I was playing a few instruments and had classical vocal training; as an adolescent I had performed parts in children's operas.)

Lately, I have started using my texts reciting in my performance practice: I read out the phrases which are then transformed via PC programme and sound through a PA system as altered material, flowing, massive soundscapes that are manifold with the layers of pronounced text phrases. The soundscapes grow in mass and soon take up all the performance space, forming overwhelming sound canvas; soon there is no space for a pause, a sound wall is taking up all available resources. I am often using recitation, list of phenomena or concepts, appearing in my texts, as an example of post-conceptualist poetry practice, allowing uttered sentences to be short, to allow maximum overlapping of sonic structures – here is an example of such a text (English translation by Laura Hendrickson):

* * *

a glossy child's figure
emerges from darkness
shimmering like a 3-D hologram
sparks flicker in his eyes
must be static in the transmission
his mouth stays closed
but from somewhere in his throat comes
a sweet childish voice
softly reciting –
fear of poverty
fear of old age
fear of impotence
fear of infertility
fear of venereal disease
fear of ostracism
fear of war
fear of the electric chair
fear of aids
fear of cancer
fear of medical error
fear of corpses
fear of terrorism
fear of dying in a nursing home
fear of being buried alive
fear of earthquakes
fear of floods
fear of getting laid off
fear of offing yourself
fear of car crashes
fear of weapons
fear of wrongful conviction
fear of prison
fear of coma
fear of plague
fear of syphilis
fear of ghouls
fear of satan
fear of zombies
fear of the atom bomb
fear of being raped with a strap-on
fear of obscurity
fear of transparency ... (...)
the transmission continues
as we walk down a dark corridor
and finally come out on a cliff
overhanging the sea
my buddy rummages in his pocket
and holds out a capsule
i take it and the sea vanishes
the cliff recedes
and the childish voice falls silent
is there another way?
i ask my buddy
but he only shrugs
his head ripples slightly
like there's a bad signal

I became interested in philosophical issues of sound self-sustainability (John Cage, La Monte Young, etc.), historical origins of drone music (Ancient Eastern musical tradition), minimalism, especially mentioning inspiration from work of Eliane Radigue (an example of combining Eastern philosophy with the Western minimalist practices) and twentieth-century avant-garde and experimental music tradition. I consider drone as a metaphor for the eternal flowing development of 'primordial', 'primary' matter on the macrocosmic level as opposed to human body development's physicality. My sound is also formally inspired by sound poetry tradition of using human voice (Dadaism and Futurism practices) that is linking my sound work with my work as a poet.

Nuppe Nappe (Dva original)
Barbora Ungerová
Halabala (CZ)
Higgledy-piggledy (EN)
adverb
Synonyms:

disordered, disorganized, chaotic, slapdash, sloppily, anyhow, messy

Meaning:

This word describes something, what is in confusion or disordered. When we do things without thinking or when we do something randomly, lightly and easily. Something that's in the space above and below, right and left.

Application:

'I don't understand free jazz, I feel the tones are *Nuppe Nappe* in it'. 'We placed the furniture *Nuppe Nappe* in the room'. 'Dadaists compiled words *Nuppe Nappe* into their poems'.

Expressions from Nuppe Nappe Derived:

Nuppsnapp means doodle, child's drawing.

Nuppsnapp-art is the art style of Jackson Pollock.

Nuppnapp modi means sloppy, careless fashion style.

Nuppstopf is special sweetly salty dish cooked in one pot.

Nuppofonnik is music style of cacophony bordered on dissonance.

Nuscheln [ˈnʊʃln or ˈnʊʒəln] (German)
verb. Translation: *to mumble, to mutter.*
Malte Kobel

There is a certain embalming warmth when you hear someone *nuschel*. When I think of the softening of the tongue's articulatory functions, I imagine a speaker from the southern area of Hessen, somewhere close to Frankfurt or Wiesbaden. In the mouth of such a speaker, the word *nuscheln* performs its own sounding and the tongue becomes a brushstroke that slurs and smudges any rough consonant edges. This Hessian *Nuschler*in*[10] grumbles with their mouth closed. *Nuscheln*: *n* on its way to an *m*; consonant infinity, *nuscheln* knows no beginning or end. And so too, the following *u*, absorbed by the vastness of the deep *n*, barely emerges from the throat. The faint weight would lie on the *sch*, cloaked in a hush of a soft ʒ sound, as if a gentle breeze rustles through dried leaves in a forest. There is little articulatory precision in the act of *nuscheln*; it comes to life in a murky murmur. Vowels vanish in the mouth of the South-Hessian *Nuschler*in*: from *sch* to *l*, the *e* is swallowed and merely exists on the written page, turning *nuscheln* into a moan that would spell *n sch ln* or *nuscheln*. When a *Nuschler*in* mutters the word *nuscheln*, you can hear their tongue dissolve some delicious cotton candy. It gets carried away by the rush of sweetness, articulation withers and what emerges from this mouth and what is heard is a self-pleasing moan that speaks volumes.

Etymology

The English translation of *nuscheln* is *to mumble*. Mumbling, again, seems to relate to the German word *mümmeln*. *Mümmeln* differently to *nuscheln*, however, does not connote any notion of speaking or vocalization but refers to a specific way of eating. Rabbits are known to *mümmel*: they churn over their food in the mouth rapidly and continuously in order to break up bigger chunks into digestible bits. *Mümmeln* thus demands a well-functioning jaw that can perform the strenuous task of repetitive chewing. Other than the English word *mumble*, however, which to some degree asks its speakers to open their lips in order to utter the soft plosive *b* but also the initial letter *m* – positioned much closer to the front of the vocal cavity than the deep lying *n* – *nuscheln* can be grumbled with almost no lip movement or lip opening. Etymologically, *nuscheln* hints at another opening that allows sound to leave the speaker's body: the nose.

In the act of *nuscheln*, the mouth is often bypassed in favour of an uttering through the nose: for reasons of speaking with a mouth full, physiology and sinusitis or for the joy of playing with sound and speech. *Nuscheln* derives from the Early Modern High German *nuseln*, *näseln* (Kluge, 2012b) or *nüsselen*, 'referring to *nose*' (Pfeifer, 1989, S. 1184).¹¹ Particularly *näseln* brings into play and into speech the word *Nase*, engl. *nose*. To *nuschel* is to speak through the nose and not solely through the mouth. In etymological dictionaries, it is here not a rabbit but a horse that is asked to demonstrate the activity of *nuscheln*. The horse's *Nüstern*, that is, its nostrils, relate to the word *nuscheln* by way of *nuseln* (see Kluge, 2012a, Pfeifer, 1989). The German *nuscheln* activates a physiological function of communication that is usually reserved for olfactory perception. Where horses use their nostril's sensitivity for olfactory communication, the *Nuschler*in*'s nose has less immediate communicative functions but enables speaking as a sensing of oneself, a self-pleasing murmuring. What this extension of the senses brings forth is thus not speaking as a form of outward-directed communication but rather a sense of self-consumption that is perhaps always already part of any enunciation. When I *nuschel*, I eat my words.

The joy of *nuscheln*

Nuscheln can be defined as an utterance whose function is not primarily intelligibility, communication or signification. Rather than obeying the dictum of communicable speech, *nuscheln* takes pleasure in its own obscuring of meaning by privileging sound over sense. *Nuscheln* is an act of speaking that disregards the congruence of verbal language, if just for a moment. The *Nuschler*in* indulges in the sonorous feeling of juggling bites of speech in the mouth – softening consonants, touching syllables with tongue, teeth and lips and even swallowing whole chunks of words. This is a play with a verbal language where words live inside the mouth and its cavities and are only partially projected out into the world. In contrast to *proper* communication models that are based on intelligible and successful communication and that have a directional relation between sender and receiver, the enigmatic figure of the *Nuschler*in* is both sender and receiver and renders meaning secondary (see Figure 1). The feeling of one's own sonorous flesh, the vibrating of nasal cavities, the murmuring of phonemic matter and the sensual moving within the vocal cavities bare joy, just like the horse that sighs or snorts in comfort and that indicates its joy through nostril sounds.¹² Where *nuscheln* is a pleasurable utterance directed mostly to oneself, less so to another, it functions as a form of consumption of speech and self. *Nuscheln* allows for a private vocal act in the public of speaking.

The confounding of mouth and nose and their distinctive perceptive and productive functions in the act of *nuscheln* is also highlighted in another encyclopedic entry of the word, this time in the Brothers Grimm's dictionary of German (Grimm and Grimm, 2022). Their entry on NÜSCHELN, NUSCHELN not only discusses mumbling as a form of speaking through the nose 'or otherwise incomprehensibly' but also lists another meaning of the verb that emphasizes again the involvement of the nose (ibid.). *Nuscheln* is here defined as '*schnüffeln, wählerisch suchen*', that is, *sniffing* or *selectively searching*, in particular, 'mit der nase worin herumwühlen', to rummage or burrow for something with the nose (ibid.). This version conjures not a horse but a pig or a boar, where the snout's rummaging would signify the gesturing of searching for articulation. Here, the *Nuschler*in*, nose ahead, digs not for truffles but for similarly valuable goods: words. *Nuscheln*, after Jacob and Wilhelm Grimm, could be thought as a ruminating before and for the word.

Sound and sense

When *nuscheln* troubles successful and directional models of communication and instead emphasizes the sonority and jouissance of unintelligible uttering, it also brings forth the question of aesthetics and its possible potentials for disrupting the grasp of linguistic signification. What to make of such a vocal act that is not in the service of communication?

Michel de Certeau has discussed the functions of inarticulate voices, such as glossolalias – fictitious languages – and other non-sensical or gibberish vocal acts (Certeau, 1996). Intelligible speech, Certeau argues, depends on non-sensical utterances; they make the articulation of speech and its institution possible and meaningful in the first place. The mumble can be included into this 'field of statements' (Certeau, 1996, 30) that falls outside of the 'institution of speech' (Certeau, 1996, 40) because it 'escapes the control of speakers and [. . .] violates the supposed division between speaking individuals. It fills the space between speakers with the plural and prolix act of communication and creates, mezza voce, an *opera* of enunciation on the stage of verbal exchange' (Certeau, 1996, 30, my emphasis).

The singer and songwriter Mark E. Smith, the only consistent member of the band The Fall, is a notorious *Nuschler*, both in his speaking and singing voice. A short video interview that was recorded as part of the BBC Culture Show in 2007 demonstrates this particularly well.[13] British comedian Mark Skinner, a confessed The Fall fan, talks to Mark E. Smith for his fiftieth birthday in a pub in Wolverhampton. Skinner represents the BBC with all of its institutional and hegemonic modes of speaking. Mark E. Smith, on the other hand, defies what Certeau calls the 'institution of speech' (Certeau, 1996, 40) and indulges in being the enigmatic figure of the *Nuschler*, mumbling to himself unintelligibly. As listeners, we can only gauge what Smith is trying to say, but it seems his *nuschelig* speaking voice is less interested in *saying* anything because it is already on the verge of becoming Smith's murmuring singing voice.

Nuscheln, after Certeau, has a utopian quality, a potential for the 'devaluation of institutions of the word (ecclesiastical or social), the deterioration of customs and practices, the debasement of linguistic convention' (Certeau, 1996, 41), arguably also because *nuscheln* is already a speech act on its way to becoming musical. The operatic voice, like any musicking voice, diverges from linguistic intelligibility, it escapes – even if only temporarily – the control of speech, meaning and signification. Similarly, what I hear in the act of *nuscheln*, its self-pleasuring consumption and the auscultation of vocal cavities, is not just a voice 'on the verge of speech' (LaBelle, 2014, 129) but perhaps a voice on the verge of music.

References

Certeau, M. 'Vocal Utopias: Glossolalias'. *Representations* 56, no. Autumn (1996): 29–47.

Grimm, J., and W. Grimm. 'nüscheln, nuscheln, verb'. *Deutsches Wörterbuch von Jacob und Wilhelm Grimm*, 2022. Accessed 31 July 2022. https://www.dwds.de/wb/dwb/nuscheln.

Kluge, F. 'Nüster'. *Etymologisches Wörterbuch der deutschen Sprache*. 2012th edn. Berlin, Boston: De Gruyter, 2012a.

Figure 30 NU Performance festival Tallinn 13 11 2020 © Madis Kurss.

Kluge, F. 'nuscheln'. *Etymologisches Wörterbuch der deutschen Sprache*. 2012th edn. Berlin, Boston: De Gruyter, 2012b.

LaBelle, B. *Lexicon of the Mouth: Poetics and Politics of Voice and the Oral Imaginary*. New York; London: Bloomsbury, 2014.

Pfeifer, W. (ed.) *Etymologisches Wörterbuch des Deutschen: H-P*. Berlin: Akademie Verlag, 1989.

Om (Sanskrit)

Budhaditya Chattopadhyay

Recent events in the world have been showing that nations and cultures are tending to turn inward. Does this sociopolitical tendency of going inwards contribute to deeper self-awareness and personal freedom within a social structure? The primary aim of the right-wing politics tends to proliferate a sense of protectionism and conservatism in the society, hindering the sense of freedom in the social formation. The inward-looking tendency then is actually a closure of the self rather than opening it up to the s(urr)ounding world. Such an approach stems from a nostalgic longing for the past in a search for the revival of a grand narrative (e.g. a colonial and imperial past for Europe and America – the Global Norths, and a pre-modern glory for the Global Souths). These narratives neither exist nor have the affordance, legitimacy and validity in a new world order. In what possible ways, then, one can imagine a self-aware social situation that aims to sustain its systems and mechanisms for times to come, not via exclusion and closure, but through reciprocity and exchanges with others outside of its borders and fences. My contention is that, this mode of self-awareness can be developed from a celebration of the selfhood and fostering the subjective formation, where being aware of oneself within today's planetary constellations is empowering, as opposed to an ego-driven idea of a closed political collective (e.g. state- or nationhood). How can a practice of genuine self-awareness be nurtured and sustained in an increasingly divisive and hopeless world? It is this context, in which the unpacking of a word like *Om* and visiting the concept hold some timely relevance.

Om (or Aum) is a widely known and well-practised Sanskrit sound word. It is an onomatopoeic word that is pronounced the way it sounds: *Om* starts with a somber 'o' and rests at 'm' for as long as the resonance in the throat stays and the larynx can hold the breath. Adding a 'u' between *o* and *m* may prolongate the sound and add a reverberant dynamics. Therefore, the single syllable Om is composed of three sounds – a, u and m. As per Sanskrit grammar, when the sounds 'a' and 'u' come together, the resulting sound is 'o'. Thus, a + u + m results in Om. The utterance of Om is attuned to 136.1 Hz known as 'The Om Frequency'. Arguably, the frequency of 136.1 Hz resonates with the earth and has been associated with light, warmth and joy. Thus, practising Om helps experiencing a restful state of the mind sometimes described as self-aware, meditative and serene. This tone also corresponds to the sacred expression 'Amen' exercised in the Christian religion to allegedly bring out spiritual sensations. Used first as a mystical sonic symbol in the Vedic chants dating from 1800–1000 BCE and in the major Upanishads dating from 1000–200 BCE, Om takes on a concrete ontological purpose in the later Upanishads and Tantric texts that form the sacred sound philosophy in Kashmir Shaivism from eighth to twelfth century CE. Om has been understood to contain human knowledge to help a listener unify with *Brahman*, the Absolute Reality, as a higher form of speech evolving into a definitive *mantra*.

What is the ontological foundation of this claim about sonic spirituality? Given a phenomenological account from a personal experience, I can describe the sensation of pronouncing Om. When I practice Om closing my eyes, the meditative and transcendental sounding of the word through voice transmission channels of my body (e.g. throat, larynx), it does engage both mind and the body and triggers an embodied unification of the two where the sound becomes the connecting force. A repetitive performance of the sound word creates a rhythm that feels grounding in the sense that the body slowly opens up and re-attunes itself to the innately natural forces usually dormant in the everyday social and cultural bounds. As the rhythmical vibration passes through the body turning it into a resonant chamber, the instrument of the body performs the natural music found in tree murmurs, winds, clouds, water and other elementary sources. The body thus feels

Figure 31 OM [Public Domain].

at peace, finding the communion with nature it always seeks for. Practising Om makes it possible for the body to become sensate.

In essence, what the practice does is to allegedly consecrate the body through a wash of ambient vibrations – hold in a breath by the resonant vocal cord. In doing so, an intensified sense of self-awareness is awakened through a sonic meditation that allows for an intensified attunement with the surrounding world and thereby enhances the capacity to connecting with nature and other elements that constitute nature more inclusively. As a Vedic ritual, the utterance of Om produces a distinctly unifying reverberation in the body that creates a harmony within the random, contingent and chaotic movements of the world around. The moment one pronounces Om, it produces a cyclically repetitive sonic chord, which lasts for several seconds as long as the breath lasts – long enough to touch the healing centres (or chakras) in the body. The moment an attentive listener voices the Om, he/she/they enters a state of trance where the listener is self-aware and sensitive, thereby empowered, and receptive to the surrounding environment. This trance state is the one with inner peace – Om works as an antidote to the prevailing chaos preparing the listener for a spiritual contemplation. The vibrations of the interconnected mind and body produce a multiplicity of sounds by generating a sense of collectivity, generating the apparent oneness of the universe. Attuned with the phenomena of natural worlds, Vedic poets of Om chants developed a strong reverence for occurrences in nature. Examples of this include the breaking of the dawn in light and sound, mysterious power of wind and the movement in water.

There is a strong esoteric quality in how the word Om is defined in Hindu religious texts, aesthetic discourses and Sanskrit literature. Religion scholar Azalea Tang suggests, 'the sound of Om was the means by which divinity descended into the human world. Made intelligible to humans, Om became an aid of unification and was used as a way of establishing and maintaining a connection with divinity'. (2014: 2). Among the multitude of elements associated with the religious experiences, the sound is one of the most intriguing senses in characterizing the subconscious and often incomprehensible aspect of the religiosity and divinity. Many religious traditions across the globe regard the power of sound to be creative and evocative. The sacred sounds are used to communicate the core ideologies and rituals as well as focus on the personal aspects of religious practice. In the Hindu and Buddhist religious traditions, Om is an embodied methodology of connecting with the divinity that is embedded in the personal sense of becoming. In the religious texts like Vedas, Om can be understood as an entry point, or a mantra, to engage with the essence of the text. When chanted or sung repeatedly, Om serves as a unifying support for the meditative thought-stream to emerge from self-study and self-understanding. Om signifies the essence of *Brahman*, or the ultimate reality, consciousness or a realization of the *Atman* or the universal self – the eternal core of the personality accommodating and reflecting the universe in it. Fundamental to this perspective is the belief that 'word and consciousness, or the divine will to relay meaning, are inseparable. Because of this, spoken word has important ramifications for both the divine and empirical worlds. In Hinduism, the specific sonic relationship between the divine and empirical worlds can be illustrated in one phrase: Om' (Tang 2014: 1).

Music and sound practitioners, particularly the ones working within a South Asian context, are aware of this sonic inheritance. In an interview Oscar-awarded sound designer Resul Pookutty informs,

> There was one thing called Aryanaadam – the first sound, which is 'Om'. There

was something preceding by silence and followed by more silence. We are the only civilization who believes in it. My Oscars speech was about that. I come from a country and civilization that has given the universe a sound. A sound preceded by silence, followed by more silence and that sound is 'Om'. That's why I thrust upon that. Today, we are sadly the only civilization in the world, which has completely forgotten where we came from. (Chattopadhyay 2021b: 227)

This lamentation denotes the serious lack of careful and nuanced sound works often found in modern Indian aural cultures, e.g. film and contemporary music production (Chattopadhyay 2021a). Revisiting the word Om also enriches the underexplored field of aural cultures in the Global South (Chattopadhyay 2023) to provide a helpful interpretation of the element of sonic meditation in the light of contemporary times and conditions, which demand returning to inner sanctums for reconnecting with the planetary self. The word remains as a constant but esoteric reference and keynote, from which sound practitioners, artists, and musicians often draw their inspiration.

References

Chattopadhyay, B. *Sonic Perspectives from the Global South: Connecting Resonances*. New York: Bloomsbury Academic, 2023. (forthcoming).

Chattopadhyay, B. *The Auditory Setting: Environmental Sounds in Film and Media Arts*. Edinburgh: Edinburgh University Press, 2021a.

Chattopadhyay, B. *Between the Headphones: Listening to the Sound Practitioner*. Newcastle upon Tyne: Cambridge Scholars Publishing, 2021b.

Tang, A. *The Power of Syllable OM in Hindu Thought: Creative and Unifying Qualities of Sound*, 2014. Senior Thesis for Partial Fulfillment of the Requirements for the Religion Major. Prepared for *Religion 401: Senior Colloquium* at Davidson College.

'ÖÖ' (Estonian)
Robert Jürjendal

'ÖÖ' means *night* but sounds really odd. To pronounce it properly, one needs to put his/her lips into tube position. Because 'ÖÖ' consists of two vocals, you can let it sound as long as you need to breathe. Some more – if you look at these two letters then you probably will see eyes. And if you see this kind of eyes in the darkness then you might think you have met an owl. Owl in Estonian is 'ÖÖKULL'. If you are working in the night time then your job is called 'ÖÖTÖÖ' (*night job*). English *night* and German *nacht* sound both elegant and sexy. Estonian 'ÖÖ' is absolutely far from this. For example, Estonian word 'ÖÖKIMA' means in English *to vomit*. 'ÖÖ' is a powerful word. Estonian popular podcast is called 'ÖÖÜLIKOOL', which means *night university*.

ørenlyd (Danish)
Jacob Eriksen

'At en Forfatter kan beslutte sig til at skrive saaledes, kan vel synes snurrigt, men lader sig dog forklare. Medens Literaturen i vor Tid, viser, at der saa godt som Intet præsteres [...], kan man næsten ikke høre *Ørenlyd* for Løfter, Trompetstød, Subscriptionsvræl, Skaaler, Bebudelser, Forsikkringer, Becomplimenteringer o. s. v'.[14]

The now antiquated but still used Danish term *ørenlyd* is composed of the two words *øre* (ear) and *lyd* (sound). It is often used in the sentence 'jeg kan ikke få ørenlyd' (I cannot hear myself, or, I have no space for my voice to be heard by others), which would be felt in a very noisy environment.

Figure 32 ÖÖ © Signe Jürjendal.

The sound of oneself that cannot be heard in the situation would rarely refer to a specific sound. Often the sound of oneself would be understood as one's own thoughts, utterance or speech, which then cannot be thought nor communicated because of other louder voices that occupy busy ears around.

Ørenlyd is thus both an actual physical fact about difficult sonic conditions in a noisy place, where one's voice or thoughts cannot be heard, but also, and more importantly, a psychological situation of power relations where the loudest voices get heard and quieter voices drown between them. To hear someone, you need *ørenlyd*, you must have that specific amount of silence it requires for the sound of someone's voice to reach another's ears. This means being able to stay quiet, to listen, to give someone *ørenlyd*. A sonic space for listening.

Thus, you would unconsciously consider your or someone else's need for *ørenlyd* less when you actually have it yourself. Contrary to the American proverb 'the squeaky wheel gets the grease', where the loudest voice attracts the attention, *ørenlyd* focusses on the frustration of being unheard or unable to voice. An utterance spreads into existence because of its given *ørenlyd* and thus differentiates itself as something more than idle chatter.

'otonai (おとない)' (Japanese)
Kazuhiro Jo & Maho Fujimoto

In this entry for the almanac of sound words, we would like to describe a Japanese word 'otonai (おとない)'.

'otonai' is both the title of a group exhibition with five artists including one of the authors (Jo) and a curator, another author (Fujimoto) (Otonai, 2020), and a 'sound word' with the following meanings.

'otonai'

1. a sounding and the sound/acoustic itself. ('hibiki')

2. a sign/indication/touch ('kehai')

3. a visit ('otozure')

4. a fame/rumour ('uwasa')

As the meanings state, 'otonai' represents both the central theme of this exhibition, 'sound', and 'visit' at the same time. And, for the latter, we intended to have the meaning in a double sense.

One is the 'visit' of the acoustics to the museum, a place mainly focuses on the visual arts. The other is the 'visit' of the artist living in the present to the place of the 'mueum', which has a 'mansoleum' character at its core, as Theodor W. Adorno has articulated (Adorno, 1967).

For the exhibition, we aimed to revitalize the art museum and the art scene in Fukuoka through these double 'visits' and encounters.

According to a Japanese kanji ideograms (Chinese characters) scholar, Shizuka Shirakawa (1987),

'Sound is "otonai" (a sounding/visit) of a god'.

It is one of the properties of art to be a medium for capturing things that are invisible, untouchable and inaudible in a visible, tactile and audible way.

As Paul Klee describes,

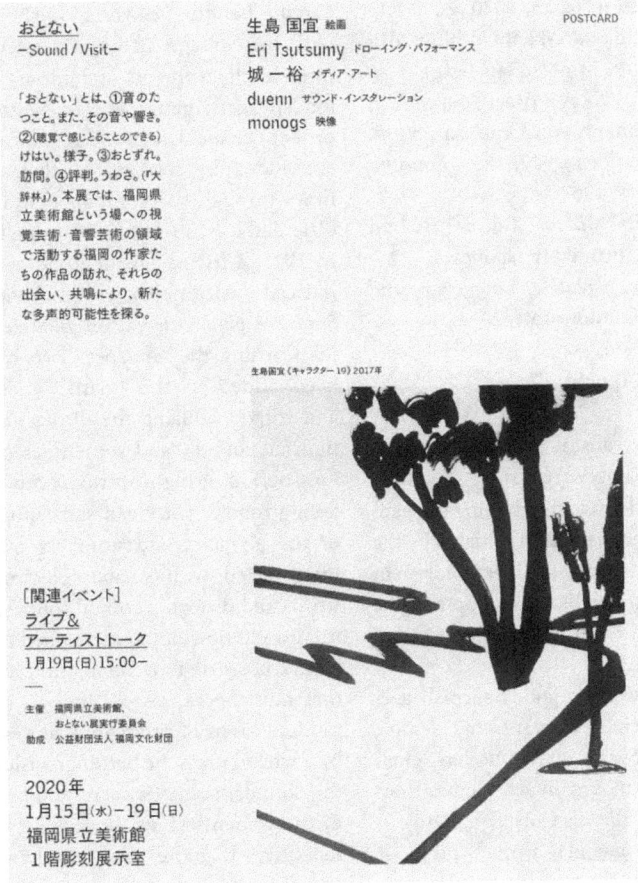

Figure 33 otonai © Daiki Goto.

'Art does not reproduce the visible; rather, it makes visible (Kunst gibt nicht das Sichtbare wieder, sondern macht sichtbar.)' (Klee, 2014).

If we take the quote literally, then confronting 'sound' in a museum could be an opportunity to reconsider the nature of the visual arts, or even of art itself.

As a result, we have investigated polyphonical possibilities of exhibition and museum itself in combination with paintings, installations and sounds through the exhibition.

References

Otonai-Sound/Visit-Exhibition. Fukuoka Prefecture Museum, Japan, 2020. 2020.1.15 ~ 1.19. https://fukuoka-kenbi.jp/blog/2019/12/23_kenbi11049.html (in Japanese)

Adorno, Theodor. 'ValŽry Proust Museum in Memory of Hermann von Grab'. In *Prisms*, edited by T. Adorno, 175–85. London: Garden City Press, 1967.

Shirakawa, Shizuka. *Jikun*. Tokyo: Heibon Publisher, 1987. (printed in Japanese)

Klee, P. *Paul Klee: Creative Confession and Other Writings*. London: Tate, 2014.

Patasurréalisme (French)

David Nadeau

translation: patasurrealism

phonetic writing: patasewrrealisme

In the field of sound art, I am pursuing the path of 'patasurrealist' reconciliation initiated by the Czech writer and collagist Albert Marenčin (1922–2019): a member, like me, of both of the Surrealist Movement and the parisian Collège de 'Pataphysique:

'Je suis une des rares exceptions: surréaliste et pataphysicien en même temps, suivant l'exemple du fameux POISSON qui, tout en étant SOLUBLE, reste toujours intact'. (letter from Albert Marenčin to Etienne Cornevin, 2015).

These two movements work, more or less in the shadows, towards a desirable re-enchantment of the world through poetic and analogical thought. Many are the Pataphysicians who ignore themselves and among surrealists, I must say that the Pataphysical, Faustrollian temptation is very strong. Some surrealists have been and are Pataphysicians (Marcel Duchamp, Bastiaan Van der Velden, Jean-Pierre le Goff), and vice versa. More and more, for me, the two are inseparable. I believe in this bringing together of the pataphysical 'principle of equivalence' and the 'Point Suprême' of the Surrealist quest.

Circuit bending, Black MIDI and electroacoustic percussion are thus used as tools for exploring the unconscious and searching for 'imaginary solutions' (Alfred Jarry, Gestes et opinions du docteur Faustroll, pataphysicien). Circuit bending consists of short-circuiting old[15] low-voltage, battery-operated electronic musical instruments (children's toys with loudspeakers, guitar effects, synthesizers), in order to create new sound generators. Switches are added by hackers so that the current flows through the components of the circuit differently than what was originally designed. In 2015, a friend gave me one of these noisy musical instruments, made from the *Little Smart Alphabet Desk*, an old electronic toy for learning the alphabet. Two buttons have been added to the board, whose pressure and rotation during the ditties generate new unusual sounds, and sometimes over a fairly long period. A high-pitched, deep or strangely failing robotic voice can start spouting letters of the alphabet and numbers out of order, interspersed with various electronic noises, words and distorted animal sounds. Above all, there are times, all too rare, when the machine seems possessed by something very precise that must be expressed through it, since the random loops of prodigious noises, generated by it when I press the button in order to modify the sounds, seem to correspond strangely to the movements of my inner life. The complex, repetitive or, more rarely, evolving rhythms, and the rich textures generated by the hacked toy, from which I create my pieces of electronic

Figure 34 Electroacoustic Percussions © David Nadeau.

sound art, correspond to certain aspects of the 'real functioning of thought' (André Breton, *Manifeste du surréalisme*). Inner speech is made up of not only discursive language, however symbolic or metaphorical it may be, but also the most concrete characteristics of the sound phenomenon. The discoveries are numerous; it's about staying on the lookout. During recording sessions, the toy is placed on a plugged-in electric guitar and speaker towards the microphones, and the gain and reverberation effects of the amplifier can bring out certain subtle sounds and arouse quite a bit range of new textures.

In the field of electroacoustic percussions, my search for personal rhythms, both naive and incantatory, is close to rhetoric and speech. I explore the rhythmic and timbral possibilities of metallic objects and structures using a contact microphone plugged into an electric guitar amplifier. The contact microphone, pinched on an object, captures vibrations that are not audible to the naked ear. I don't use editing very much, and the main mixing job is the 'spectral' superposition of the same track at several different pitches. The pitch of the track is changed to get several other lower-pitched tracks, at regular intervals, of five or eight semitones, and a few more high-pitched ones, which are then layered and mixed together. In studio work with rhythmic loops generated by my circuit-bending instrument, the same processing is applied, but only with lower-pitched versions of the original track. In fact, the sounds coming out of the toy's speakers are already saturated with high frequencies. By lowering the pitch of the sound loop, the quality of the loop changes substantially and some frequencies become more audible, while others are hidden. The final mix is the sum, as harmonious and balanced as possible, of the chosen possibilities.

The instrument used on the piece 'What You Sing Comes' To Life[16] was invented for the surrealist exhibition *The Archeology of Hope*, organized by Merl Fluin and Paul Cowdell, and which took place on Small Hope Beach in Shanklin (England) from 7–23 June 2017. For this project, each participant was invited to create an exhumed object from the future, a fragment or a document linked to it, from a notice written by another participant. I still don't know who wrote the leaflet I received or who got mine!

'What you sing comes to life / / We believe this object to be part of what is known as sounding treasure, which is a contemplative / expressive surrealist nurturing art'.

Figure 35 Sketch for What You Sing Comes To Life (2017) © David Nadeau.

After receiving this archaeological notice, I very quickly drew a sketch, of which I sent a copy for the exhibition. Then I searched in small shops and flea markets to find pieces that might be suitable for the construction of the object. I found almost all of them, with the exception of a long elongated shape (15–20 cm) which could have recalled a tongue.... Once at home, I discovered that all the chosen pieces (an electronic board with potentiometers, a metallic sun with rays ending in a spiral, a bell and a mask for crafts) fit perfectly.

The object, which was originally conceived as an imitation of an electronic musical instrument, a kind of *oral theremin*, quickly showed the potential of a true electroacoustic musical instrument. This is because each of the rods, or rays of the sun, vibrates in a particular way, which can be picked up and amplified by a contact microphone plugged into an electric guitar amplifier. For 'What You Sing Comes To Life', I layered three versions of the same track, at different pitches. This fifteen-minute piece, in three parts, was shown during the 'ritual performance' evening which closed the exhibition *The Archeology of Hope*.

My piano compositions are akin to Black MIDI, a genre of music that uses MIDI files to create remixes of musical pieces, containing a large number of notes. The name refers to the visual appearance of the scores, on which the large number of notes makes the blackened page more or less illegible. My book *Partitions Pour Piano/Piano Scores* includes 14 solos and 1 duet, or 286 pages of sheet music. The pieces are sheet music generated automatically using online software, from transpositions into MIDI files of some of my electronic and electroacoustic art pieces. In fact, I don't know how to write scores.... To create 'The Egg Hatches At Dawn'[17], the MIDI file was converted to wav, which was reconverted a second time to MIDI, in order to result in a much more stripped-down composition. To mark the publication of this book, I have invited artists to perform certain pieces among those which are transcribed there. They could interpret the pieces on the piano, synthesizer or any other instrument, freely draw inspiration from notations and work from recordings of these pieces on the keyboard or from MIDI files. This project, titled *Davidurgic Neadors: Playing David Nadeau's Compositions*,[18] was released on the French netlabel Camembert Électrique (formerly called No Records).

Figure 36 David Nadeau, a page from The Egg Hatches at Dawn, Partitions pour piano/ Piano scores, p. 13. © David Nadeau.

I am, or have been, an active member of a few communities of experimental sound or noise artists, such as Classwar Karaoke, Institute For Alien Research, Electronic Cottage, and I participate in various netlabels regularly publishing compilations (Paracelsian Records, No Records, etc.). As part of the Generative Loops Compositions project, sound artist Thomas Jackson Park created for me,[19] as for the other participants, a 'live mixing console' using eight short sound clips of some of my electroacoustic and electronic music pieces. It is thus possible to create online your own mix, from these eight extracts playing in a loop or from some of them.

The tactile qualities of a descent into the Underworld combine the elements of a vibratory architecture. Stereophonics adjusts vertigos to each other. The microphones capture the structure of the overwhelming manifestation. Strange intensities brush against the Orphic sounds, to the rhythm of the recreation of the world in oneself.

References

The Archaeology of Hope (exhibition catalogue). Head Louse Press, 2017.

Corrales, Miguel Pérez. *Surrealismo : El Oro Del Tiempo*. Teneriffe: Ediciones Del Archibrazo, 2016.

Pflotsch p͡flo:tch (Swiss-German)
Johannes Binotto

A sonographic state of matter in between.

I fear I was all too quick in accepting to write about this sound I know so well but do still not really have a concept or even an idea of how to work and what to do with it. I just thought it was a funny choice of subject. I already regretted it the next day. But then, only now, by writing about it, by translating (or rather attempting to translate) a disturbingly obscure acoustical object into readable letters on a page I started to become aware of how central it is to me, precisely in its peripherality.

The noun 'Pflotsch' and its derivatives like the adjective 'pflotschig' are expressions that are at the same time extremely common in as well as highly specific for the Swiss-German dialect. Interestingly enough, these words that no one in the German speaking part of Switzerland will fail to understand, quite certainly sound enigmatic in all the surrounding countries. Although more recently a Swiss software firm has adapted and anglicized the term for their weather app 'Pflotsh', which is aimed at the whole middle European market, it remains doubtful that the term it picks up on will really find traction outside Switzerland.

So what is it? Pflotsch – like its English counterpart 'slush' – designates the mixture of partially melted snow with ice, water and dirt. In the nineteenth century, the word also designated wet soil and street dirt in general according to the Schweizerische Idiotikon, the dictionary of Swiss dialect expressions.

Obviously, there is an onomatopoetic quality to the words 'Pflotsch' and the adjective 'pflotschig' as they, when spoken aloud, remind one of the sound that is produced when walking through wet and melted snow. So as the onomatopoetic name already instructs us, the auditory quality of this natural phenomenon is one of his major aspects. Or to put it differently: the substance of Pflotsch is always already auditory.

However, it is worth to further consider also the physical substance of Pflotsch, namely its peculiar properties as a mixture of ice and water. Solid ice and liquid water are what in physics are called different states of matter. Pflotsch, as situated oddly in between the solid and the liquid state of H_2O, is thus also physically a dubious object. In thermodynamics this state between solid and liquid is called soft matter and in this particular case more precisely 'liquid crystal' – a state of matter which combines contradictory aspects like the fact that it may

Pflotsch pflo:tch (Swiss-German)

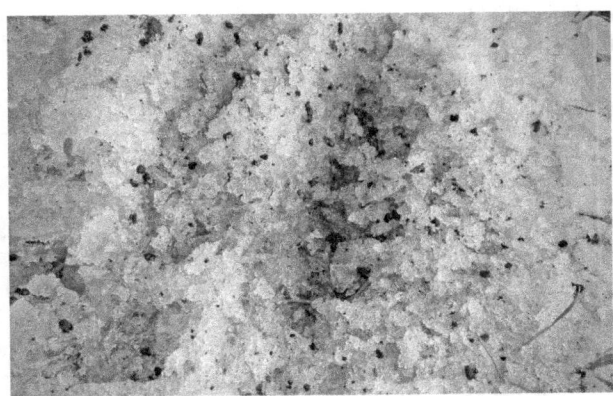

Figure 37 Pflotsch © Johannes Binotto.

behave like a liquid but has its molecules oriented in a crystal structure. These unique properties are also what eventually lead to its usage in liquid-crystal displays, the so-called LCDs. As we learn, the substance of Pflotsch and media technology are closely related.

Like the neither fluid nor solid but soft matter of liquid crystal so too can Pflotsch as an acoustical phenomenon be considered as hovering between different states, namely between the indexical and the symbolic. Listening to Pflotsch as only indexical would mean to reduce it to an objective event (like walking in slush) that produced it. Listening to it as only symbolically would, on the other hand, reduce it to what it means to me and what subjective associations it evokes in me. However, rather than just remain in one of these two realms Pflotsch seems to constantly move back and forth between them: as much as the sound of Pflotsch reminds of actual events like, for example, of how as I child I used to enjoy to stamp through the heaps of slush accumulating at the side of the road, I at the same time experience how the sound of Pflotsch becomes detached of any natural source and seems to take a life of its own.

Pierre Schaeffer in his *Treatise on Musical Objects* discusses the two listening modes of the indexical and symbolical to then differentiate them from what he calls 'the sound object':

> When I listen to a galloping noise on the gramophone, the object I target, in the very general sense we have given the term, is the horse galloping [...]. When I listen to speech, I target concepts, which are transmitted to me by this medium. [...] There is a sound object when I have achieved, both materially and mentally, an even more rigorous reduction than the acousmatic reduction: not only do I keep to the information given by my ear [...] but this information now only concerns the sound event itself: I no longer try, through it, to get information about something else (the speaker or his thought). It is the sound itself I target and identify. (Schaeffer 2017, 210–11)

Pflotsch becomes a sound object precisely then when it is no longer clear what produced it but when it still remains so concrete that it does not allow to assign symbolic meaning to it. It is, therefore, very fitting that my favourite audio recording of Pflotsch was quite certainly not done in actual snow, nor was it even done intentionally: some day in January 2020 I got informed that on the voicemail of my phone is a five-minute message from a hidden number. When listening to it I quickly realized that I must have received a so-called 'butt dial', an unintentional phone call with the phone of the caller probably sliding around in their pocket or bag producing all these 'pflotschy' sounds. To this day I have no idea who tried to call me then nor can I know what exactly the source of these sounds was. So both the indexical and the symbolic route to make sense of this sound are blocked for me and what remains is instead a pure mysterious sound object that I can nonetheless revisit and listening to without ever completely understanding it. There is a distinct rhythm to it that may remind me of someone (or something) walking and the different timbres may give me the impression of wading through a wet, slushy substance while at the same time I am rather certain that this is not how this sound came to be but more likely that the wading through slush is rather a microphone brushing against fabric while also picking up muffled environmental sounds.

Like in my example of an accidental recording, sent from an unknown number, we hear Pflotsch appear most insistently not where we might expect it, not in actual winter situations outside, but most of the time suddenly and surprisingly elsewhere. And not as an intentional product of musical production but as an aleatory event and not as something picked up by recording devices but as an accidental side product by those recording devices themselves (like the butt-dialled phone sliding around in your pocket).

So we often encounter it in liminal situations, at corners and borders between different actors, and between different media. Like in the case – my second favourite example – of a vinyl record has been played through and the needle brushes against the closed groove on the inside that prevents the stylus from crossing over the paper label.

As we know the closed groove was also one of those crucial 'experiments in interruption' (Chion 1983, 20) used by Pierre Schaeffer in order to isolate and free the sound object from its supposed source:

> The closed groove did, indeed, give an object in the sense of a thing, hidden away, as it were, by destroying another object. We have just observed that this involves not so much an objective discovery as putting the participant in a different situation. [. . .] Breaking it [the record] up informs him [or her] about the object, which he [or she] has – momentarily – destroyed only to hear it better. (Schaeffer 2017, 311)

This typical repetitive sound signalling to us that we should stop the turntable or put the stylus back to the beginning is another instance of the sound object we are interested in: Pflotsch! Pflotsch! Pflotsch! Once more we find ourselves in an odd in-between state: the music has come to an end but the record is still playing on. Does the sound of the locked groove belong to the record or not? What is its status in relation to the rest of the record? In literature we might call this a paratext – a textual instance that both come with the 'main' text but still is not really part of it, guiding towards while at the same time resisting interpretation (cf. Genette 1997). So too the brush of the needle against the end of the record remains forever at the border between record and not-record. As if trudging on an endless street covered in Pflotsch with nowhere to arrive. Forever trapped in Pflotsch, but continuing, always going on, aimlessly, ploddingly, in one word: pflotschig.

References

Chion, Michel. *Guide des objets sonores*. Paris: Éditions Buchet/Chastel, 1983.

Genette, Gérard, *Paratexts: Thresholds of Interpretation*, translated by Jane E. Lewin. Cambridge: Cambridge University Press, 1997.

Schaeffer, Pierre. *Treatise on Musical Objects: An Essay across Disciplines*, translated by Christine North and John Dack. Oakland, CA: University of California Press, 2017.

Parafonie (Dutch)

Mark van Tongeren

As an émigré from the Lowlands for more than ten years, I became aware that English will never be my native language (let alone the local Mandarin tongue spoken here in Taiwan). Every month I would come across a word that I really only just knew in Dutch, like *waterpomptang* ('adjustable-joint pliers' according to my dictionary), or a word that may be untranslatable (not to mention useless in most countries) like *binnenvaartschipper* (sailor on an 'inland navigation vessel'). Both qualify as sound words in the sense of their unique, obscure syllabism.

As soon as I became an émigré a strange longing for things Dutch took hold of me. For example, I began to wonder where those incredible place names dotting the Dutch landscape came from, which cause similar syllabic rapture and even conjure up exotic destinations.

It's a small step from there to onomatopoeia, that treasure house of lush, poetic, quirky expressions found in any language around the world, an eternal source of inspiration for nursery rhymes and folk songs. Music at the edges of your tongue and your brain. But no, that's too easy; there must be something more specific. Besides, when you start with them, you cannot stop.

What about the words that act as a gauntlet for any newcomer to Dutch? Due to a diphthong between a highly uncommon and a common vowel, the succinct *ui* ('onion') instantly identifies the immigrant from the truly native speaker. (Secret: the initial vowel is not one of the fourteen vowels that exist in isolation in Dutch, except in The Hague dialect; it is also harder to pronounce than *sproeiauto*, despite the confusing sequence of all cardinal vowels).

The expression *keel schrapen* ('throat clearing') is guttural in form and content, as it literally translates as 'rasping the throat:' Picture it! With its horrendously sounding *sch* combined with *r*, it is the fright of every foreigner learning Dutch and responsible, I presume, for a dear composer-friend telling me that Dutch 'sounds even more appalling than German'. *Ouch*.

That brings me into the territory of words about sounds – conventional and, if I may put it

Parrega

Rucphen

Nuth

Tzummarum

Suameer

Rooth

Sexbierum

Kadier en Keer

Parregea

Figure 38 Some time after coining 'my' word, I found this little 1918 booklet, entitled *Strange Words in Music*. Its fifth print brought the total amount to no less than 60,000 copies! As many people might have stumbled upon the word *paraphonie*, meaning 'progression in fourths and fifths'. © Mark van Tongeren.

that way, *non-onomatopoeic* sound words. Like the poetic *omfloerst* ('veiled') . The comical *grinniken* (chuckle). The musical *grasharp* ('grass-harp', from Anton Quintana's wonderful children's novel *Bodpa*). Or the remotely sonical, scientific *vagale syncope* ('fainting due to a disturbance of the nerve feedback system that guides the heartbeat and blood pressure'). But in the end none of the words and sounds mentioned qualify. I can only think of one word that is worth sharing in this volume because it has absorbed me so much. That is a word I invented to describe a musical-sonical evolution.

The chosen word did not exist when I began thinking about it: it was a feeling as well as an acute awareness and a realization. It was the sense that there had been something going on in my mind and in the functioning of my body as the primary source for receiving signals from a so-called 'outside world'. Something puzzling, because of its strangeness, and inspiring, for the vast panorama of listening possibilities it suggested, within and beyond the imaginable.

As a student I had learned to hear out, and gradually to amplify, to single out and to select different overtones from the spectrum of my voice. What started out as a daily practice of listening to my own vowels became hearing the faint melodic leaps between a pair of them (like you can hear between aa and oh, or oh and oo), and from there onward to making melodies with the overtones of my voice. I had dug into the very matter of sound colour, or timbre, in order to find what it is made of, and discovered its building blocks. But neither overtones nor overtone singing was new, and those terms sufficed to describe the acoustic principle and the vocal technique. What kept my enduring interest is the question of the reorientation of the mind so that it can start to hear the voice in its full spectrum. What was the proper way to articulate this new field? Overtones are essentially part of acoustics and psychoacoustics (though some cognitive scientists might now claim it as theirs). Overtone singing was merely a new singing technique and a rather obscure one at that. What I thought about was not limited to this obscure vocal technique, but something that applies to all educated, well-informed, curious listening. That is, all listening that does not stay in the same grooves but actively looks for change.

I was concerned with the way in which several questions converged in a single, relatively new phenomenon: those of the art of musicking (making music by actual people and listening to it); those of knowledge of music and sound from a theoretical perspective (be it acoustics or musicology); and those of embodied perception and cognition, such that it showed their adaptable, dynamic nature, their ability to reset some internal parameters and focus on a timbre's spectral content.

I began the search to construe a word containing an element signifying that we are dealing with the entire sound spectrum and its harmonic and inharmonic components as a playground, and an element signifying a ramification of musical knowledge that hitherto did not acknowledge this new terrain. It soon became clear that one of the signifying syllables, the confix, would be -phony. Derived from Greek phonos, *–phony* features in a widely used system of musical sounds and concepts: monophony, homophony, polyphony and a host of other terms. Each of them fences off one mutually exclusive segment of musical procedures, yet none of them describes the key point I want to add, which is the role of perception, cognition and awareness to change the content of the procedure or element of sound. The missing element turned up while browsing the *Encyclopedia of Language*, where David Crystal writes, 'The laryngeal, pharyngeal, oral and nasal cavities can all be used to produce "tones of voice" which alter the meaning of what is said. These effects are sometimes referred to as effects of "timbre" or "voice quality", and studied under the heading of vocal *paralanguage*'. Though I wasn't interested in language as meaning, I had found my prefix: *para*, to form *parafonie* or *paraphony* when spelled in English.

Parafonie is not a static descriptor of sound like those that can easily be recorded and analysed by electronic tools and computers. Parafonie is dynamic, changeable and sometimes unpredictable or unrepeatable when the listener makes a breakthrough through hearing. It primarily concerns itself with the way in which similar patterns (like a piece of recorded music you hear again and again) are experienced differently, not in an emotional sense, but in the details of the sounds themselves. These can reveal different aspects of the quality of the sound and effectively turn the listener into a co-creator of any sound experience. It is the abundance of sonic elements present in even the simplest of sounds (a human voice speaking, an instrument playing a simple melody) that gives rise to this parafonie. We can record a sentence and then say of course, 'well here you are, everything is there, the hisses and clicks of consonants, the sound spectrum of vowels, the meaning of words, the pitches or movements of the tones of the voice, the dynamic differences . . . everything is there'. But repeat a short phrase multiple times (using your normal speaking voice, you can try it out now . . . you can try it out now . . . you can try it out now . . . you can try it out now . . . you can try it out now . . . you can try it out now . . . you can try it out now . . . you can try it out now . . . you can try it out now) and words become melody, rhythm, in other words, music . . . in other words, music . . . in other words, music . . . in other words, music . . . in other words, music . . . in other words, music . . . in other words, music . . . in other words, music . . . in other words, music. The silence you hear where you read the comma gives a very different feel to this last sentence compared to the first one, which has a continuous flow. You'll probably become aware of the tonal shape and other qualities of sound that were initially 'hidden' behind the meaning. It is the way your mind changes its perception that takes *this* -phony beyond the *other* -phonies.

The grammar of musical sounds can be taken apart and grouped together, for example, as monophony (one melody carried by all parts) or polyphony (two or more parts moving in diverging but related patterns); or in rhythmic elements such as tempo (speed of the underlying pulse) or metre (division of emphasized and un-emphasized beats). Parafonie applies to all of these. It cannot be 'taken apart', because it never is 'a part'. All the partial elements of all voices, instruments, rhythmic and dynamic aspects, environmental sounds and so on make-up the totality that is embraced in the idea of parafonie. These elements can be actual 'partials', that is, harmonics or overtones; or hissy, noisy sounds; or psychoacoustic effects that are the result from the way our brain processes acoustic signals, to name a few examples. Listening to two or three different parts sounding together, as in a Bach chorale or a piece played on a thumb piano (mbira, likembe), can be heard and understood as polyphony, but also as parafonie. A woman's speaking voice can sound 'monotonous', but also be heard in its parafonic aspects. Parafonie must be understood as an umbrella term; it envelopes other *-phonies* and is not mutually exclusive in the way these other *-phonies* usually are.

No matter how much deeper we are able to penetrate into music and sound with the parafonic mindset I describe here, it would be futile to think that it could somehow be the final, last or ultimate word about what we hear. To become a *parafonist* warrants a multiplication of sensory impressions and leads to many new questions.

References
Crystal, David. The Cambridge Encyclopedia of Language, 1997. Cambridge: Cambridge University Press.
Bouman, Leon C., Vreemde Woorden in de Muziek, 1918. Amsterdam: Seyffardt's Muziekhandel.

Psyphony (English)
Daniel R. Wilson
Psyphony derives from the Greek ψυχή psychē, meaning 'breath, spirit, soul', and φωνή phōnē, 'sound, tone, voice'. The neologism defines a supernormal listening ideal in which human sound perception is wilfully pushed beyond its limits. Psyphonic audio recordings attempt to capture intangible essences of thought, idea or spurious hypothetical energies. The term 'psyphony' was first deployed in an August 2017 review of artist Aki Onda's 'Space Studies' as a means of destabilizing the supposedly complete gamut of sound types defined by soundscape ecologists Stuart Gage and Bernie Krause: geophony, biophony and anthropophony (geological, animal and human/machine sounds, respectively) (Wilson, 2017). The case for establishing psyphony as a definition was elaborated in March 2018's *The Wire*, tracing psyphonic precedents in historical romantic notions of music as constituting a supposed conduit for otherwise 'occluded messages' (Wilson, 2018). Early clinical attempts to explicitly embed thoughts within sound via psychical processes are detailed in Delawarr Laboratories' 1949 monograph *Acoustic Therapy* (De la Warr, 1949). Contemporary instances of psyphony can be discerned in the occult soundwork of percussionist Z'ev, field recordist Chris Watson, and also in the sonification of symbolically loaded raw data as employed by Ryoji Ikeda (Z'ev, 1992).

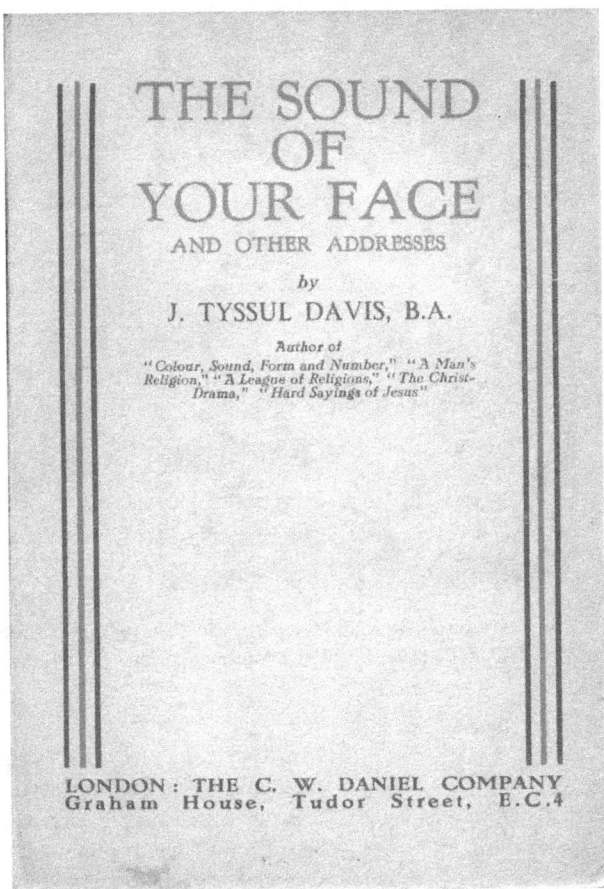

Figure 39 'The Sound of Your Face, and other addresses' (1928) by John Tyssul Davis. London: C.W. Daniel Co. Scanned in 2013 by Daniel Wilson.

References

Wilson, Daniel. 'Aki Onda: Space Studies'. *ArtReview.com*, 2017. https://artreview.com/reviews/online_review_daniel_wilson_aki_onda/ [Published August 2017. Retrieved 13 March 2020].

Wilson, Daniel. 'Further Listening'. *The Wire* *#409*, March 2018.

De la Warr, George. *Acoustic Therapy*. Oxford: Delawarr Laboratories, 1949; Wilson, Daniel. 'Radionics in Relation to Acoustics'. *Radionics Radio: An Album of Musical Radionic Thought Frequencies*. Sub Rosa, 2016.

Z'ev. *Rhythmajik*. Brighton: Temple, 1992; Watson, Chris. *Stepping Into the Dark*. Touch, 1996; Ikeda, Ryoji. *Dataphonics*. Paris: Dis voir, 2010.

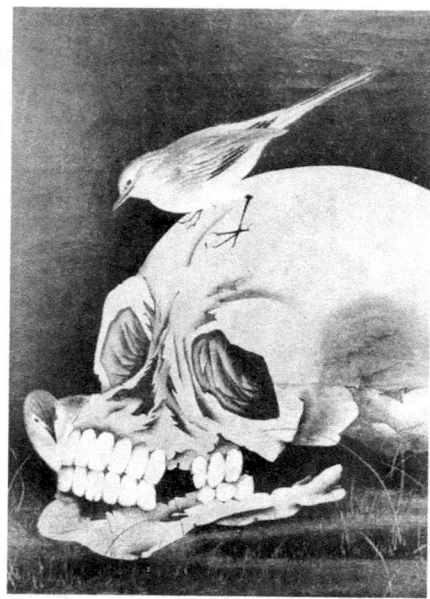

Figure 40 'The Broadcasting Experiment in Mass-Telepathy' (in 'Proceedings of the Society for Psychical Research' Vol. XXXVIII) (1929) by V. J. Woolley. Scanned in 2013 by Daniel Wilson.

Ragaireacht (Irish)
Jimmy Eadie

Ragaireacht – *to revel in the night, listening in solitude. (pronounced: rag er recked)*

Introduction
This article will explore and discuss how at night, our sonic perception shifts dramatically. It will ask what traditions and rituals we have developed for this unique experience and, more precisely, how in Irish Gaeilge we have a unique word for a person who loves the solitude of such a nocturnal listening experience – *Ragaireacht*

Gaeilge is a Celtic language, believed to have originated as Indo-European. However, English has been widely spoken throughout Ireland for many centuries. As of 2020, only 5 per cent of the population speak Irish fluently and on a daily basis. There are three main Irish Gaelic dialects, which originate within three distinct geographic locations: Munster, Connacht and Ulster. The main difference between the three is pronunciation. We have several words for sound, each with a slightly different meaning and appropriate usage. Some have the diacritic mark called a *fada* or great accent. It indicates that the vowel is to be pronounced 'long'.

1. Fuaim – (Feminine) sound: pronunciation – foo am
2. Torann – (masculine) noise: pronunciation – thur in
3. Fothram – (masculine) din: pronunciation – fuh ram
4. Glór – (masculine) sound voice: pronunciation – gloore
5. Callán – (masculine) noise: pronunciation – cal awwn
6. Gleo – (masculine) sound clamour:

pronunciation – glow
7. Trup – (masculine) sound disturbance: pronunciation – trup

Ragaireacht

Ragaireacht is an Irish term that does not have a precise English translation; literally, it means to enjoy the early hours through the night. *Airneánach* (could be considered the opposite of *Ragaireacht*), also another distinctive Gaeilge term, is a person who enjoys visiting at night; essentially being with people, celebrating. My focus here is within the sonic domain of the *raqaire*.

It is well known that there are many perceptual differences in our experience of day and night; obviously, vision is limited due to lack of light, but our awareness of sound is often enhanced specifically because of the lack of visual cues. However, phenomenologically sound changes its characteristics due to environmental and physical effects. I will discuss how within the Irish language *Ragaireacht* is a concise word used to describe a person who revels in the night precisely because of these phenomenological changes that can enhance our sonic perception.

Aesthetic of night

Music and night have always had a close association; the lullaby, for example, is written exactly for this nocturnal world to help children sleep. Many Western composers have celebrated 'night music' but perhaps most notably was Mozart's *Eine Kleine Nachtmusik* 1787 (Abert, 2007). There is also Mahler's *Nachtstücke* in his *Seventh Symphony* 1905 (Fischer, 2011). There is also the form of *vigil* celebrated in Rachmaninov's *All Night Vigil* (1915).

Traditional music within Ireland is also usually played at night particularly the Seannós (old style), which is a highly ornamented unaccompanied form of traditional Irish singing based around lamentation (Canainn, 2005).

Writers too apparently seek the mystery of night. Henry Thoreau posited 'night is certainly more novel and less profane then day, I shall be a benefactor if I conquer some realms of the night' (1863: 579). Shelley wrote the haunting line, night makes 'a sound of its own stillness'. Virginia Woolf (1816) claimed that there was a personal psychological change within the individual at night and suggested that 'the irresponsibility which darkness and lamplight bestow, we are no longer ourselves' (1927: 177).

What is it about walking alone at night that seems to conjure up images of the insomniac, the homeless, the deviant, as Bryan Palmer suggests 'the night has always been the time for daylight's dispossessed' (2000: 16). There seems to be a sense of the deviant and vagrant about nightwalking or wandering; it has had suspicious social and moral connotations for years. The individual who takes these nocturnal strolls is consciously rejecting diurnal logic in favour of the poetic character of night. Situationist Guy Debord considered that our sense of comfort and relationship with space is undermined when walking at night (Debord, 2009).

Physical changes of sound – Temperature inversion

A temperature inversion occurs at night or during periods of dense cloud cover; the air temperature increases with elevation, and sound waves are refracted back down to the ground. The reason why sounds can be heard much more clearly over longer distances at night than during the day is temperature inversion (Hannah, 2006). Another phenomenon that is experienced at night is that there will be less ambient masking and there is also less atmospheric attenuation and so sound is perceptually amplified. Listening at night can dramatically increase the auditive domain. Our ears also have a type of variable gain that adapts to the levels of sound. Our internal gain increases as the base sound level of the external environment reduces, so our ears can then perceive much more nuanced and softer sounds from further away.

Nocturnal listening
At night everything acquires a subtly different form, particularly that of sound, which seems to be magnified and brought all the more closer to us. We find that nocturnal sound has auditory information distinct from that acquired in the cold light of day. As Stephen Feld noted 'darkness intensifies sound in space' (Feld, 2012: 180). Listening at night is soaked in a sort of fragile spatial tension. Night soundscapes are dense, complex and layered. They have no source; they arrive from a delicate type of unstructured background hum, an underscore. To borrow from Christoph Cox (2018), sound is more of a 'sonic flux' – a material flow that carries us on and within it. Is this the *ecological silence* that John Cage referred to, we the listener organizing the sonic stream into an aesthetic experience. The microsonic details provide the ontological framework from which this non-teleological *nightscore* originates. It comes, endures for some time and recedes, gone, never the same, complex.

Distant sounds come alive but are shapeless; they emerge unexpectedly from the blackness, ephemeral and fragmented, and we accept them mutely and move on. There is something *otherly* about the enveloping night; it feels heavy within our ears, and it has mass and its own sense of history, primordial. It brings us into an unspoken embodied dialogue that activates our surroundings with acoustic and spatial dimensionality that outlines the dark contours of the barely seen. The *ragaire* seeks this universal deep quiet-solitude and seclusion that is associated with the night. The nocturnal realm is perceived differently. There needs to be a sensory adjustment whereby vision becomes subordinate to hearing; aural sensation is heightened to enjoy what R. Murray Shafer defined as 'macrocosmic musical composition' (1977: 30).

There is outer complexity with the soundscape. The sounds have both aesthetic value and social meaning. If we attend to these sounds as a musician or composer would and let them *perform* we become composer–spectator listening to our personnel orchestrated *Nacht Muzik*. Chance and indeterminacy are at play in this ever-emerging ethnographic real-time event. As Robert Morris considered, there could indeed be an art made of 'mutable stuff which need not be finalized with respect to either time or space' (Morris, 1993: 68).

When situated rurally we hear distant trains and traffic, animals and the odd singing reveller. They puncture the base night-tone of internal tinnitus and the external sound of night crickets. This fleeting, 'site-specific' work unfolds continuously, simultaneously arriving and receding, but always in the present. The urban nightscape is a little different in its orchestration: harder, reverberant, threatening, unique and unrepeatable. Disembodied voices reflected off concrete surfaces instantaneously relational and symbolic come and go, as if part of a scripted narrative, with us as the main protagonist. Both urban and rural soundscapes ask the listener or 'sonic-tourist' to open their ears to the inherent environment with no preconceptions. The nocturnal durational sonic collage requires participation, agency and above all acceptance. The aesthetics of soundwalking, listening and place are well documented (Westerkamp, n.d.; Truax, 2008; Suzuki, 2005; Oliveros, 2005; Neuhaus, 2000; Lefebvre, 1974), but there is scant literature on 'night-listening' as a practice within the broader sound studies domain, could we then define this practice of night-listening as *Ragaireacht*? It could be said that the *raguire* accepts the nocturnal sonic landscape above the diurnal for its symbolic and phenomenological qualities. The subjective private moment of focused listening articulates an ever-changing sonic sensibility that swings from the mundane to the transcendental.

Conclusion

The uniqueness of any language is in its ability to describe a multitude of actions in a singular or succinct expression or word. Irish Gaeilge is no different, an ancient language that is beginning to grow again within the island of Ireland. The Irish language because of its lyrical and musical quality has been associated with beauty and romanticism. There can be multiple interpretations of a single word and it may be used to define simultaneous but separate events. The linguistic and philosophical aspects are also deeply rooted within its representational and symbolic qualities. As with many other ancient languages, Gaeilge has the ability to provide a wide range of interpretations and meanings within a single word. Ragaireacht a unique Irish word has many meanings and connotations depending on its application and intention. I believe it nicely articulates a practice of enjoying the night and particularly that of the nocturnal soundscape.

References

Abert, Hermann. *W.A. Mozart*, edited by Professor Cliff Eisen, translated by Mr Stewart Spencer. New Haven: Yale University Press, 2007.

Canainn, Tomas O. *Tomas O Canainn: Traditional Music In Ireland*. Cork, Ireland: Music Sales America, 2005.

Cox, Christoph. *Sonic Flux: Sound, Art, and Metaphysics*. Chicago: University of Chicago Press, 2018.

Debord, Guy. *The Situationists and the City: A Reader*, edited by Tom McDonough. London and New York: Verso, 2009.

Feld, Steven. *Sound and Sentiment: Birds, Weeping, Poetics, and Song in Kaluli Expression*. Durham: Duke University Press, 2012.

Fischer, Jens Malte. *Gustav Mahler*, translation edition. New York: Yale University Press, 2011.

Hannah, Lindsay. 'Wind and Temperature Effects on Sound Propagation'. *New Zealand Acoustics* 20, no. 2 (2006): 8.

Lefebvre, Henri. *The Production of Space*, translated by Donald Nicholson-Smith. Malden: Wiley-Blackwell, 1974.

Maes, Francis. *A History of Russian Music: From Kamarinskaya to Babi Yar*, translated by Arnold Pomerans and Erica Pomerans, first edition. California, USA: University of California Press, 1915.

Morris, Robert. *Continuous Project Altered Daily - Notes on Sculpture*. Malden: Cambridge University Press, 1993.

Neuhaus, Max. 'Sound Art? - Max Neuhaus'. *ART THEORY* (blog). 2000. http://theoria.art-zoo.com/sound-art-max-neuhaus/.

Oliveros, Pauline. *Deep Listening: A Composer's Sound Practice*. New York: iUniverse, 2005.

Palmer, Bryan D. *Cultures of Darkness: Night Travels in the Histories of Trangression: Night Travels in the Histories of Transgression*, Illustrated edition. New York: monthly review press, 2000.

Schafer, R. Murray. *The Tuning of the World*. New York: Random House Inc, 1977.

Shelley, Percy Bysshe. *The Oxford Handbook of Percy Bysshe Shelley*. Oxford University Press, 1816.

Suzuki, Akio. 'The Akio Suzuki Website - Sound Artist 鈴木昭男'. 2005. https://www.akiosuzuki.com/en/.

Thoreau, Henry David. 'Night and Moonlight'. *The Atlantic*, 1863.

Truax, Barry. 'Soundscape Composition as Global Music: Electroacoustic Music as Soundscape'. *Organised Sound* 13, no. 2 (2008): 103–9.

Westerkamp, Hildegard. 'Hildegard Westerkamp - inside the Soundscape'. Hildegard Westerkamp - inside the Soundscape. n.d. http://www.hildegardwesterkamp.ca.

Woolf, Virginia. *Street Haunting: A London Adventure*. London, England: Symonds Press, 1927.

Rauschen (German)
Pia Palme

An excursion across the border between the wanted and the unwanted – and then back again.

> Rauschen – *I look down from the bridge into the swollen river below. The roar of the brownish churning water rattles me entirely, from my ears to my intestines, as it thunders down from the Bernina mountain range. My fingers are numb as they fiddle with the camera and recording gear.*

Rauschen is an ancient German word with no direct and precise translation into the English language. Within the vocabulary of sound, it is my favourite. In its noun form, *das Rauschen* is an impartial expression for a mostly broadband texture of noise. As a verb, *Rauschen* is often used to describe the action of emitting/making/generating that specific kind of broadband noise.

> *It has been raining for days and the water level of the Poschiavino, the river that cuts right through the small town of the same name, has risen considerably. The ever-present Rauschen of the river has changed its register: it is much stronger now and appears to be moving faster. Lower frequencies dominate and occasionally there is a deep and very heavy rumble as large rocks tumble along the riverbed. The noise completely fills me up. I'm present with the noise. Rauschen is inseparable from what I perceive as 'me'.*

Rauschen[20] invades us, penetrates us: we have no choice but to surrender. Rauschen takes over. As the sound artist and theorist Salomé Voegelin articulates, Rauschen magnifies the fact that there is no distance between the sound and the listener.[21] Rauschen can be perceived at any volume, from the deafeningly loud to the nearly inaudible. It can arise from any kind of source, for example, from natural sources, human or inhuman sounds, instrumental, mechanical or technical occurrences. In a scientific context, Rauschen describes an unwanted signal, such as the noise of a distorted radio signal.

German nouns often describe states or situations in their dynamic form, yet within certain limits. Rather than defining static conditions, they communicate inherent activities or processes – conditions which are changing, evolving and progressing: conditions with lives of their own. This is the case with Rauschen: the term implies the notion of a swift and ongoing movement through, or within, a certain space and time. It involves a peculiar sense of moving forward – as is the case with a body of water which flows unerringly in one direction and which cannot be stopped. Although Rauschen seems to appear as a steady stream of noise, it is able to gradually – yet never too abruptly – evolve. Altogether, the term 'Rauschen' signifies a nexus of sound, space and movement.

My interest in Rauschen was sparked by the texture of the sound itself and by the ambiguity of the perceptional concepts behind the term. In the listening process, Rauschen, like a signpost, marks the borderline between the wanted and the unwanted. That emotionally laden frontier is fortified by the listener's own social surroundings as well as their personal tastes. When experiencing Rauschen, individual and cultural modes of hearing perception interfere with one another, stimulating levels of awareness and imagination within the listener. In closely directing one's ear into Rauschen, subtle sonic textures can manifest: small irregular shifts in frequencies constantly occur. In particular, a listener might begin to identify vocal productions, like ghost voices, emerging from the sonic stream.[22] Human perception is oriented towards the gathering of insight and the recognition of knowable content; if this is not possible for a given situation, the

Rauschen *(German)*

Figure 41 Rauschen, © Pia Palme.

mind will attempt to re-create the phenomena of perception. It is not always easy to decide whether a specific kind of Rauschen is pleasant or unpleasant to the ear. This is one of the main reasons why I like using Rausch-like textures in my music.

It is noteworthy that Rauschen is one of the most commonly used sound words in German literature. It appears in medieval poetry by Walther von der Vogelweide as well as in works by Schiller, Kleist, Goethe, Uhland and, somewhat later, Rilke. Over the centuries, the conception of Rauschen has evolved. From early on, Rauschen was coloured with violence, intensity and power. The Canadian composer R. Murray Schafer argues that in the ancient times penetrating noise was associated with the sacred.[23] In the medieval period, Rauschen was associated with the roar of fierce winds and stormy seas, or with the noise of battle. At that time, Rauschen meant to storm ahead in an uncontrolled manner, as would be the case with warriors who are enraged, excited or beside themselves. Rauschen was therefore conceived as being compelled vigorously forward, driven by a strong force. Jacob and Wilhelm Grimm mention in their 'Deutsches Wörterbuch' (German Dictionary)[24] that 'in the old language', the verb Rauschen had been used for the ferocious wild movements of untamed animals or living beings.

This idea implies that there is a borderline which must be crossed before entering the state of Rauschen. An edge within. Step beyond the border of civilised behaviour into the untamed wilderness of emotional power. Surrender and step beside yourself. In Rauschen, life is out of control. Mind, voice, and body running wild. War, love, and religion make human beings give up control – and so can music and art. Rausch, the shortened version of the word, stands for intoxication, fever, furore, or just plain drunkenness. Ecstasy, rapture.

From around 1800[25] in the German Romantic period, Rauschen became associated with the more gentle noises of nature. The pleasant sound of a brook, a waterfall, the sea, the sound of long grass moving in a soft breeze, leaves rustling in a tree and a forest's whisper at dusk would be described as Rauschen. Writers used the word Rauschen to describe natural sites while exploring the complex relationship between nature and mankind. Writing about Rauschen, authors evoked not only an atmosphere of freedom and openness but also hinted at obscure worlds that cannot be expressed by language. Literature adopted Rauschen as a screen onto which to project the unknown and the opaque. Here again, in the Age of Enlightenment, another borderline was transcended: nature and culture became separate dimensions. Only from a distance did humans observe natural phenomena or landscapes, from a distance did they listen to the sounds of trees, grass or water. Domesticated and tamed, nature became a scenery. Rauschen slipped to the background of awareness. Civilized society crafted nature into a metaphor for their longing. The frontier between nature and culture became the rectangular golden frame enclosing a painted nature scene, used to decorate a stylish living room.

In the twentieth century, with the advance of technology and industrialization, Rauschen became a technical term denoting a disturbance in a signalling system.[26] Authors like Kafka, Musil and Mann were inspired by the possibilities of acoustic media, such as recordings, radio telephones and gramophones. Rustling and repetitive tapping sounds or distorted voices appear in their writings as modern forms of Rauschen.[27] Contemporary and electronic musicians also discovered and explored Rauschen and its artistic potential. The use of Rauschen as an element in the arts evolved in parallel to the development of psychoanalysis: for the analyst; it became important to listen to every scrap of sound and every distorted uttering of a patient. In the psychoanalytic process, all vocal productions are equally important as signals, contributing to reveal and heal the patient's mind.

In my own artistic practice, I explore the varied concepts of noise, particularly the cognitive partition separating accepted (wanted) inner states or perceptions from those that I tend to reject (unwanted). I find the mental, emotional and cultural implications of Rauschen interesting and important subject matter for my artistic research. This brings me to feminist and queer activism. The concept of Rauschen becomes a tool to scrutinize mental, emotional and cultural boundaries that are habitually – and tacitly – imposed on one's thoughts and thought processes. I experiment with deconstructing, shifting and re-composing the boundaries between signal and noise-in-mind: Rauschen allows me to compose the personal as the political.

Rauschen is associated with processes that continue over a long duration – over hours, days, a lifetime or longer – that is, beyond human imagination. A waterfall crashing down over a cliff edge appears to thunder on forever, with the water's roar hammering into one's ears, into ears that cannot be closed off from the noise. So too does the Rauschen of machines never come to an end: in the industrialized world, the steady hum of motor noises continues (rauscht) day and night. In the digital age, Rauschen proceeds invisibly as an ever-present undercurrent of algorithms, controlling mechanisms and surveillance. Regardless of whether or not I pay attention to it, the flow of digital Rauschen surrounds me. And there is yet another kind of border closing in on me: the border between life and death, the border between what I can measure as moments in life against the endless Rauschen of time. That final demarcation that all living beings must, at one point, pass. The Rauschen of analogue and digital rivers and waterfalls will continue, even when I, as an individual, can no longer perceive it.

Listening to the river, I step across the border and become one with the roar. I am part of nature, nature is part of me. Rauschen is an ancient German word. Within the vocabulary of sound, it is my favourite, I think. I'm freezing in the rain.

Retinir (re-ti-nir) (Portuguese)
Inês R. Amado

To produce a strong sound, a metallic and acute sound to resound to echo. All of these,

Retinir (re-ti-nir) (Portuguese)

but none can really say in truthfulness and in its entirety RETINIR!

Ex: In the forge the blacksmith beats his iron, its sound vibrates in your body and its retinir pulses through your ears . . . your eardrums resonate deeply with musical notes. This retinir shakes your whole body from head to toes and somehow a connection is made between you, this energy sound and the earth.

I was about seven or eight years old, I lived in a house, in a small village, surrounded by pinewoods, the sea was just a few kilometres away. In winter I could hear it's murmuring and sometimes it's roaring . . . I loved being in the woods, mostly by myself, I would pick up needles and pine cones and make strange things with them and with some clay.

One day I was deeply immersed in making my little objects, when I heard a vibrant sound, which startled me and made me jump. I looked for the place, the cause of the sound, but couldn't find anything. So I continued my assemblage of clay and pine needles. However, within about ten minutes I heard the sound again, but this time it didn't startle me, it came in through my ears into my eardrums and filled my whole body with it, as if I, myself had become the sound itself. I was vibrating with and in the sound.

This sound was so beautifully overwhelming that I had to find its source. In the village lived a blacksmith who had his forge at the very edge of the village; we lived far enough not to hear his constant beating of metal. However, I had always been fascinated by his labour, his amazing craftsmanship and some of the noises which sounded good to me. So, from time to time, whenever I passed by his place I would peep in and watch him from a distance for a little while. It was always extremely hot, so I wouldn't stay long. This particular day, having heard the sound twice and having become extremely curious, as I had never heard this sound before, I decided to walk to the

Figure 42 Retinir, © Inês R. Amado.

blacksmith's place, as I felt that this amazing sound had to come from his forge. Actually, I didn't walk, I run, run all the way there. As I arrived at the forge there wasn't anybody there, I was so surprised and disappointed, I just thought and was so very sure that the sound had to emanate from there . . . my upset was so intense that I just sat down at the entrance and had to hold back my tears. Suddenly I realized that I was perspiring buckets, gosh it was so extremely hot, I looked in again and saw the red ambers in the kiln, it was as if that corner of the forge was completely on fire, I was scared, I had never been as close as this to the furnace. What to do next, should I call Ti António? His name was António, but all the kids called him Ti António. I was just at the point of shouting his name, when a heavy but friendly hand rested on my shoulder. So, what are you doing here little girl, aren't you too hot? he asked. My words just tumbled out of my mouth; yes, it's really hot and I think your shop is on fire, look there inside, I was just going to call you –

Well, well, he said, yes you are right, my forge is properly on fire, but that is just what I need to do my forging, actually I have a very special object to repair and I have to have all the heat I can get out of my kiln.

You are such a curious little girl, and I do like children who are curious and who like to learn new things, so I am going to show you something very special, would you like to see it he asked. Oh yes please, actually I came all the way here thinking that I would find a sound I said. A sound? Maybe you are right, this is a place with many sounds, but most of them could eventually break your eardrums, so one has to be careful and wear some protection. But anyway, wait here and I will bring out something for you to see. He was pushing a big trolley and on it he was carrying an enormous bell. I opened my eyes in pure amazement; this bell was just incredible and it must have weighed a tonne, as he was holding the trolley with great care and with some effort. Can I touch it, I asked? Yes of course he said. As I touched it I had goosebumps all over, I just knew that this wonderful object, which I had only ever seen from below as it belonged to our little church, had to be the magical object which had produced that most intriguing sound I had heard a while ago.

Ti António, what are you doing with the bell from the church, I asked? Good question indeed 'menina' (little girl)! I will let you know a secret; this bell has got a great history; it was made many, many years ago, before I was born and before my parents and grandparents were born. It came all the way from a far, far away place, a place called London. Oh yes, I know, the capital of England, I said. Oh, you really know your geography, he said. Well then, this bell was made in a place called the Whitechapel Bell Foundry. This is the place where Big Ben's bells were made. Do you know what Big Ben is? Yes, I do I learned that from a book my mother bought me, I love Big Ben, it is so tall and beautiful.

So as you see this bell is a very special object with history and memories in itself. It was brought all the way from London in 1845 as a present from Queen Victoria and Prince Albert to Ferdinand II, the son of Prince Ferdinand of Saxe-Coburg-Saalfeld, cousin of Albert, who married our Queen D. Maria II.

So, you see, if this bell could talk it would definitely tell us a great deal. Anyway, coming back to actuality, Sr. Padre Manuel, our priest called me two days ago and told me that the bell had a large hole and it needed repairing . . . so I together with three lads went up the belfry and brought down this beauty we have here.

Ti António, I said, I think you need to come to my school and tell us all about this bell and its history; actually I don't think my teacher knows anything about bells and about the stories they have to tell us. Where did you learn all these things Ti António? 'Menina', as I told you before, being curious about the world we live in is very important. Everything has got a beginning, I beat up metal, that is in essence my profession, but metal has also got its own beginnings, its history. So apart from doing my objects, which I love, I also immerse myself in the study of things and if there is any object I have never seen before, I will go and find out where it came from, what its function is today and was in other times, like this beautiful bell made of bronze in a foundry established in 1570 and rebuilt after the Great Fire of London in 1666.

Bells are normally made, cast from a type of bronze; this is because this metal has got very particular resonant qualities. Of course, not all bells are made of this metal, smaller bells can be made of other types of hard material.

So our Bell came to me asking for my services and I am grateful for that, as it has been talking to me and telling me of its existence, it's travelling and it's sound, talking of which, would you like to listen to its sound? Ti António, I said, I thought you'd never ask! Ok, ok here it goes, at this point he picked up a metal bar and made that amazing sound I had run towards in an intuitive manner, knowing deep down within myself that that profound sound had had to come from here.

So Ti António in a very reverent way touched the bell with the metal bar and made once again this profound, unique, magical sound that once again made me shake from feet to head and once again I felt that I was the sound from within, I was vibrating and re-vibrating, the energy from that sound was part of me, but I had no words to express what I was feeling, I just could say: Ti António that is the most beautiful thing I have ever seen. 'Menina', he said, one doesn't see sound. Oh yes I do! I said.

Ritselen (Dutch)
Esther Venrooij

The translation is *rustling*. A very soft sound, often produced by leaves, branches or paper. It is a sound which comes close to *white noise*. *Rustling of leaves* reminds me of the poplar tree you can find in the open landscape in the Netherlands. This tree often functions as a natural wind breaker near a farm house, along a grassland or a dike. The slightest breeze is enough to make the leaves twinkle, shimmer and tremble. *Rustling of paper* can cause very different sensations. Within the field of ASMR community and sound art, it is one of the most popular sound effects, but it can also be experienced as 'noise' or an 'annoying sound' within voice recording. The sound of *rustling paper* brings me back to my school years. I think, for example, of my speech-language therapist, softly turning pages through his book, or my French teacher leafing through the exam papers.

Roar (Yorkshire dialect)
Mark Fell

I was really struggling to find an interesting word for sound in my language. Actually although I'm an English speaker I grew up speaking something quite different. And if I spoke to my international friends the way I did as a child, I'm sure most would not understand. So like many of my friends, when travelling I resort to an internationalized version of English, using words that tend to be taught in schools and avoiding the more unusual bits. And over time I have lost most of my accent - even though most British people would still recognize where I came from (both geographically and in terms of class). Actually the minor regional dialects were so strong when I was a child that it was quite easy to recognize which part of South Yorkshire a person came from, often with striking accuracy. The word I have chosen will be familiar to most readers: roar – to make a kind of deep animalistic howl. Interestingly, although I knew this word as a child, there was another roar – literally pronounced like the German river Ruhr. 'Stop roo-ering parents would say to children', or 'look at him roo-ering for his mum'. However, I didn't know that *roar* and *roo-er* were actually the same word until I was about twenty-four. I remember being puzzled as a child why the word *roo-er* was never listed in any dictionaries and how it never featured in any literature that I read. There were more words like this, and other anomalies: why were there two alternate spellings for *are* – 'are' and 'or', both of which were pronounced exactly the same where I grew up, and when I grew up. The situation reminded me of a story told to me by an Indian friend. As a small child in the community of Keralan Brahmins he grew up speaking a language that had no name or written form. When he started at school he was asked to write something, and then he immediately realized he could not. To this day the meaning and usage of the two versions of *roar* are quite different and anything but interchangeable: to roo-er, the sound of roo-ering, is something quite different than the roar. Somewhat related to this, I have friends whose young daughter is fluent in English, Italian and German and often switches between each of these. If she wants to say and absolute 'no' to her parents – the stubborn form of an absolute no that children are expert at – she resorts to German. In terms of how this relates to my practice it is hard to say. Of course, we can point to correlations between my background, the culture, place and time that I am from, and the musical vocabularies that surrounded me as a child: working class with an extended family of politically aware miners and steelworkers, a small town in the north of England, the wanton dereliction of society and social infrastructure. The way we spoke, the rhythm of our speech, its speed and changes in direction. These things seem to fit closely with a way of relating to one another – relentless piss-taking was the basic fabric of all social encounters. Maybe there is some kind of connection between the flow of patterns and structures in the music I make, and the flow of patterns and structures of the linguistic, psychological and social relationships that I grew up with.

Sähinä (Finnish)
J-T Vesikkala Wittmacher

I

Among the marvellous sound words in the Finnish language that imply conscious agency, *sähinä* is one of the most vital and aggressive words. One that should alarm the average listener and at least call for a reaction or reassessment. With Finnish, I have the luxury of summoning and closely describing this particular onomatopoeic word from a range of sophisticated sound words.

These words are of the everyday kind I use when I wish to report the conditions in the middle of a snowstorm, falling leaves, rain, wind or when at sea, although fetching the correct word requires trivial fluency on a native level on which all other ancestral languages are lost to me. These words are remnants of life forms past in the present. I cherish them, as a composer, as my grasp to a more rudimentary humanity.

Although archaic, Finnish sound words are far from obsolete – idiomatic speakers still distinguish between related variants and apply them as intended, verbalizing prey, pets, enemies and friends. In visually crowded yet sparsely populated environments like Finland, sound remains the main channel of communication. Where forests are the rule and savannahs are not, limited visuals cannot be taken for granted.

Everyday people, not only composers, treasure onomatopoeic words because they most accurately mediate between the human world and the non-human environment. Where this communication was pivotal was in hunting, for which a vocabulary of codewords was needed; each shared a three-syllable make-up of short vowel and consonant sounds. Aptly, only voicings by which animals vocalize for fleeing or, in the case of *sähinä*, for self-defence, were labelled.

Sähinä (Finnish)

Gradually, these numerous words refined into either abstracted sound or mere descriptions of physical actions, now void of any violent signalling. Still, to describe sounds, we can invent a new word, and that word will face scrutiny from the same intricate ruleset. The particular *sähinä* sound is well suited for the abstractness of music, whereas in the natural realm, we hear *sähinä* most accurately in a cat's aggressive hissing sound when threatened. I imagine *sähinä* would match the wildest sounds that skunks, beavers and snakes can make too. From a time when sound words meant survival and coordinated livelihood, they have since been domesticated and serve to enrich speech and musicians' work.

The short 's' at the beginning of *sähinä* carries a high-level energy ready to occupy any space that we were using to hide from it. This same unsettling feeling and width of frequencies is felt in the electrifying words *säpistä*, *säristä*, and *siristä*.

II

On a deeper level, *sähinä* opens our ears into its peculiar structure, workings on listeners, and how living beings have often harnessed this sound for fearmongering intentions, only to later build music and language out of them.

My active vocabulary was able to recollect seventy-five such Finnish sound words and derive sound verbs from them, using the endings *-sta* or *-stä*. An average native speaker would have intuitively grasped these words by age ten. Yet there is nothing infantile about these words, however limited their usage. Out of all the sound words, I am fascinated by *sähinä* precisely since it holds a clear link to living beings and also closely connects to non-animate yet sonically similar words. These sibling words are *sihinä* and *suhina* – the consonant combination S–H connects *sähinä* with the crowd. This word category prescribes a general morphology, a discrete energetic burst in the middle-high spectrum with temporal continuity or frequent repetitions.

If we want to push it further, the complex and subtle logic of sound in the Finnish language extends even to the spectral aspect – that how sounds were named using certain consonants and vowels bear resemblance to the details in loudness and frequency of the sound, a spectromorphological rationale.

The approximate meanings of these sound words mirror their spelling. Several logical word categories based on vowel and consonant combinations correspond to a musicianly understanding of the sound's duration, uniformity, main frequency regions, loudness and possible granularity.

The three consonants take up greatly varying space and explicate meaningful aspects for *sähinä*, whereas vowels inhabit smaller yet emphasized frequency regions or formants. The first and second formants are the strongest frequencies that together direct our spoken

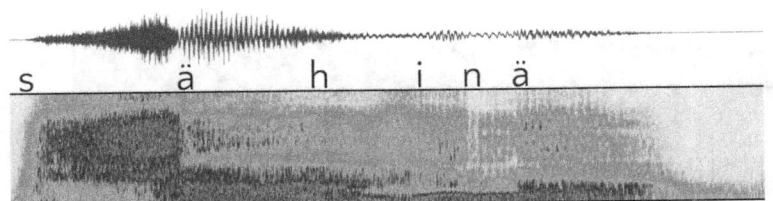

Figure 43 My spoken word 'sähinä' in about 0.9 seconds, © J-T Vesikkala Wittmacher.

vowel perception among the eight Finnish vowels. This large available space for sound doubtlessly improved communication in forests. Since the vowel 'ä' has the highest and most open first formant and 'i' has the highest and most frontal second formant possible, how could the extremeness of *sähinä* be a pure coincidence?

> The first 'ä' in *sähinä*, which differentiates it from its sibling word *sihinä*, has reached the highest energy, an open vowel that begs for attention. From this position, it machinates a rising intensity towards the next even more frontal vowel i.

Regardless of their lost and untraceable root words and lexical origins, these standard nouns are neither simple shouted interjections nor non-descriptive enough to be imitations. But there is more. With tiny yet meaningful alterations to the three syllables and their six letters, a semantic chain of kinships between similar-sounding words emerges. These small differences might have distinguished the behaviours of groups of animals that move, make noise and threaten us similarly, without having to exactly identify which fauna it is.

Most sound words today associate with inanimate mechanical objects rather than with prey, friends or foes. Nature sounds have essentially remained unchanged, giving little reason to abandon or change the words. One would expect that a composer would be up for imitating the natural origins of this vast Finnish vocabulary. Yet rather than aiming to exactly replicate anything previously in existence, it is this kinship web of sound words like *sähinä* that directs my imagination and provides inventive tools for sonic design and fine-tuning compositions.

The 'h' in *sähinä* denotes the moment of relative ease and composure, for our listening to reflect on what is happening, what led to this moment, and what is soon to come.

III

By noise-making, a subject summons the self, for the self, to hear its anxiety being voiced. Perhaps this sound is made as much for performing as for listening? If *sähinä* attempts to (re)claim space, how much can a *sähinä* vocalization extend the self, or does it only serve self-reflection? It may not be the best vehicle to either end. Rather, these sounds have evolved into threats because they electrify the space between the subjects which, prior to the sound, was clouded by courteous and benign indifference. Indeed, the most useful survival codewords reveal the presence of a conscious subject. Come to think of this auditory psychology, we cannot quite abandon that association with cats.

The *sähinä* in a cat's hissing expresses fear, a defence mechanism instead of a genuine readiness to attack. Even though *sähinä* includes two distinctly high regions of frequencies, a twofold signal of warning alongside a wish to avoid physically confronting the other subject,

Figure 44 A generated sähinä sound, © J-T Vesikkala Wittmacher.

the listener may, however, catch the fear from this display.

While *sähinä* implies an actor, sound words that also designate nature or animals might also suggest direction, rotation or unavoidable directed processes as in entropy. Our encounter with the cat's *sähinä* is neither magnetic nor predestined, however. Cats' repositioning of their body in combination with hissing unlocks both the physical and frequency space. It launches in us a primeval need for fighting, hunting, or fleeing – there is very little to this sound that would make us freeze on the spot and just prefer to listen since it drains us from our perceived safety. Paradoxically, that and the transfixed state is exactly what human listeners prefer.

> The 'i' in *sähinä* denotes the most frontal point in the mouth, which most pushes and pulls the listener. We feel comfortable again because the sound is now closing with the rather closed vowel.

Instances akin to *sähinä* in the concert realm are, however unplanned, heard in the electroacoustic repertoire, evoking the same reactions and desires. Such determined yet uncontrolled sounds make us squirm slightly in our seats, turning our heads in a civilized way. Something about the sound evades an accurate perception of its essence; the listener is bound to a continuous re-evaluation of the self, which effectively leads to inaction by both the performing and listening subjects. This strong emotional response and our avoidance notwithstanding, we can hardly imagine any sound emotionally or timbrally opposite to *sähinä*; something flowing smoothly and without agency, yet how long would we stand that either? To a musical ear, there certainly are minutiae to the sound, potentials to listen for among the painful roughness. And what makes us need to hear it, so much so that we listen silently, succumb to the emotions? Perhaps this stance as mere tolerant observers might grant us an evaluation and nonacceptance of our own threateningness?

> The 'n' in *sähinä*, the ending that is common to most of the sound words, denotes the uneasy realisation that the noise is still going on, and will go on until we actively interfere.

It is with their sheer range and energetic instability that *sähinä* and its similarly marked neighbours such as *rähinä*, *kähinä* or *särinä* can pierce through. They aim to unnerve and petrify us, and in so doing, the sound does 'sähistä' around in our mind until we finally manage to fetch the proper responses off the top of our heads.

> The last 'ä' in *sähinä* denotes the safety of returning to a vowel that was heard before, and signals a definite closure.

Schwup (Swiss-German)
Salomé Voegelin

schwup is a vernacular, everyday term that is entirely contextual, meaning it depends on the contingent circumstance of its articulation to glean or rather to generate its meaning. And it is not only the 'outer' context or time that determines what it might say. Instead, it is the timing of vowels and consonants and the context they build together: a short *u* after a long *sch*, or a sharp *p* after a short *sch*, that creates entirely different actions and consequences.

The word and its meaning, as far as it has any meaning at all, are not permanent or assured in any way: it does not mean but performs meaning that generates rather than names or describes. In that sense it is not a word that can fulfil or retain lexical criteria. The description will always fall short of what else it could mean. Thus, it shows the lexical referent to be at its limit. Not a lie exactly, but a reduction which, at best, helps us to come to meaning as a provisional sense, and at worst reduces what anything can mean, discriminating and excluding alternative possibilities to safeguard comprehension.

schwup is not a word we can learn independent of its occurrence. It is a word as event, that itself does what it says and achieves understanding not through reference to a prior use or dictionary but by being said, as a performance, in context, now. Its written form has no meaning in itself but invites articulation as action, on the body and with the body. Because it is the result of the vernacular as a radical form of expression that speaks in sound and has an effect rather than makes a description. Thus, its utterance articulates not in letters or their orthography. Instead, it draws from the body speaking a current movement and attitude, and it gains its sense as a consequence from that which it has touched.

However, it is not a riddle. It is not a word to make you guess. Instead, it brings you to articulation as movement and as causality embedded in a moment that it helps create. And it makes us appreciate that the meaning of all words might similarly not be referential; that the lexicon might be the construction, if not the conceit, of an organizational world view; to make us think we can speak in words that match a pre-existing language and through pre-existing possibilities, when instead it is on the contingent body in action that letters come to mean.

The lexicon is an effort of organization. It inadvertently creates exclusions and taxonomical uncertainties, that might just show the limit of its organization and reveal the pleasure of disorganized speech in the possibility of its sound. *schwup* is such a sound that is a word created from the pleasure of the unorganized: denoting literally and performatively a falling down, and pushing down, and rising up and hurrying along, and many other transformations, that between sounds, the breath and body get a temporary articulation that does not outline or denote, but makes that transformation.

schwup appears as an adjective but makes a verb. This is a verb that knows no tense as it is always in the present, even though this present can be a performance of the past or the future. And its speaker is not the subject of its action but part of its generativeness. In that sense it is a verb that performs without tense *or* conjugation: without the relevance of a subject, the relevance of the action generated in their articulation as an entangled movement that makes no separation between who does, who speaks and what it is called.

Figure 45 Schwup, © Emilia Mollin.

ich schwup, du schwp, er schwup, sie schwup, es schwup, wir schwup, ihr schwup, sie schwup

And so it is not referenceable within grammar either, but belongs entirely to the moment of utterance as an entangled and generative event. It is a sound that makes what it describes and leaves no description. In that sense it is an adjective that is a verb, whose sense of time and action happens on the body of the speaker in simultaneity and extension with that which is moved by its articulation, rather than from a distance, in hindsight and through letters. It has the quality of an imperative, not because it tells you what to do, but because it entices articulation as action: to make a doing that might have no subject at all. This lack of subject determination is apparent in its articulation, which is often breathy, astonishing even those who speak it, with the autonomy of its doing.

It voices the dread or joy of an always current occasion that in letters hangs together but as sound takes place. Its sonic dynamic is the energy of what is happening, or what has happened but what is always in telling happening now.

The description does not engage in a moment but makes that moment that nobody might have seen, that might remain entirely invisible but for its sound. And it is entirely ambiguous as to its benefits or harms. The *schwup* of a glass falling down to break into many pieces and the gesture of a hand moving upwards to signal a raise are all the same to its grammatical construction. Its sense exists only in sound: in plurality, porous, permeable, always different.

However, I am not referring here to a Derridean deferral, in which things move through interpretation and into new associations held in place by a horizontal chain of signifiers leading back to a root and leaving a trace.[28] Because, the différend, unlike *schwup*, remains dialectical, it retains the possibility of meaning. This is as meaning shifting in time and through mobile associations, but it remains always relative to an originary interpretation. *Schwup* by contrast demands a more fundamental letting go of the origin and structure of meaning. To find that instead of voicing a description or interpretation it articulates as 'materialization': performing a radical shift away from coming to meaning by making sensorial sense.

> Rather than asking how the past might be radically reinterpreted in order to bring to light diverse accounts, or indigenous and settler stories, or to identify new discursive subjects, we ask a question about method: what occurs when we strategically foreground the material events over their interpretation? To put it another way, we have a deep curiosity about whether the language of the material and materialization might have different epistemological and political effects from the language of interpretation and the subject.[29]

In this context, *schwup* stands as a word outside of language. It is in performance and on the body. It is an example of how else words as material can be approached and worked with not to get to meaning and understanding, but to build another route to knowledge: not via the dictionary and thus via the historical, patriarchal and semantic centre of language, but through actions on the margins; to hear how else and what else we can know from the material of words about things, the world and ourselves.

The word or rather the action *schwup* in this context is a device. It is a device to get to . . .

> . . . materialization as a possible escape from interpretivism's endless referentiality and deferral of representation, from its political inertness, from its inability to escape the threat of relativism, and from the danger of

uncertainty in the face of those who do claim to know.[30]

schwup's own otherness: its existence in performance, on the body and in gestures, permits and enables this connection and move into materialization. It helps me to think beyond the term and its interpretation of language more generally as performance and materialization. Bringing every word into the possibility of a generative sense. At the same time, its reflection in relation to a normative, referential context allows me to question the limits of this context, exposed through the appearance of the other, the strange, the non-lexical, the feminine and local, that performs in its midst the generative autonomy of the vernacular and spoken word.

Schlierig (German)
Holger Schulze

It's unclear and as if from afar. Sound events occur which I definitely can hear. However, it is not quite clear what they are. Are they acoustic effects or illusions or repercussions from other, much more distant sound events? Or are they artificially inserted into a sound production in order to provide some strange or alienating, some surprising, but weirdly distant ornaments to it? I am not quite sure, what I hear.

Unlike other moments characterized by such an uncertainty, by doubtful activities and incomprehensible articulations, this moment, however, is full of pleasure. I am actually enjoying these distant, grey and unclear sounds. What would be deemed a mistake by standards of professional sound engineering or ambitions towards an audiophile ecstasy of the highest fidelity is actually a source of my joy. I wish to remain and stay in this moment. I wish to listen further and longer to these unclear sounds engulfing me. Maybe it is precisely this distant and unclear quality that makes it so appealing?

There are various musical pieces, recordings, listening situations and also whole musical genres and subcultures that have embraced exactly this aesthetic in a more explicit and reflected or a more implicit and strictly affective degree. The range goes from genres such as *Shoegaze* and *Retro Ambient* that indulge unashamedly in the pleasures of presenting unclear and distanced sound productions to musical aesthetics in the wider area of *hauntology* (Fisher 2012, 2014, Schulze 2020), including the works by Burial or The Caretaker, even including the delightful use of vinyl static in genres such as TripHop. In all these examples a sort of distancing, grey and white noisy, masking sound is filtering all the brilliance that the original recording, made with contemporary recording equipment, would have had, supposedly. The effect this has on some of its listeners is, however, not to find these music productions unappealing or even repulsive – but the contrary is the case. The effects of sonic distancing, of framing a series of sound events in sort of a distant past or a distant location, from which a listener only is able to grasp a densely filtered rest, they activate a strong desire, an almost unbearable wish and need to listen to these sounds even more, with even more joy and delight. Withdrawal attracts: a common effect.

One might now intervene and claim: isn't this effect just a symptom of a totally idiosyncratic desire, finding an almost kitschy if not totally superficial and baseless pleasure in a rather peculiar yet unremarkable sound signature? More a kind of fad, a passing, highly idiosyncratic preference or inclination than an actual sound or a sound effect? To the contrary, I would claim, that of this nature exactly all sound effects are: they all are connected and inextricably intertwined with particular listening situations, with corporeal constellations, personal desires, fears or individual sonic experiences. Sonic preferences are, as in this case, *by definition* rooted in idiosyncratic sonic desires. So, I wish to investigate, what desires are activated or

Figure 46 Schlierig, © Holger Schulze.

amplified, in a pleasurable way, by this sound effect of a distancing of some sound sources as if listened to through a veil, a curtain or as if from another room? What is so desirable about *not* being fully present in the notorious *sweet spot* of a projected sound?

When you actually listen from afar, from a distance or through a veil, a window pane, a wall, when some sound is oozing out through only partially open doors, somewhat blurred and smudged then you are obviously safe from it. It cannot shake you up. You are in a safe distance. You can keep all by yourself. You can still have a conversation with a friend or lover, you still might even engage in an activity that requires a fuller attention – be it reading or writing, preparing a meal, doing taxes or finalizing a calculation, bibliographic references or some handicraft? Sounds from a distance are sounds that respect the personal space of their listeners. You might be having dinner or going for a walk, caressing a romantic partner or playing with your dog, redecorating the window sill or watering your plants. It is a thoroughly urban, civilizing if not bourgeois quality of sounds that one enjoys from afar. This becomes even more obvious when investigating the details of listening situations in everyday life that offer this kind of comfort: when on a balcony I can feel safe, yet included; outside, in a park, I might enjoy the company of sounds, but can still be all on myself; the same goes for the aforementioned open door; but also the earbuds that allow me to listen to music, somewhat from afar, can serve as a tool for a distanced listening pleasure. My favourite example however, in domestic and situated terms is to listen to a sound source when falling asleep: the sound comforts you, it makes sure you do not feel left alone, but it is also not too intrusive. You can listen to it, if you like. But it is alright not to listen to it. It provides a comforting and a tender sound that envelopes you. The infamous white noise machines, the *Sleep-Mates* and sound conditioners from the 1960s, all the online noise generators or the more recent calming apps (Hagood 2019) – they all perfectly serve to their users and listeners as a grounding sound of a grey and veiled, a respectfully calming presence that does not aggressively harass or even attack you. Today, some listeners might prefer to fall asleep to podcasts or tender ambient recordings. A pleasure that attaches firmly to the first half of Brian Eno's foundational criterion for ambient music he provided in the last sentence of the liner notes to *Music for Airports*: 'it must be as ignorable as it is interesting' (Eno 1978).

It is, however, a musical genre in the wider field of rock music, born in the 1980s, that is surprisingly consistent with precisely this aesthetic; at the same time it represents proto-ambient music and a calming array of white noise generators: it is the music of *Shoegaze* that is thoroughly defined by its blurred and trancelike, often drone-filled usage of instrumental sounds. In an article from 1997 a somewhat paradoxical habit of its guitar performers is taken as its starting point, performing in withdrawal:

> One faction came to be known as dream-pop or shoegazers (for their habit of looking at the ground while playing the guitars on stage). They were musicians who played trancelike, ethereal music that was composed of numerous guitars playing heavy droning chords wrapped in echo effects and phase shifters. (Prown & Newquist 1997: 237)

Shoegaze, in this sense, is a hauntological musical genre by design. In its historical time the use of guitars, effect pedals and an aesthetic of drones within the notorious *Wall of Sound* as idealized by producer Phil Spector constitutes the material and sonic substance of this genre. From a standpoint of the early twenty-first century and its expanded ubiquitous corpus of recordings, back catalogues and archival works shoegaze needs to be situated in an intersection between pre-ambient Krautrock, maybe even Trance, also between Burial and The Caretaker and, most obviously, even as an unsuspected version of radical Noise or Industrial from artists such as Merzbow or Throbbing Gristle. Bands iconic for this genre, like My Bloody Valentine, Slowdive or Ride, perform a blurred and softened amalgam of various genre constituents and trace elements. These elements then represent for me, a listener, the traces of fleeting memories, evading sensations, and vague and ambivalent, even numbed or paralysed sensibilities: an intricate and fragile mélange. I feel at the same time haunted by sonic allusions and reminders, masked behind drones and colourful noise – and I feel freed from all of these, as the greyish, smudged, blurred and *schlierige* sound leaves me be, as a listener, in my familiar listening habit and situation. The blurred and the grey are, in this case, true markers of individual freedom, of autonomy.

This experience is not so much a phenomenon of retromania, following Reynolds (Reynolds 2010). It is also not possible to explicate it fully with Fisher's notion of hauntology. It is definitely not a secondary or subordinate phenomenon of listening. To the contrary, this listening experience of a distanced, slightly distorted, but still agreeable, pleasurable yet smudged sound, grants us listeners the room to breathe, to think, to drift and dream, to imagine and, also, not to listen. It is, quite clearly, an openly white and a bourgeois form of listening. But it is also a weak, an unstable and an insecure specimen of listening. It is an aesthetics of listening that stands in harsh opposition to all the massively advertised ideals of perfect listening in the sweet spot, being in the focus of the most brilliant and clear and immediate sonic events. *Schlierige Klänge*, smudged sounds are tender and caring as such.

When listening to them, one is granted the pleasure of enjoying the musical, the referential, also the sonic and especially the masking and shielding effect of sound – without the violent, and often inhumane demand for full and unlimited attention. These sounds do not wish to overwhelm anyone listening to them. They do not intend to overpower you. One is granted the gift of inattentiveness, of being distracted or drifting along, into different territories, of times and moments, doubts and idiosyncrasies. Your sensibilities and your experiential listening body are respected here: you can be the *sonic persona* you are right now (Schulze 2018). These sounds respect you being, in most of the cases, potentially careless about their existence – as if from a civilized distance. Smudged sounds offer you a moment of reconvalescent listening, deeply recreational or even rehabilitating listening: an instant of sonic healing and an outstretched experience of audible care.

References
Eno, Brian. *Music for Airports. Ambient 1.* London: E. G. Records, 1978.
Fisher, Mark. 'What Is Hauntology?' *Film Quarterly* 66, no. 1 (2012): 16–24.
Fisher, Mark. *Ghosts of My Life: Writings on Depression, Hauntology and Lost Futures.* Winchester: Zero Books, 2014.
Hagood, Mack. *Hush: Media and Sonic Self-Control.* Durham: Duke University Press, 2019.
Prown, Pete, and Harvey P. Newquist. *Legends of Rock Guitar.* Milwaukee: Hal Leonard, 1997.
Reynolds, Simon. *Retromania: Pop Culture's Addiction to its Own Past.* London: Faber & Faber, 2010.
Schulze, Holger. *The Sonic Persona: An Anthropology of Sound.* New York: Bloomsbury Academic, 2018.
Schulze, Holger. *Sonic Fiction.* New York: Bloomsbury Academic, 2020.

Schwätza (Swabian: to chat, to gabble, to talk, to speak)
Friedemann Dupelius

Swabians like to *schwätza* and at the same time they don't. Whereas the verb *schwätzen* in High German is a colloquial synonym for chatting or gossiping, in Swabian it is the general term for holding a conversation and for verbal expressions. The Swabians are proud of their dialect, which manifests itself in the tourism slogan 'Wir können alles. Außer Hochdeutsch'. ('We can do everything. Except High German.') At the same time, the inhabitants of the south-western German area that covers most parts of the former Kingdom of Württemberg (now part of the state of Baden-Württemberg) and some adjacent western parts of Bavaria, are infamous for their sparing use of words. In addition to their frugal use of money they are also economic when it comes to talking. This doesn't stop at the kitchen table, where eating in silence is already considered as praise for the cook's skills ('Net gschempft isch gnuag globt.' – 'Not scolding is enough praise.')

At the said table, one can find an interesting alternative use of the verb *schwätza*. One of the most famous dishes in the Swabian cuisine is potato salad (*Kartoffelsalat*). A popular saying goes: 'Kartoffelsalat muss schwätza', that is, 'potato salad must talk'. This refers to the smacking and flicking sounds a well-prepared potato salad utters. Here, the agency in *schwätza* exceeds from humans to food, and at some discreet Swabian lunch tables the salad may even be the most talkative part of the table society.

In 1596, the English botanist John Gerard described the potato, which has been imported from America to Europe since the early sixteenth century, in his book, *The Herball or Generall Historie of Plantes*. Besides an accurate scientific description of the potato plant, he also put down the first documented recipe for a potato salad in Europe: 'The Temperature and vertues to be referred unto the common Potatoes, being likewise a food, as also a meate for pleasure, equall in goodnesse and wholesomenesse unto the same, being either rosted in the embers, or boyled and eaten with oyle, veneger, and pepper (..).' This is basically the recipe for the classic Swabian potato salad that was expanded with salt as well as parsley or chives and sometimes chopped onions.

It took some time for the potato to arrive in Württemberg. After the Thirty Years' War and some military conflicts with the French, the country was poor and people were starving. Fearing a population shrinkage, Württemberg offered Vaudois refugees – Protestants persecuted in France – the opportunity to settle; some of them even founded their own villages like Perouse. Most of them were farmers and skilled in making abandoned ground fertile again. In 1701, Vadouis seed supplier Antoine Seignoret brought the potato to Württemberg and, in addition to Schupfnudeln (Swabian potato noodles) or roast potatoes, also the Swabian potato salad developed in the simple and poor circumstances given at that time. Back then, vegetable oil was costly, so the first Swabian potato salad presumably was prepared with hot pork lard. This was probably a stiff and stodgy affair that soon led the Swabians to use broth to dilute the dish. Vinegar instead was cheap and easy to afford, so it was heavily used for giving the salad its characteristic sour taste.

It's this way of preparation that enables the potato salad to *schwätzen*. A Swabian potato salad, like other dishes of this cuisine, has a soft and glutinous consistency, which in Swabian is described as *schlonzig*. This dialect term refers to the perfect in-between consistency of a meal that is equally not too runny and not too solid. When you dig your fork into the sliced potatoes and they make a smacking and fizzling sound, this is a sonic prophecy of an enjoyable meal. For even more pleasures, the potato salad will continue *schwätzing* as it is chewed in the mouth.

The perfect *schwätza* sound is achieved in finding the right balance of broth and potatoes. The potatoes should absorb the broth and equally release starch when dressed. Pouring the broth over the still-warm potatoes makes them absorb more of it and therefore creates more *schlonzig* and *schwätzend* sound. But it's just as important to let the boiled potatoes rest a little – when too hot, the starch escapes and they become crumbly. Dousing the salad with oil at the end helps the dressing soak in even better. So, it's all about the permeation of potato matter and liquid. A potato salad *schwätzes* when there is contact and exchange. It's about taking and giving – absorbing and releasing. In these special circumstances, communication is happening.

Figure 47 Schwätza, © Laura Weber www.lauraweber.net.

A good, smacking, *schwätzing* potato salad makes a Swabian person feel safe and home. It's mumbling to their subconscious: 'Don't worry, you are fed and nourished.' Usually, a potato salad is the number one side to the famous Swabian *Maultaschen* – dumplings filled with meat, spinach and breadcrumbs – and also popular in combination with other meat and vegetarian dishes as well as it is the most popular component of any Swabian salad bar.

Protestant refugees brought the potato to Württemberg about 300 years ago, which directly links Swabian potato salad with Protestantism. Around the same time, the Protestant belief movement of Pietism spread in Württemberg and has shaped the mentality of its inhabitants ever since. Pietists were critical of both secular and ecclesiastical authorities. They saw Christian values such as charity and altruism on the wane since the wars and advocated in-depth Bible study. Pietism shaped people's sense of both democracy and criticism of authority, as well as the work ethic and entrepreneurial spirit which led to the founding of big companies in Swabia, such as Daimler, Bosch or Porsche. At the same time, Pietism is said to have had a certain degree of prudence, abstinence and frugality.

Potato salad manifests the development of a region from a poor farmer's country to one of the most prosperous areas in Europe. It's a simple dish, quick and easy to prepare and still it stands for humility and simple pleasure (and pleasure is not a given in Swabia). It's a simplicity that actually doesn't correspond to the wealth of the majority of Swabians. There are some more interesting tensions in potato salad and its sound: its flicking is reminiscent of the sound of bodily fluids during sexual intercourse, which contrasts with the more disembodied prudence of Pietism. And this paradox is also found in the word *schwätza* itself: Swabians don't talk much and often refuse to engage in conversation with strangers, but if their potato salad can talk well, they feel understood and enjoy the chat a lot.

Sssshhhh (English)
Lawrence English

simplified ocean
A whisper to fill the void
promise of absence

Sssshhhh
Your world is shrinking...

Sssshhhh
You are retreating...

Sssshhhh
You are being reduced, your perspective and agency in the world is being eroded...

Sssshhhh
Sssshhhh
Sssshhhh

What is left then? In the wake of Sssshhhh. Perhaps it could be described as a horizon of audition that is submerged in acoustic fog, permitting perception that is shrouded and only sanctioned within the realm close to the body. It is a means of carving out a snug reckoning of place and engendering a state of listening that is slowly being folded ever downward into the semi-consciousness of lulled hearing.

The building block of Sssshhhh is the diagraph Sh, an unvoiced fricative that exists across a great many spoken cultures, albeit with a variation of applications. Its associations with quietening have been formalized in various language groups across the millennia. Shh, as a phoneme, without a low-frequency vowel or high-frequency plosives, maintains a unique vocal quality that is both easily repeated and acoustically dominating when used in close proximity to a listener. Its repetition across language groups is assured by the physiology of the human body.

Since the earliest days of emergent human cultures, we have sought to exclude or diminish sensory stimulation from select moments of our lives. Our ears, one of the tools we relied on so heavily during these times of lurking uncertainties in the dark nights, can filter information just as successfully as they collect it. Even now as you read this your ears are actively reducing the surrounds of your environment, the whirring of hard drives, the chirping of birds and mumbled voices from outside, all drifting underneath the blanket of conscious thought. Subliminal as it may be, your capacities to be stimulated by the world around you are in a state of near-constant shrinkage.

We can recognize stimulation as a great double-edged sword carving through the pleasure/pain dialectic. At its best, stimulation induces states of positive elation, and at its worst crippling anxiety and uncertainty. Even before the ceaseless cascade of sound from our modern urban environments, we sought (for ourselves and those close to us) a release from the demanding weariness that was required to persist in environments that presented all manner of potential dangers be those predation, encounters with less than hospitable neighbouring humans or other threats. In these places and times, Ssssshhhh worked as a way of 'not knowing' what lay beyond the edge of the campfire light. Whatever dangers were there, dangers that might only be revealed through our capability as listeners probing the very depths of the ambient noise floor for events and variation, Ssssshhhh masked them and in doing so acted as an anxiety release. It offered just enough proximate separation from the unknown fears, hidden in the dark, for unconsciousness to settled upon us.

Modern echoes of this phenomenon abound, albeit echoes that reflect a far less savage setting. In the early 1960s, James and Trudy Buckwater spent a restless evening in a rundown roadside motel. In that room, where their air conditioner was broken, they tossed and turned as uneasy thoughts pulsed through their minds. These restless contemplations centred upon the absence of the consuming whirr of the air conditioner, a whirr they came to realize quietened the escalating waves of sound from outside.

Without the perfunctory motor, gently humming and blowing on them, like some kind of mechanical evocation of Sssssshhhh, they were unable to forgo an awareness of what lay beyond their motel door; their minds were active, seeking and agitated. It was these initial moments of unease that would a few years later result in a successful patent lodgement of the *Sleep Inducing Sound Producing Machine*, a device first sold as Sleep Mate, but which is still in production today as Dohm by the Marpac company. More importantly, it was this device that formed a base upon which countless mechanical Ssssshhhhes have been and continue to be manifested.

memory comfort
This hush to erase a place
hypnogogic, dream

As singular as Sssshhhh might be considered in the first instance we casually encounter it, if we actually become attentive to its sonic character, a slightly prolonged exposure to the sound is often fatiguing to even the most seasoned listener. Perhaps this is due to partly socially conditioning – our parent's calm desire for us to be quiet is ever-present. Still unquestionably, when considering the nature of this sonic material, Ssssshhhh is an emphatically *vertical* sound.

Vertical here refers to what a sound invites from its listener. On the surface Ssssshhhh appears deceptively simple and dimensionless; it is seemingly uniform and unwavering but upon casting our ear into the sound, it creates an abyss of complexity – an overabundance of information that captives and excites, while simultaneously fatiguing and finally subduing our interrogations. It's little wonder the sound can be used interchangeably (with some pitch variation), for the sound of wind in the trees or

Figure 48 Ssssshhh 'Hush! He sleeps' engraved by J. Franck after a picture by J. H. S. Mann, published in *The Art Journal*, 1866. Steel engraved antique print with recent hand colour. Good condition. Size 19.5 x 27 cm including title, plus margins. Ref H3616 – public domain.

surf caressing a sandy shore. These sounds too maintain a tremendous capacity to overload our audition; they are deceptive and provoke in us a reductive appreciation that speaks strongly to the habits of our everyday listenership. We often find ourselves opting to associate these sounds with white noise, a fitting reference as it maintains a promise of an infinite zone of audition, a theoretically possible universe of frequency and tempered amplitude stretching across the sound spectrum without limitation.

Ssssshhhh's multiplicity of functions also speak to the materiality of sound, both in terms of creation (through its utterance) and its reception. The sound's timbre, a somehow all-encompassing upper frequency blanket, has a way of consuming all sound in its wake, not just those sonics that share the frequency band of the emission. Ssssshhhh's mimetic relation to white noise is evident, but moreover it's the capacity of this sound to create reflection and acoustic backscatter that is both distinct and profound.

As any parent would attest, Ssssshhhh when delivered to an infant in arms reflects off their face and body, creating a kind of affective feedback loop that can be as therapeutic for the parent as for the child. This is perhaps doubly present for the emitter of the sound, as the internal resonance of the sound within the mouth and into the skull combined with the faint vibrational massage-like quality that tempers the lips is an unusually satisfying combination of sensory interactions.

Tides swallow the shore
Each wave articulated
Ocean alone, speaks

For many on the receiving end, Ssssshhhh is a sound of reassurance, an affective relation to a time and place in which they were positively enveloped, not just in an acoustic way, but also in a physical one – in the arms of a parent or loved one. Ssssshhhh here, in these moments of consolation and reassurance, is acutely reductive. It affords a plunge into the cushioned interiority of our protected and loved selves. The sound then is received as an invitation to close down external stimulation, reducing the capacity of the senses (in this case the auditory) from being disturbed by the events surrounding the listener. It's a positive disassociation from the exterior, in favour of an interior attachment. A singularity of intense externally generated, but self-actualized pleasure. A provocation to remember: less can be so much more.

Within this blissfully reductive reading of Ssssshhhh, however, lurks a baleful undercurrent. That reductive sensation, that closing off of a potential means for communication in the world comes to us ghosted by an evil twin. This twin not only refuses any affective consolations but simultaneously seeks to disconnect us, gripping those in its clasp tightly and hurling them into an abyss of isolation, frustration and *languagelessness*. Even if words are found, language actualized, these words are eroded by a spilling forth of frequency that is emitted by those who, *Ssssshhhh*.

We must be cautious; silence is violence and Ssssshhhh as an utterance inherently seeks to mute. In situations of domestic violence and abusive relationships, racial intolerance, misogyny, political struggles and many other locations of desire for something more than is present in those moments, Ssssshhhh is often used to quash hopes for change. It is used to eviscerate enunciation, sometimes doubly cruel when offered with an all-knowing 'quiet, I know better than you'. It is not just a refusal to let speak, but a refusal to listen, a complete disavowal of an agent's wills and aspirations to be recognized. Ssssshhhh may exist then as a vulgar display of power.

Drawing upon a reading of the absolute potential of noise to consume sound in all directions at once, Ssssshhhh becomes imbued with the potential to shut down and collapse the capacities of individuals and groups to interact effectively in the world around them. The legitimization of this strategy is ubiquitous – aspirational autocrats such as the forty-fifth president of the United States used this technique with a flagrant disregard for anyone seeking to interrogate his questionable capacities at leadership and policy development. A casual listening to parents engaging with their children in a shopping mall reveals a seemingly innocuous but aligned use of this technique. Even when offered as a sympathetic soothe for a weeping baby, Ssssshhhh carries a secondary meaning of 'please be quiet, I am not in a position to hear your feelings just now'. Ssssshhhh, like the ideals of noise it emulates, creates a complexity of potential meaning (and obfuscation) that may carry both positively and negatively charged denotation, within the same utterance. A sound in the absolute.

Skoskespringe (Dutch)
Jan Kleefstra

There have been winters in Friesland, the northern part of the Netherlands, in which all the water in the area I grew up was frozen. The lakes, canals and ditches. For waterbirds and birds that had to find their food in the water, these were days of starvation, for people the short days were filled with nostalgia. We skated for days on the waters we knew from swimming in summertime. But fortunately, these periods of ice always ended in days of thaw. Slowly the ice was getting thinner and started to break. It meant that spring and warmer days were coming. Wind was getting a grip on the water again. The ice was falling apart in ice floes. Literally 'skoskespringe' means jumping from one floe to another. When they are big enough you can walk/jump on water as long as you don't fall. These big foes have violent sometimes unearthly sounds. When they rise up to the shores through strong wind they even get threatening. But when the wind is gentle, you can risk a wet suit and jump from one floe to another all across the water.

For me 'skoskepringe' has another and a more gentle meaning. That is when the floes are getting really small and very thin. Mostly these floes appear in small canals or wide ditches. There is only a bit of ice left and there is a very gentle wind on a sunny day that promises spring in the light it carries. When the small waves shove the small pieces of ice against and over each other, they make the most amazing sparkling sound. It is almost the sound we think the light could make if we could hear it or sounds that surround us in heaven. It is as if the sound is not coming from the pieces of ice but from the lights that glitter from the waves and the ice in a joyful celebration of liberation from the heavy ice-covered days.

The sounds are very small and short but are numerous and continuous as if dancing on the boundary of the water and the remains of the ice in the light that gets no grip on this untouchable beauty. It is most similar when a lake is covered with hundreds or thousands of wigeons. When they start to whistle by many at the same time and continue to do so, it approaches almost the same experience of the sounds of the leaving ice. For me the sound then jumps from floe to floe in a very vulnerable way. The sound 'skoskespringt' in accordance with the light and the waves and the wind all together in the most gentle and liberated way sound can free you from all the sorrow and time. It is an unearthly sound, though it appears on earth. It is a sound that must be there when you enter Nirvana.

Most kinds of art mimic the natural world. Only abstract art tries to keep away from that, but hardly ever manages to do so, because also the natural world is in its smallest and biggest parts abstract itself, and also because

we humans are nature, we are connected to the natural world, so everything we do is always part of her. We are trapped in our own mistake that human and nature are two different phenomena. Therefore we think art is a human expression, but it isn't. It is an expression from nature through the existence of human beings. That inner truth draws us to nature and causes the fact that arts are mostly a mimic of nature itself. It is a circle we cannot escape even if we wanted to.

In music we also witness the desire to mimic sounds from the natural world, for instance, by making field recordings to catch the sounds of nature and use them in the parts of music being made. I have only heard a small part of the music ever made on this planet, but I haven't heard any music that is similar or comes close to the sounds of the little floes of ice on the boundary of water and ice. A few pieces of music try to come close. For instance, there is *In the White Silence* by John Luther Adams. In this music there are these small bits of sounds that connect to the sound of the floes of ice. But, moreover, there is the general atmosphere of the music that connects to the feeling you feel in all your senses when you are there on the edge of the water near the boundary and you hear the sounds in a light and time in which winter turns into spring.

Another piece is *Imperial* from Unrest. The first part of the piece visualizes the small, gentle waves on the water. And then around five and a half minutes suddenly the waves enter the boundary where the sound of the floes of ice comes in. And when they passed that boundary there is the one tone of the remaining layer of ice on the other side of the boundary. A sound that left the water and now waves upon the air that is in the hands of the wind.

The third piece is *How I Blew It with Houdini* from Long Fin Killie. This is more about the sounds we don't hear, but must be there under water just below the boundary. It is a bit darker sound, but with the uplifting small sounds that

Figure 49 Skoskespringe, © Jan Kleefstra.

must be there above the water and of which small echoes must be heard under water. And the disappearing of Houdini is similar to the slowly disappearing of this boundary and the sounds that it makes and are soon to be gone even from your memory, because the memory is never capable of preserving such amazing beauty. In all these pieces the tones and chords 'skoskespringe'.

As far as I'm aware the air's the sea
and my knife scrapes the wind to waves
again and again

with unheard brushes
smoothes fables through her stiffness
lift a little light
closer to the glass house
to trace the shadow I cast yesterday

crawl little by little into the crooked constitution
that by an invisible thread hangs
from a thundercloud

break the reed in two
have a nightmare
hurl a stone into her eye

This boundary is only there for a very short time. Thaw creeps its way in and only leaves a very small amount of time for this boundary to be there to witness. In this little while the two worlds are visually also clearly separated. On one side there are the remains of the ice. A part of the canal is still covered with the disappearing ice. A small layer of water on top of it causes a mirroring in which the sky is almost as beautifully covered as on a windless lake. This captured side of the boundary is in full, but dying peace.

The other side is already liberated and shows a cautious joy of the wind and the water. It still has some fear for the frost and the ice, so it stays gentle and friendly, but the outburst is soon to come when all the ice is gone.

The sound appears in the surrendering of the ice to the thaw, the wind and the water. There is definitely the appearance of joy in the sound, but, on the other hand, there is also the disappearing sound, a sound maybe never to be heard again and very much related to the circumstances in which it can appear and survive for a small amount of time. So the sound itself 'skoskepringt' also through time. Every now and then somewhere on this planet it appears and dies away. That connects here to the cosmic sounds that are everywhere but rarely to be heard outside in nature by the human ears.

It has become a rare sound though, because there are hardly ever severe winters anymore to cover the waters with enough ice. So, it is also a sound that 'skoskepringt' through my memories and longings. But fortunately, the wigeons are still here every winter and I can hide behind the reeds and listen to their whistling as if it is the melting ice and the wind playing with it, even when the lights are dark and spring is a long way away.

Šniokštimas (Lithuanian)
Daiva Steponavičienė

Šniokštimas ('shnyok-shtee-mahs', a noun) - a sound that a sea or trees make on a windy day (as well as falling water, like a waterfall or strong rain). Sometimes these words are used for something else, like the sound of breathing when a person has a lung disease, because it resembles.

Dūzgimas ('Dooz-ghee-mahs', a noun. English version would be humming) - a sound that bees make. This word is used in any other context only if it resembles bees.

Ošimas (oh-shee-maahs, a noun). A sound that only sea and trees make on a windy day. Barely used for something else.

Zyzimas (zee-zee-mahs, a noun), zyzia (zee-zyah, a verb). A high pitch, fast and dynamic sound, like a mosquito or nagging children.)

Pliumpt ('ploomt', onomatopoeic interjection) - a sound of something rather heavy falling into a somewhat-deep/big water (if you say this word correctly, it closely resembles the actual sound).

Tekšt (teh-ksht, onomatopoeic interjection) - a flat sound of something flat hitting the surface of usually water (it could be a pond, morass). Could be used for describing a slap in the face too.

So'kout (سکوت) (Persian)
Yashar Valakjie

So'kout (سکوت) (/so'kut/Iranian Persian and /sukut/Classical Persian) meaning stillness or silence is derived from the Arabic radical of the verb سَكَتَ /sakata/ meaning the state of becoming motionless, calm and stop moving.

Here the 'Silence' is referred to as a state that is tightly characterized by the absence of motion, hence the stillness.

This directly links so'kout (stillness) to the materiality of the sound waves, acted upon by the rules of physics in contrast to how in many fields – that are mostly dominated by more dominant visual thinking – sound is looked at, as something immaterial or even spiritual.

So, in this case, it is the elimination of the movement that results in silence. However, we could still go further by examining its Persian synonym khamoushi (خاموشی, /xɒːmuːˈʃiː/ Iranian Persian, /xɑːmoːˈʃiː/Classical Persian) and we could argue a case for the leakage and expansion of the 'silence' into other dimensions. Khamoushi referred to a state of silence, an absence of sound, either for a person to remain silent or as in silence, that is, for a place to be quiet – the implication of what is quiet is far beyond the scope of this text; but as a hint it could refer to a state of absence of 'noise', for example, being in a calm environment, or we could think of a more radical case of absence of sound, for example, in an anechoic chamber or ultimately, the absence of adequate medium, for example, in the vacuum of space – however the actual difference between so'kout and khamoushi is that the latter could also refer to the absence of light, for example, darkness, and to be fair, in contemporary use cases, khamoushi is often used in this sense. But as an adjective 'khamoush' refers to a place that is extremely quiet to point that it could even mean – in the case of atmospheric description of the place – it is also dark, for example, a dark silent house, valley or sea. It is also used to describe a person or any other living creature's

Figure 50 Tehran Moon, © Yashar Valakjie.

desire to remain silent as well as the state of being dead or figuratively said: to lie still in death.

We could argue that in the case of the khamoushi the silence that generally resulted due to the stillness of motion takes a broader scale from the easily perceptible mechanical motion to the ceasing of functions on a microbiological level – in case of the death – and over to the electromagnetic spectrum, that is, the absence of vibrations of particles of light or simply put darkness.

Finally, it is worth mentioning that the word 'khamoushi' has been frequently used by many poets and writers over many centuries, hence its archaic quality in today's contemporary Persian language.

Šup (Czech)
David Livingstone

- **The Czech Word You Can't Live Without**

One of the frustrations of living abroad and learning the local language is to realize that there is a whole new 'undiscovered country' when you have children. At least this is my experience having lived and raised children in the Czech Republic. Words needed for encouraging your toddler to produce a poo on the potty or close its eyes and finally go to bed are not usually included in your language books. Czech, unlike English, is extremely rich in diminutives to be used under these circumstances as well as a number of onomatopoeic words which come in handy when dealing with uncooperative children, animals and so on.

Among the Czech words I learned from my child-rearing days, and which I continue to use actively, is the onomatopoeic interjection 'šup' (shoop) meaning a quick movement or a fast activity. On a side note, zvukomalba (literally sound-painting), the Czech word for onomatopoeia, is quite charming. The word 'šup' is short and efficient and can be used in many contexts: giving instructions to move to a child or dog; encouraging someone to get off their fat ass and do something (useful with teenagers); and even in an erotic setting (or so I've been told).

There are various theories as to its etymology. Czech, although a West Slavonic language, has many words from German and one explanation is the origin being in the word 'schub' meaning to push or shove. Other sources claim it to have Slavic roots, while the most intriguing would be it having its origins in the Italian 'subito presto' (right away soon), which would link it with the English usage of 'presto' (suddenly), which is often used by a magician when performing a magic trick and is of course also a technical musical term for speeding up the tempo. The word 'šup' is also used in Slovak and in Polish, the latter sounding the same, but spelled 'siup'. I do not know of an English equivalent (the closest might be 'chop-chop' or 'spit-spot', only having heard the latter spoken by my first love Julie Andrews in the film *Mary Poppins*) and certainly not one which is so short and nifty. The French borrowing 'voilà' might have some affinities, at least in certain contexts, when something has successfully turned out right.

Regardless of the origin, the word is used extremely frequently in Czech with one friend with small children stating that is the most common word used by parents in the changing room at kindergarten. Czech, like most Central Europeans, tend to have unwritten rules concerning outdoor and indoor clothing. Upon arrival at kindergarten, parents have to assist their often protesting five-year-olds to change into their school uniform, which consists of slippers for both boys and girls, usually tights and a T-shirt and sometimes a cute apron for the ladies. You might throw in some 'šups' while encouraging your child to pull on their tights themselves instead of passively resisting or when finally sending them into the classroom after tears and clinging. At the end of a hard day, you might also employ 'šup' when encouraging your child to finally get into bed after endless delays for drinks of water and pees.

Figure 51 The author having a slivovice.

Sticking with the bed setting, 'šup' could also be used in an erotic context when, for example, a woman encourages her husband/lover to join her in bed before the sexy mood fades or the sheets grow cold. In my own case, 'šup' is usually only used by my wife, when in bed, to encourage one of our two (or both) over-affectionate dogs to join us, on my side of course. Despite all of my 'šups' directed at them to move over so I can extend my legs, they don't seem to understand my Czech. My wife and I also make use of the word profusely when trying to compete for the attention of our cat. When sitting on the couch watching a film while sharing a blanket, we both attempt to coax the cat over for a cuddle with the words 'domeček' (small house), indicating our competing comfortable spaces, and 'šup', spoken for some reason in a high squeaky voice; the cat inevitably stares off into space and begins licking itself.

I have found myself using 'šup' quite often of late during my online lessons, usually with discouraging results. When teaching on zoom, I struggle mightily to successfully share screen powerpoints, videos and so on. While my students are waiting for me to demonstrate my talent, I enthusiastically say 'šup' (and here the origin in magic would seem most appropriate) expecting my technical skills to show fruition. Tragically, my efforts are often in vain and my students (if I'm lucky) point out that they are still staring at my desktop picture of Elvis with a banjo.

To end on a positive note, I am now pouring myself a shot of Moravian slivovice, usually translated as plum brandy but better served by the lovely Americanism moonshine, and 'šup', down the throat it goes.

- **Tapedropping**
Daniel R. Wilson
Tapedropping refers to the deliberate placement of home-made audio cassettes in public places for people to find. It was introduced on the radio series 'The Exciting Hellebore Shew' on Resonance 104.4FM airing in late 2003, showcasing the guerrilla cassette soundworks of sound artist and theorist Daniel Wilson from 1996 onwards.[31] According to Wilson's manifesto on this practice (published in 2006) dropped cassettes typically contain challenging, comical or confrontational home-made sounds, words or music to elicit reactions from anonymous people who discover them.[32] Email addresses provided on the cassette sleeves enable responses to be harvested, and the response-eliciting effectiveness of tapedropped music can be refined further by drawing on such communications. The wider term 'mediadropping" was implemented around the time of the cassette's decline as a mainstream audio format, *c.* 2005, to accommodate CD-Rs as a droppable format, but this was found to be an inferior medium for the practice, generating lower response rates[33].

Thủy: Water in the sea
Nguyễn Thanh Thủy

1. Thủy
I was born in Hà Nội. When my parents chose a name for me, they thought of a famous verse from the epic poem *Truyện Kiều* (*The Tale of Kiều*) by Nguyễn Du.[34] This is one of the verses which describes the beauty of Lady Kiều:

> Làn thu thủy nét xuân sơn
> Hoa ghen thua thắm liễu hờn kém xanh[35]

Truyện Kiều was written in 3254 verses in Vietnamese traditional *lục-bát* form. *Lục-bát* is Sino-Vietnamese for six–eight, referring to the alternating lines of six and eight syllables. It will always begin with a six-syllable line and end with an eight-syllable one (Vũ, 1956). Rhymed verses in Vietnam are related to proverbs. It is not only the abstract and metaphorical-typical language of poetry but also the rhythm, and the combination of both rhyme and tone in Vietnamese makes this traditional verse form impossible to translate into other languages.

So my parents chose the word *Thủy*, as my first name. *Thủy* means *sea* or *water in the sea*. Today, as an adult, sometimes I think of my name and Kiều's poem. Often my name appears in my mind as an image. But since I am not good at drawing, I described the meaning of my name to my eleven-year-old daughter and asked her to help me visualize it. Below is her drawing; an image which also conveys how my daughter perceives my name (Figure 52).

The Vietnamese tone system belongs to the pitch-plus-voice quality type, that is, the tone is not defined solely in terms of pitch: it is a complex bundle of pitch contour and voice quality characteristics (Michaud, 2004). Hà Nội Vietnamese is typically described as a tonal language which distinguishes between six tones (see Figure 53), although some researchers have identified more variants, for instance, adding two additional variants in pitch and tone colour (see, for instance, Brunelle et al., 2010).

The six tones of the Vietnamese language are

ngang A1 – (level)
huyền A2 – (mid falling)
sắc B1 – (rising)
nặng B2 – (low glottalized)
hỏi C1 – (low falling)
ngã C2 – (broken)

My name, *Thủy*, has a low-falling tone, *hỏi*, also characterized by breathy voice quality.[36] If you just slightly raise your voice, *Thúy*, or fail to make your voice fall low enough, *Thùy*, you would call someone else's name. The chart above only indicates Hà Nội Vietnamese. Vietnam is a long country and the dialectal variations in the tonal structure of the language shift as you move south, from region to region through the country.

2. Việt Cộng

I do not need to travel very far to experience that I can't hear the sound of my name the way it would sound to me if I were in Hà Nội. In 1995, during my first year as a junior in Hanoi Conservatory of Music, I travelled to Hồ Chí Minh city the first time to attend the *National đàn tranh competition*. The train ride took almost thirty-eight hours and I slept most of the time on the train because of being train-sick. Hereby, I missed all the stunning landscapes, shifting continuously as the journey unfolds from the north to the south. When I got off the train, there were so much people everywhere, the noise from all the vehicles on the streets, many high buildings and the sound of people talking was so different from Hà Nội where I came from. I thought I had just arrived in a new country. There, in the south, the sound of my name appeared with a different tone, more of a broken tone rather than a low falling tone. I remember I felt hesitant when I needed to talk to people since my voice sounded so "out of tune". One day, I needed to go to the school of music. I went outside of the guest house to where there were several motorbike taxis standing and waiting for customers. I told a motorbike driver where I wanted to go. He gave me a little longer glance (I thought) and said (I wasn't sure he said it to me or to himself): 'a, con nhỏ Việt Cộng!'[37] (ah, a little Việt Cộng girl!).

That trip to Hồ Chí Minh city was an eye-opener for me, and that was the first time I began to grasp the division of my country, which was the result of the civil war. That memory now remains as a scene in my mind with my name as part of the script.

3. Rượu vang

And here I am in Sweden, the country I now regard as my second home.[38] I don't hear Vietnamese often in everyday life, and if I would hear it now and then, it is definitely not the same sound I would hear if

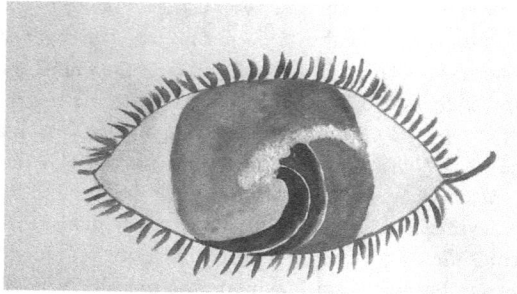

Figure 52 The image of my name, visualized in a drawing by my 11-years old daughter Đặng Lan Yên.

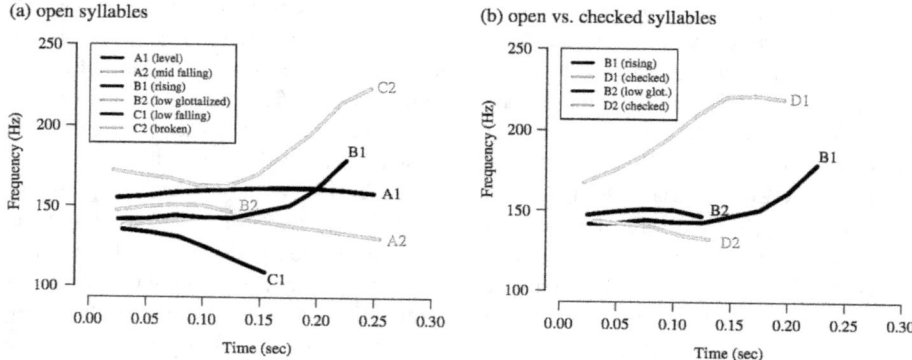

Figure 53 Tracks of tones for a male speaker of Hà Nội Vietnamese. Panel (a) shows the six tones found in open sonorant-final syllables; panel (b) compares the pitch of rising and low glottalized tones in open or sonorant-final syllables (black lines) with their checked counterparts (grey lines) (Kirby, 2011, p. 386).

I were in Vietnam. But in the work with my Vietnamese Swedish group *The Six Tones*,[39] I try to experiment not only with Vietnamese music but also with Vietnamese language. One example is a collaboration I made with the composer Henrik Frisk in 2014, a piece for my instrument – *đàn tranh*, my voice, and electronics, titled *Drinking*.[40] The way the working process was designed, the chosen poem – *A Drinking Song* by William B. Yeats in a translation to Vietnamese, was recited by me, and it was the sonic trace of the reading that constituted the point of departure for the composition *Drinking*. Following the instructions in *After Yeats*, I had to practice and develop my reading, based on the text and a recording of Yeats's own recitation (Brooks, 2013). When one Vietnamese word is read slowly and articulated for longer than it should in normal speech, it creates a clearer melodic pattern for each word. The word (as well as its meaning) is formed slowly from the beginning of the pattern until the end at the final pitch. In this case, the meaning of the words is of less significance than the melodic structure. This recording I then passed on to Henrik Frisk, who took the recording and—according to the instructions in *After Yeats*—composed the piece according to the implications of the declamation from my recitation. In an audio paper[41] in 2019, Frisk and I discuss the process of making this piece, and what we found in this process of translation, from English to Vietnamese, from text to sound, and how emotional responses that arise from engaging in artistic practice operate in a space beyond signification, similar to how Cobussen (2008) discusses listening, which 'involves an opening of the senses that is not necessarily enfolded in conscious meaningfulness, by sense. It also takes place outside, before or beyond sense; it also refers to a sense that operates outside, before or beyond signification' (p. 131) (Figure 54).

4. Quê[42]

When I was a child, in Mai Dịch, at the outskirts of Hà Nội in the 1980s, I heard my name every day from people around me, from my parents, my brother and my grandparents; from my neighbours; from my friends and my teachers in school; and so on. Life in Mai Dịch in those days was so different from today.[43] Back then, when people were at home, every door was always open. People spent much more time outside. My mother could be chatting with her neighbour next door while cooking. After school, kids often gathered and played in the open, around the many ponds and near the rice fields. My mother could just call her child's name from a distance when she wanted her child to come home for a meal or to go to bed. My friend could whisper my name from her window towards my window when it was time for us to skip the nap after lunch and sneak out to play. In those days, my name only appeared as a sound to me, outside of its semantic signification.

My name was one with its sound, which also filled it with emotional associations. As a musician, grown up in a small community in Hà Nội but now living in Sweden, I have sometimes addressed the soundscape of Hà Nội in academic writing, as well as in artistic projects. But I had never thought of how the

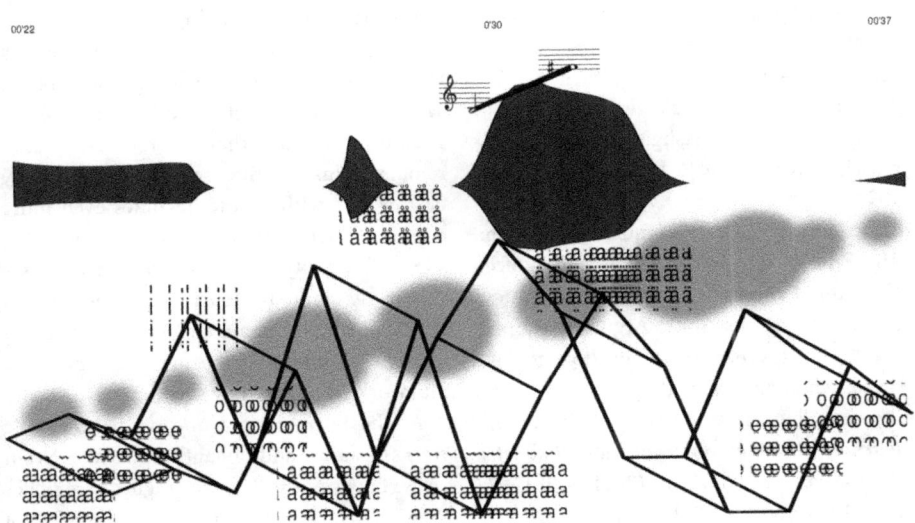

Figure 54 Example from Henrik Frisk's composition *Drinking* for voice, đàn tranh and electronics.

sound of my name also belongs to the memory of that soundscape, that as soon as I travel outside of Hà Nội, that sound still remains there. As Trịnh Minh-Ha (2011) observes in her book *Elsewhere, Within Here*, one may doubt whether "Mother's language at home – or Language – will ever be able to withstand the mobility of the journey" (p. 28). In my journey across the sea, I could only manage to bring fragments of my name with me. Other soundings couldn't travel with me, but stayed back home with my parents, with my childhood friends. Some perhaps only remain in my (fragmented) memory.

References

Allen, T. 'The Wooing Of Kiê`u By Kim'. *Poetry Review. Cosmopolis*, 99, no. 2 (2009). http://www.stephen-spender.org/SSMTrust/times_ss_prize_08/ssmt_evPrizeOpen_03.htm.

Brooks, W. *After Yeats for Performer and Composer*. Published score. Frog Peak Music, Lebanon, 2013.

Brunelle, M., D. Nguyen and K. H. Nguyên. 'A Laryngographic and Laryngoscopic Study of Northern Vietnamese Tones'. *Phonetica* 67 (2010): 147–69.

Cobussen, M. *Thresholds: Rethinking Spirituality in Music*. Ashgate Pub. Ltd, 2008.

Counsel, M. *Kiều*. Hà Nội: Thế Giới Publishers, 1994.

Frisk, H. and T. Nguyễn. 'Found in Translation: The Process of Making A Piece for Voice'. Vietnamese zither đàn tranh, and electronics. Seismograf, Fokus: Sonic Argumentation I, 22, 2019. https://seismograf.org/fokus/sonic-argumentation-i/frisk_thuy.

Kirby, J. 'Vietnamese (Hanoi Vietnamese)'. *Journal of the International Phonetic Association* 41, no. 3 (2011): 381–92. doi:10.1017/S0025100311000181.

Michaud, A. 'Final Consonants and Glottalization: New Perspectives from Hanoi Vietnamese'. *Phonetica, Karger* 61, no. 2–3 (2004): 119–46.

Östersjö, S. and T. Nguyễn. 'The Sounds of Hanoi and the After-Image of the Homeland'. *Journal of Sonic Studies*, 2016. Retrieved from https://www.researchcatalogue.net/view/246523/246546.

Pham, A. H. *Vietnamese Tone: A New Analysis*. New York: Routledge, 2003.

Pham, H. *Vietnamese Tone: Tone is Not Pitch*. Toronto: Working Papers in Linguistics, 2001. Retrieved from https://twpl.library.utoronto.ca/index.php/twpl/article/view/6507

Thompson, L. C. *A Vietnamese Grammar*. Seattle: University of Washington, 1965.

Trịnh, M.-H. *Elsewhere, within Here*. New York: Routledge, 2011.

Vũ, N. P. *Tục ngữ ca dao dân ca Việt Nam*. Hà Nội: Nhà Xuất Bản Văn Học, 1956.

Ti (Turkish)
Ilgın Deniz Akseloğlu

- **Tinking Thinking: otherwise, how everything is some-ti-ing**

Earplugs can be like joke glasses in the way they steer perception to an unusual place. They blur the characteristic lines of specific sounds until only their vibrational quality remains. Inside the semi-blindness they bestow ears with, sound becomes even more haptic. Starting with tides smacking the soles of the city, moving with the tramway slithering along the surface of the square, the sound waves come all the way up to the windowsill, climbing the floors gripping the pipework. What do they say?

At the beginning of one of his essayistic works,[44] author and philanthropist Aziz Nesin writes how verbs in Turkish language are richer than nouns. He argues that this is the result of living a nomadic life for thousands of years. Verbs that describe actions have emerged as the result of having always been in motion. In contrast, in the languages of sedentary societies, nouns are richer than verbs. In these languages, verbs are usually derived from nouns; since there was more time to produce names by abstracting. 'To think', Nesin writes, 'is to stop, to be still, to be slow. A person cannot think intensely in rapid motion'. Two centuries before Nesin penned his insight, philosopher Johann G. Herder argued that language was first an activity of assigning sounds for actions, not for things. Herder thought onomatopoeic verbs are 'the first elements of power', because 'the sound had to denote the things as the thing gave rise to the sound. From verbs nouns were derived, and not verbs from nouns'.[45] From these perspectives, language as we know it seems to have taken shape as an onomatopoeic articulation. Many onomatopoeic words are technically untranslatable, but nevertheless they do not need translation. Since they are sonic descriptions, they are easily understood by the non-natives – perhaps *all*-natives – of any specific language.

Verbs are names for movements, for concrete actions. Looking at the variety of verbs and deverbatives, it is noticeable how Turkish grammar structures itself by obeying what vowels summon. As a result of their breathless chase of vowels, to be able to camp as words, consonants must transform into their hard or soft versions. It seems like it is the motion-savviness that shapes Turkish grammar with a vowel-hearkening tendency, while at the same time it is making it an onomatopoeically rich language.

Almost every crossword puzzle in Turkish asks what the pipe sound is, granting two white squares for the answer: *ti*. Ti[46] is the onomatopoeic root for the family of words that describe the sounds for wind instruments, for tooting, blaring and so on. Having one of its derivatives as *titreşim* (vibration), *ti* seems to be the mother sound of many motions. The vibrational force *ti* identifies in many instants as/in sound, works like a universal code. The Latin *tinnire* is the root for 'tinkling, ringing', which describes the resounding effect in the ears. What is called 'eardrum', the membrane that vibrates when sound waves reach creating the experience of hearing, is also called the *tympanic* membrane. When tinkling in the ears becomes the cause of a psychopathological condition, it carries the name *tinnitus*. When a sounding membrane is placed in the body of an insect that 'sings', it is called *tymbal*.

Vibrations move through air, water and ground. We say *tingling* to describe the sudden sensation of prickling under our skin. Touch is the sense of the paradoxical journey of ever-approximating, never-fully-arriving atoms.[47] The pipe sound *ti* points at the sensitive qualities as diverse modes of undulations of the same sort. We keep sculpting sonic forms, from within an everlasting mortar of sound. Sound does not only skim over surfaces or reach us by the physical ears. It penetrates our skin, sometimes pierces and passes through, sometimes settles in. In the sound, we float sometimes and sometimes sink. We are compositions of vibrational chords and sound plays us. When the wind blows, it is the wind's sentiment. When someone sings, it is their breeze. Feelings are climates. Bodies undulate in response to changing weather. Kept together with the gravitational waltz, there is ongoing movement between particles of matter. We navigate in porous nests, vibrating in waves.

Acoustic waves morph into names, according to how we perceive their behaviour. Thinking sound as vibration through *ti* makes sound not only as something heard but as a force, an extension of a source so deep one cannot immediately identify; something that is not only the *ti*p of an unclear beginning but the process itself. The sound waves of the *ti*des smacking the soles of the city, climbing the floors gripping the pipework say *ti*. The perceptual change the earplugs make turns into an encounter with the continuum between all that vibrates and music. This might at first sound like an attempt to subtract meaning from the musical. In effect, it is an attempt for an immersion in sound beyond and through the simultaneous way *ti* does; when finitude is taken from the sound to define it, it becomes a continuous and layered openness. Gauging this openness in acoustic terms corresponds to *ti*me, and this time, I dare to think, what time does – or how time is done – is *ti*. We did not objectively resolve this very old and very long *ti* that is time, even though we are rhy*t*hm – as well as arrhythmia. The journey of two letters tuned in-and-through time, hacking the seeming foreignness of contemporary languages, *ti* encapsulates what composer and philosopher of sound Pauline Oliveros meant by the practice of sonic relationality in the form of Deep Listening.[48] *Ti* materializes time so that it *is*. *Ti* identifies the terrestrial vibrancy, linking our fragmented, humane perceptions.

In many cultures, primordial time is the water element depicted as creator goddesses. Like the biblical Hebrew *tehom* or *tohu wa bohu*, the Sumero-Babylonian goddess mother *Ti*amat is the personification of deep time and the 'flux', a state of formlessness between manifested universes. Among many forms water takes, perhaps the river exemplifies the best the single lifetime each human seems to be experiencing. Along the riverbank of lifetime, the way waters move in one direction only, we move towards ageing and death. Even though the river seems to be moving in one direction, water moves in cyclicality in all directions; being all that has ever been, and that will ever be.

Artist and composer Laurie Anderson asks, 'What time is it?' during her talk 'The River',[49] pointing at the pandemic and the unpredictability and inaccessibility of the social instant as 'shared reality', a shared experience in space-time, and how in solitude, consciousness experiences reality almost like a mirage. Like the waters of the river reach the ocean, in contemplation, dreams and reality merge, like life and death. During the time I was thinking *ti*, I have spent weeks by The Tiber River in Rome, realizing it is the Aegean word *tifos* meaning 'still water' that names these ancient yellow waters, and their god Tiberinus, the son of Tethys and Oceanus.[50] In a place like Rome where thousands of years are knitted organically in the urban landscape, this time, the human lifetime becomes a mirage, getting smaller and smaller on time's horizon.

*Ti*nk is a newly derived verb, 'knit' spelled backwards, referring to unknitting, undoing one stitch at a time.[51] Tinking describes well the way I work with/through language. Since the first moments I caught myself thinking, writing has been a way of speaking to/about other worlds, and not only the one where you are reading these words now. The places where we read words and the places where we hear the words we read are listening to each other with our mediation. I am wondering as I write, what other words can sound the glimpses of the synchronicity of these worlds, once they are assembled. So perhaps, by tinking language, I am working towards a strip-*tea*se of meanings – until only the *ti* remains.

The effect of playfulness in the ritualistic art and music in the mythical religion is described by anthropologist David Graeber as 'time out of time', where humans and gods transact. If time is out of joint today, thinking out of time and place proves to strengthen imagination as resistance. What other thing it is, than the imaginary, which resists imagination? 'What war is this?' Anderson asks in *The River*, mentioning words can cause wars. Is it a war of imagination? I ask, wondering about a beginning where there was not a word, but *ti*.

Tjöh! (Meänkieli and Lule Sámi)
Torbjörn Ömalm

'Tjöh!' or 'Tjeh!' is an interjection that is still used quite frequently in both Meänkieli and Lule Sámi. The usage, situation and functionality of the word differ somewhat between regions and villages, yet its main function is to drive, steer or force an animal to move in a certain direction, most often forward or away from something. The word itself has no meaning in Meänkieli; it is a sound tool practised by reindeer herders and mushers, as a method of regulating movement. I remember my father using it when communicating with his dogs when I grew up. I also recall my grandfather using it during reindeer calf labelling and 'poroerotus/porokaarre' (the procedure of separating reindeers in a mixed herd according to different owners) within the Forest Sámi village he was associated with. In some villages in the east Torne Valley area, 'Tjöh!' is used in an opposite manner, for instance, to attract dogs. The sound of 'Tjöh!' is supposed to be loud and clear, strict and short. It is pronounced and shouted, somewhere in the border between talking and screaming, with a sharp and accentuated pitch.

ТОПОТ (Russian: топот [ˈtopclea])
Andrey Logutov

The word makes part of a group of sound-related vocabulary ending in an archaic suffix -ot / -et: ropot 'murmur', tsokot 'clatter', shopot 'whisper', rokot 'roar', lepet 'babble', khokhot 'loud laughter', stryokot 'chirping' and a few more. These are mostly onomatopoeic and, thanks to their shortness and the repeating vowels, have a tapping feel to them.

* * *

The reason I chose to write about this particular word is there's a family with two small kids living in the apartment upstairs. The kids produce *topot* – they stomp, thud, thump and pound their feet on the floor; this is a familiar sound, and it's, of course, annoying.

Figure 55 Tjöh https://commons.wikimedia.org/wiki/Category:Woodcuts_by_John _Savio#/media/File:John_Savio_Dælve_2_SKU.K.00037.jpg.

Figure 56 TOPOT, © Andrey Logutov.

It falls in the category of sounds that let you in on somebody else's private living, oftentimes against your will and without the other person's knowing. The sounds of a family fight, a bed being too creaky, the banging of utensils in the sink, doors slamming, a stay-at-home telephone whose call remains unheeded. This auditory leakage relates a home to a home, a schedule to a schedule and a human to a human. Our shared existence is permeated not only by arteries of support or ducts of hostility but also by a finespun web of little annoyances.

In the case of the children, the annoyance seems fairly large to me. They rise at around 8:30, when I'm usually asleep. If my head is touching the wall near my bed, the thud is transferred through the concrete slabs right into the bone of my skull, and I wake up. I would not go as far as Kafka in declaring my bed 'the headquarter of noise' of the entire building, but there is a sense of an unsolicited contact, as if somebody touched me, where and when I don't like to be touched, and, despite my grunts, would continue to.

'Topot' can also refer to the sound of a crowd moving or the patter of a horse's feet. It is a nomadic sound, chaotic in itself, but with a sense of direction and power. At the waking moment, my fantasy is unchecked enough to imagine myself a member of an ancient sedentary tribe disturbed by the 'topot' of migratory hoards approaching the village. But in a jiffy my head pulls away from the wall, the sound fades somewhat and the hoards recede back into being two energetic kids.

I remember myself doing the same when I was their age. My family lived in a much feebler structure, where soundproofing was almost inexistent. One could hear a loud conversation in an apartment next door. I stomped away, and I can only imagine the people downstairs felt. My parents told me to stop, but there was something about *topot* that made me want to continue, and they weren't particularly insistent.

I crashed my little body into the floor, and it felt bigger, more massive, more resilient and more powerful. Small things try to look larger in triumph or danger. For me, it was a moment of triumph. If you throw yourself into something hard, and you don't break, you are therefore just as hard. A point can be made that perhaps I was so eager to prove my powers because I was also insecure and not entirely happy? Of course, I was. Just like the nomads of the past, enveloped in the *topot* of their horses, didn't travel merely out of the feeling of superiority and freedom; they were often motivated by fear, famine and death.

Topot is what animals do more often than people. However, in fear or ecstasy, our human nature subsides, and we step into the territory of genetically wired reactions universal to animals like ourselves. We flee or fight, shrink or swell, pale or flush. Is there a natural instinct to thump? There must be, as I don't believe the two kids or myself in the past were ever taught to do it. Is it a specific impulse or is it part of a larger desire to produce rhythmic sounds that ultimately leads to music-making? On a less lucid morning, when I hadn't had enough sleep, for the first few moments I couldn't tell whether I was hearing the usual thudding, or it was a backbeat from a dance track played a few floors away. It sounded a bit too wobbly for a proper beat; and yet again it lasted long enough to amount to something musical.

As Wikipedia kindly suggests, many cultures perform something called the 'stomp dance'. I think traditional Russian dances have at least elements of stomping referred to as *pritopyvanie*, produced from the same root as *topot*. Such pieces are typically performed by male dancers wearing high metal-shod boots. The resulting intensity of the sound and the straightforward 2/2 or 2/4 metre give an aggressive, almost belligerent, flavour to them, which I remember I disliked as a child.

What's different and fascinating about the 'topot' of the kids in the flat above, is how they're trying to play around with the rhythm and the articulation. There's nothing aggressive or particularly 'manly' about it (I strongly believe girls and boys to be equally able to disrupt my sleep). You almost never hear a steady thud that one can easily produce by jumping in one place. They prefer accelerating or decelerating patterns, which oftentimes sound like drum breaks, intros or outros. There are unwarranted pauses, odd off-beats, attempts at syncopation and neat little motifs too good to be true.

One of the obvious reasons why *topot* is annoying is that there's a game going on behind it that I'm excluded from. Why the weird pause? Why the crescendo? Why is this particular trajectory more popular than the others? Why has the sound stopped? It's Kafka's 'The Burrow' all over again, a never-ending attempt to figure out the outside world and its intentions through sound, which works better as a conveyor of presence than that of understanding.

* * *

As an onomatopoeia, *topot* aspires to reproducing its referent sound. As a palindrome, it points to a multiplicity of ways it can be read and also, perhaps, to its indifference to the arrow of time. If the word is the same in reverse, would this apply to the sound itself?

Attached: A reversed recording of TOPOT.

T'sé (Québecois)
Mitchell Akiyama

Ce gars là, il a l'aire anglophone, t'sé? That guy over there, he looks like an anglophone, y'know?

Although I graduated high school with a certificate attesting to my English–French bilingualism, any competent French speaker would have had reasonable questions about the Toronto District School Board's linguistic standards. I had a decent handle on how French dealt with gender, and I could comfortably conjugate verbs, even the irregular forms that we were convinced had been devised to specifically mess with our learning of the language. *Je sais, tu sais, il/elle sait, nous savons, vous savez, ils/elles savent.* But conversation isn't information retrieval, and speaking French felt like looking for index cards in a rusty filing cabinet. After I graduated high school, I moved to Montréal to study creative writing at Concordia University, where I was reminded of my poor French every time I tried to speak the language with a waiter or a grocery clerk who would inevitably and wearily answer back in English.

My first apartment was in a high-rise complex, blocks away from the downtown university campus; a cosmopolitan, English-friendly niche in a predominantly Francophone city. I barely left the area during my first year, and, consequently, I had few opportunities to practice my French. I was optimistic that I'd be able to improve my fluency the next year when I moved in with my friend, a bilingual American from Detroit whose parents were both Québecois, and her cousin from Sept-Iles, a small, northern city in a predominantly Francophone part of the province. As it turned out, his English was excellent, and the household's linguistic path of least resistance was established. My friend moved out the following year, and her cousin's friend from Sept-Iles took her place. This new roommate spoke barely any English. He was also impressively messy. I developed competence for talking about household items and chores, along with confidence in expressing my frustration in French, an aptitude honed by exasperation. I also quickly became familiar with Québecois profanity, a repertoire of swears primarily consisting of taking the names for various Catholic paraphernalia in vain – *tabarnac* (tabernacle), *calice* (chalice), *hostie* (host). I was neither raised in Québec nor in religion, and I couldn't feel the force of these words, but they were the only tools I had for communicating my frustration. *Hostie, mon gars, fais ta vaiselle! La salle de bain est déguelasse, tabarnac, et c'est moi qui l'ai nettoyé en dernier!*

It first occurred to me that I was functionally bilingual one day on the metro. I usually had my head and attention in a book or a magazine, but I found myself distracted by the conversations around me; I could fully understand and follow French subconsciously, without effort or intention, and I couldn't block out this novel comprehension. And as I got more comfortable speaking the language, I found myself both consciously trying to become and unconsciously becoming a more natural, fluent speaker. I had no illusions about passing as Québecois, which is arguably a racial as well as a linguistic category. As a mixed-race person in an ethnically insular province, I experienced a lot of low-grade racism disguised as curiosity. *D'où viens-tu?* Where are you from? Toronto. *Non, mais vraiement, tu viens d'où?* No really. Toronto. And so on without ever giving anyone the satisfaction of knowing that I'm a fourth-generation Japanese Canadian. I suppose on some level I wanted to fit in, but I was more interested in the aesthetics and the challenge of fluency. As I became more comfortable with the language, I started to pay closer attention to the idioms and mannerisms of native speakers – the semantically extraneous parts of speech, the filler words and the unconscious vocal tics that written language rarely records. In Québecois, many filler words are contractions – take *faque*, which is a shortened form of *ça fait que*, which loosely translates to 'so'. Or *pis*, which is a truncation of *puis*, which means 'then'. But the filler word that I heard most often was *t'sé*, a contraction of *tu sais* – what y'know? is to 'you know?' In one sense, *t'sé* functions as a disingenuously interrogative closure to a sentence in the declarative mood. Or, it can have what the anthropologist, Bronisław Malinowski, called a phatic function. Philosopher of language, Roman Jakobson described the phatic function as a class of utterances whose purpose is to verbally call attention to speech itself, to open the lines of communication between people engaging in conversation (Jakobson 84). Ending a sentence with *t'sé* suggests that one is fishing for affirmation, y'know? And, y'know, beginning a phrase with *t'sé* implies priming one's listener, making sure that they're ready to hear what you have to say.

It's ironic to me that an ease with filler words and idiomatic nonsense speech only tends to arise as one becomes fluent in a language. I vaguely remember the effort it used to take to deliberately scan my memory for vocabulary, conjugation and agreement. There wasn't any extra mental space or processing power, conscious or unconscious, to dispense filler words. That only came when I no longer had to think about each new word successively, when French magically started to flow from my mouth without my brain struggling to supply vocabulary and grammatical rules in advance. It felt a little contrived or disingenuous, at first, to deliberately introduce these pauses and almost-extraneous parts of speech to my repertoire. I was performing a more fluent, integrated version of myself by un-refining the way I spoke, y'know? I felt self-conscious, a poseur trying too hard to fit in. But even my studied stammer eventually became natural to me.

Around the time that I could finally, in good conscience, call myself bilingual, I began travelling frequently to Europe to tour as a musician. On an English leg of my first tour, I reconnected with a Canadian friend who had moved to London a few years earlier. She had picked up – to my ears at least – a pronounced British accent since we had last spoken. Her intonation followed the rise and fall of the English lilt, and she now chewed her t's. How did you get here? *I took the chube.* I was silently judgemental and told myself that if I were to spend significant amounts of time in the UK, I would be immune to the subtle peer pressures that had taken hold of her tongue. I had to soften my position the next day when I tried three times, unsuccessfully, to order a tuna sandwich. Defeated, I ate *chuna* for lunch.

After shows in Spain and Italy, where conversations were laborious and organized around my inability to speak the local languages, I travelled to France and Belgium, imagining the pride I would feel when I got to show of my French. I don't remember my first conversations, but I can recall my sense of shock when virtually nobody understood me. It wasn't a matter of competence or confidence as far as I could tell, *t'sé*? *T'sé*, it was my accent. I had been so immersed in the Québecois dialect that, even though I could easily hear the difference between it and Continental French, I had somewhat unwittingly become fluent in a vernacular that European Francophones found difficult to understand. I then understood that I could, or maybe should, think of Continental French as a dialect that I might learn. This didn't seem pretentious or forced to me in the way that I imagined it would feel to deliberately don a British accent when speaking to a Londoner. I practised modulating my voice in new ways. I studied Belgian slang and Parisian filler words. As I mentioned before, Québecois profanity is very Catholic (in the literal sense), while French swearing is more sexual and scatological in nature: *bordel* (bordello), *putain* (slut) and *merde* (shit). French and Québecois speakers also use very different Anglicisms. Continental French speakers leave their cars in *le parking* when they do *du shopping* on *le weekend*. Québeckers park their cars in *le stationnement* when they *magaziner* during *la fin de semaine*. Even filler words are different, which I learned when French interlocutors asked me what that strange sound was that I kept making: *t'sé*. I eventually figured out that I should be using *tu vois* (you see) as a substitute.

I moved from Montréal to Toronto almost a decade and a half ago. There are few French speakers here. But on the rare occasion that I end up in conversation with a francophone from Québec, it takes a few minutes for the linguistic fog to clear. I'm always surprised how much I've retained and how I spend less time retrieving words the way I once did when I was learning the language. And all of the tics and mannerisms of fluency are still there, tacitly seeking assent, communicating pauses and finished thoughts, t'sé?

Reference

Jakobson, Roman. *The Framework of Language.* Ann Arbor: Michigan Studies in the Humanities, 1980.

צְלִיל (Tz-lil) (Hebrew)
Eyal Hareuveni

The Hebrew word צְלִיל (Tz-lil) means sound, but according to the Israeli Academy for the Hebrew Language, the word צְלִיל has a few more meanings:

In its phonetic usage, it can mean a phone.

When attributed to info-tech it means sound, as in recognizing sound.

Obviously, it is used in relation to acoustic, electronic or electroacoustic musical sound.

It also references a note, a musical note or the sensation of listening or tone or even resonance of air density as by touching a surface or a key of the instrument.

This word encompasses the meaning of sound, tone and note in theatre, music and songs.

And it also covers the term 'timbre'.

A more liberal interpretation of the word צְלִיל (Tz-lil) can include more meanings as follows:

The word מִצְלוֹל (mitzlol) may be translated as the colour/shade of a specific tone or an instrument and also used in poetry to mark the qualities of rhyming words or the rhyme in general.

Playing more with the tz.l.l. Root, we can refer to other words that – poetically – refer to other qualities of sound.

For example, הִצְטַלֵל (hitzlalel) means to become clear, as of not only a vision but also a musical idea or theme.

צָלַל (tzalal) is a verb that means to dive, usually into the water but metaphorically also into an issue or a composition/soundscape, and so on, but its onomatopoeic sound can also hint about the resonance qualities of a distinct sound.

צֵל (tzel) means a shade but its plural צְלָלִים (tzlalim), which is often borrowed to describe a glimpse of light or hope, carries also the connotation of echoing-resonating qualities of sound.

Sound is defined by the Hebrew word צְלִיל (*tzlil*), based on the root tz.l.l., but *tzlil* also means tone or even resonance of air density as by touching a surface or a key of the instrument.

uid uid (racoonese)
Lasse-Marc Riek

contact sound between adult "raccoon" and puppies (Procyon lotor)

When nature comes into the studio. . .

. . .by chance, on 21.05., from the roof terrace, I saw a raccoon rising from the fireplace of the sound studio.

when the raccoon was on the move again the next evening around 21.30 pm, I drilled a small hole above the chimney and fixed a small electret microphone in it. I put on the headphones and assumed to check the signal with the knowledge that the raccoon was on the roof or already on the way to find out in surprise that there was more inside the chimney . . . it sounded like a whole family.

Young animals were born and were suckled there continuously. I think that the young animals cannot climb out of there? The male – or maybe it is also the female with young animals – goes in and out.

We now had an acoustic permanent line, a listening window into the social intimacy of the raccoons like a kind of telephone into the heart of a family. I connected the recorder every day and recorded at different time windows, between three and six hours a day.

Slowly, I thought about starting a rescue operation, because I couldn't imagine that the animals could get out of there without help. You are not allowed to do anything about it, because the species is already protected by a hunting law.

At 02.06 am, the time had come: the mother and her three children came in from the fireplace late in the evening. for approx. two hours, a small drama played itself out. The children were very frightened and the mother seemed overwhelmed. She had to instruct the children individually to climb from the roof over the tree and plants of the building. The whole thing lasted for about 2.5 hours and then the little ones fell into and onto the hut of my children. They took one or the other things with them. There was falling, breaking and even a bell was struck by the animals. . . .

I recorded the process from above and below

Around 5.45 am, the mother brought the animals back into the fireplace one by one and spent the day sleeping and awake until late in the evening. At nightfall the mother brought the young ones out of the fireplace and from the roof, one by one; this time almost without a sound. Since then, they have never returned to the fireplace. One night later, they visited the hut and the garden again and have now moved on.

My last recording is the moment when the mother inside carries the last child in the neck up the chimney and pulls it. At first you hear the animal (very close) to the microphone in the wall, then it very slowly becomes quieter and quieter the higher it climbs up the chimney shaft. At the end you only hear a few pebbles falling. . .

Undu: of *vindur* in Iceland
Halla Steinunn Stefánsdóttir

It is a summer's day, and I am filming and recording cairns in the Þjórsárdalur valley in South Iceland. The valley is named after the river that runs through it: the Þjórsá River and the cairns, created and maintained by the locals, mark the outset of a path over the highland plateau Sprengisandur. I often get an eerie feeling on this site; one reason perhaps being its vicinity to the stratovolcano Hekla, whose eruption in 1104 ended all farming in the area. I am working on an installation for a festival in Scotland, set to draw on the common culture of cairns as a key to look at how humans navigate their immediate surroundings. At the same time the work is set to invite its participants to reflect on the notion of being lost. And so I find myself among straws and pumice, on a rare *blíðviðrisdagur*, or day of gentle weather, and watch as the breeze or *gola* plays with the straws.

> My grandparents had all been farmers and their vocabulary sprung out of that. They could read the clouds and the weather. They often personified the wind, called him *Kári*, 'he is being noisy' or '*Kári* is raging today'.
> (Árný Inga)

> You would talk of *stólpaþurrkur* when steady wind reigned and dried the hay. *Mó* is when the wind hardly moves, and the hay dries just slightly. Then when it finally dried there could be such *rok* that it just blew away and we had to pick it out of ditches and from fences.
> (Kristín)

> It was always *him*. I do not know who he is. Maybe God almighty, and as we know he can move in mysterious ways.
> (Halla)

My microphones are resting inside one of the mossy-clad stone structures, catching how the *gjóla* plays with the cairn's surface. The idea came to me some years back, as I was recording above the Þakgil canyon, close to Mýrdalsjökull glacier on what was a day of *hvassviðri*. The English-Icelandic dictionary translates it as 'windy, blowing hard', but I do not think this definition captures it. *Hvass* means sharp or harsh; that combined with a sense of unpredictability and pushiness starts to approach some verbal description of the feeling of *hvassviðri*. Growing up on this island you get your fair share of it. It feels like your life is spent in *hvassviðri* to such an extent that one sometimes calls Iceland a *rokrass*, which can be freely translated as a windy hole. On that day in the highland by Mýrdalsjökull glacier, as it was *hvasst*, the wind travelled uninhibited across the mountain and wrecked all my recording attempts; when I spotted a small cairn I felt as though it presented the perfect windshield. But I was also curious: what does it sound like inside a cairn that is battered by the wind year in and out? I wanted to listen from within a cairn; this could be made possible by my recording device and miniature microphone setup.

> I think what most characterizes this island is not its landscape or size but rather how its blessed *vindur* constantly engulfs you. A day may on rare occasions start and end with *stilla*, but you almost never get through an entire day of *stilla*.
> (Helena)

> *Útsynningur* comes from the southwest, when low-pressure passes through and the temperatures drop. It is accompanied by *hryðjur* that come and go or slacken up. So *útsynningur* is not a *vindur* but rather a certain type of phenomenon.
> (Stefán)

> The *vindur* is a movement, when it appears you must seal or shelter your body from it. Close the *vindur* out. I feel it is harder to tackle him the older I get; I freeze more easily.
> (Ingólfur Björn)

The *gola* in the Þjórsárdalur valley feels like a blessing, as she does not shake my video camera nor threaten to damage its lens by whirling the pumice around. I can sit nearby out in the open instead of seeking shelter. Occasionally I hear a sheep bleat, and I spend some time watching a spider crawl through the vegetation. The sound of a car in the far distance travels to me over the plane: it is like a river of white noise, for on this day the type of wind allows sounds to travel. The cars might be heading to the highland or the Búrfellsvirkjun hydropower station. There are new utilitarian plans on the drawing table for this longest river in Iceland; plans that turned my grandmother into an environmental activist at an old age. She uttered sounds that I had never heard from her before: she cursed.

> I have strong memories of the *vindur* and it is usually the good ones that prevail. Such as standing on the top of mountain in *logn*. But I also remember watching my grandfather fight his way in front of the car to lead us through a *snjóstormur*. There were no marker posts back then on the heath.
> (Árný Inga)

> The environmental sounds travel differently depending on the wind, if there was *sunnanandvari* you could hear the sounds from Þjórsá river and even the voices of the men singing down in the meadows.
> (Kristín)

> We feel that *staðvindur* reigns more than it used to. If a direction starts it stays on, for days on end, like it has entered a certain gear. It can start raining in May and rain for 5-6 weeks. It was never like that. We also get rain when the wind is from northeast and the north. That was unheard of. (Halla)

Some eight months later the cairns oscillate as projections on the exterior walls of Kirk of St Nicholas Uniting in Aberdeen, Scotland. The

Figure 57 *Að Vörðu / To Cairn*, © Ian Wilson.

sonification of *gola*, caught with my microphones inside the cairns, blends with other sounds of the piece: these sounds are testimonies of people living in Aberdeenshire, sharing their daily routes but also their wayfinding through life. The work also extends one of the questions that the participants received, to the visitors of the Spectra festival, 'Have you ever felt lost?'. The sonification of the *gola*'s movements and timbre, through another sound, enables it to be heard as it otherwise would have disappeared in the auditory space of the city.

> We hooked our arms together and strode through the snow, carrying a flashlight because the electricity kept going out in our village. Then we had to regularly turn our bodies away from the *vindur* to catch our breath.
> (Katrín)

> The *vindur* was not my friend. My cheeks were always red. I think it was because of him, that I was marked by him. We also built igloos as a way to seek shelter, and you took great care to start digging from the right direction in order not to get the *vindur* into your house.
> (Halla)

> I loved to play with the *vindur*, I would pull up my coat and use it as a sail. You also used him as 'motor' when skating, he pushed you forward. I did in fact spend a lot of time wondering about the *vindur*'s direction. My friend was also asthmatic, so it mattered which way you chose on your way to school. And sometimes we had to be accompanied by grownups when he raged.
> (Árný Inga)

The work, titled *Að Vörðu / To Cairn* is one of my works that engages with wind. As I composed the text-driven part of the audio, the sonified movements of the *gola* guided and affected its construction, and so the *gola* continued to shape the atmosphere as it had done on-site. Similarly, the movements of *gola* were visible in the atmospheric video material, where she stirred straws under the slow drifting of clouds. In other work the *vindur* has become a co-creator of scores, driven aeolian violin performances or led to wind-like inspired performances. I have also continuously captured its movements through further video and audio recordings, a sensorial material used later in scores and installations. *Vindur* also shapes the atmosphere, which is so essential to my environmental performance. Yet at the same time I am aware that it is utilitarian policies related to wind, alongside other geo-forces, that enable my digitally driven creativity.

It was almost never calm in our fishing village, the *hafgola* would always appear during the day. If there is sun, the earth starts heating, which creates a rising current and triggers the wind. Then in wintertime the *rok* brought sea salt with it and coated the electric transmission lines so we would go for days without electricity and had to cook with primus. The infrastructures were weak.

(Hjörleifur)

At sea, in times of *bræla*, the wind would grab you and throw you along the deck and you had to hold onto things.

(Ingólfur Björn)

Our word usage does not always coincide with the charts from the meteorological office. It is a feeling what is *rok* and what is *stormur*. Rok is not all that bad as it is made out to be in those charts.

(Stefán)

In our everyday life the movements of air, in its mild or raging state, are at times accompanied by snow, fog, pollution, ashes or rain. Its movements are visible in the drifting of clouds, shuffling of leaves, gliding of birds or undulation of light as the wind plays with the sunbathed ocean. Its movements of varying degrees (degrees of direction and of force) are also perceived by us through sound as it encounters a surface. As such, they sometimes make our dwellings whistle or moan. What is being moved – air – is the essence of our existence. Thus, as we breathe, we are always already more-than-human, a process which prompted Tim Ingold (2007) to describe our encounter with air in terms of our bodies being *enwinded*. And so, we live in a weather world where we habitually read the wind and the weather by sensing; in return we categorize and describe them through words. These words continuously become a part of the culture that surrounds us.

I have started using other words by moving here to the South although I still tend to use *þræsingur* instead of *belgingur*. But yes, you start using the words that circulate.

(Katrín)

I remember that I had to exit the car on Holtavörðuheiði heath to move the snow from our window. The door almost went off the hinges and if I had not been able to clutch onto it, I would have been blown into the *bylur*. It reminds you that the man is small.

(Stefán)

I can also link confusion and despair to *vindur*. Grownup men could get so angry when rounding up the sheep. They kept screaming instructions at me but they were blown away by the *vindur* so I could not catch them. It caused me anxiety. There were such expectations and they just screamed and screamed.

(Kristín)

Wind in my native language is *vindur*. But it also takes the verb form *að vinda*, which means to wring, twist or wind and unwind. Its plural past tense is *Undu*. Incidentally, *Undu* can also be traced to the word *að una*, which can refer to 'one being happy to be somewhere'. What greets you here on the pages of *Undu* is part of an ongoing processual project related to atmosphere understood as air/weather but also an independent essay. The words on wind – in its many skies and utterances – and the following dictionary spring out from my family's everyday life. They relate also to words used by people who came before us.

It can sometimes be akin to sport to find a good spot, or hollow to eat your provisions when hiking. Where is the least *strengur*. Is it under this ridge or over there? Where is the *vindur* coming from? And it affects which path you choose when hiking.

(Árný Inga)

Figure 58 *To Cairn*, still, © Halla Steinunn Stefánsdóttir.

> Suddenly I was just standing there by the garage, holding the door handle of a door which had blown off the hinges.
> (Hjörleifur)

> *Gjóla* is not just a wind denotation but also contains a certain temperature. It can be biting, travel through your clothes if you have dressed too lightly. It is not *gola*, but *gjóla* because of the temperature, so there is complex sensing going on there.
> (Stefán)

I extend *Undu* as an invitation into contemplation on your experiences of wind in the past and in the present. At the same time I live in an age where stories emerge from various directions that winds are shifting, dunes are becoming more ferocious, wind directions linger for longer, pollution rides on its wings and hurricanes and typhoons create havoc. It is therefore not merely a case of our bodies being *enwinded*: humans affect the wind's own movements.

A list of *vind* words

> brought forth by Árný Inga, Halla, Halla Steinunn, Helena, Hjörleifur, Ingólfur Björn, Katrín, Kristín and Stefán.

Andvari: gentle breeze, hardly noticeable, like someone's breath on your neck. It can be denoted as coming from a certain direction, such as 'austanandvari', that is, a gentle breeze coming from the east

Austanstæður: the wind, type can vary, coming from the east

Bál: the word means fire in Icelandic but can also be used to describe air movement. 'Bál' as a weather force is wind in clear weather, coming from the north. It is icy and dry, burns your cheeks and dries out your eyes and your skin. It is sometimes called 'norðanbál', meaning 'bál' from the north

Bálhvass: stormy. The word is, however, an adjective compound word, made of 'bál' (see above) and 'hvass' (see further down). It is, however, less of a biting frost feeling than in 'bál'.

Bálviðri: the dictionary translates it as severe winter; a severe climate. It is a compound word, made up of 'bál' (see above) and 'viðri', meaning weather

Belgingur: a word that can mean flatulence, inflation or turgidity. The word is used to describe hefty

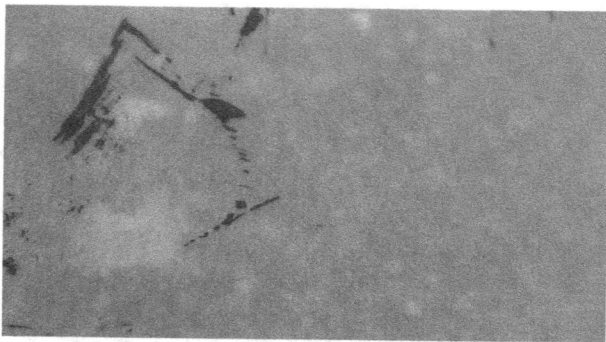

Figure 59 *strengur*, documentation from the creation of the graphic score, © Halla Steinunn Stefánsdóttir.

wind, which behaves in an inflated manner, like a bossy person

Beljandi: rush of wind

Blaka: flap

Blása: blow

Hann blæs af norðri: the wind is blowing from the north

Landið er að blása upp: the soil is being eroded; the topsoil is blowing away

Blástur: breeze. 'Blástur' can be used to describe wind during daytime but was also earlier used by some to describe wind in late summer that wakes up and stirs the morning dew following the night still. You could not start working with hay till the 'blástur' awoke

Blær: gentle breeze

Brakar: creak

Bræla: wind and rain at sea

Byljóttur: gusty

Bylur: storm or snowstorm

Byr: favourable wind

Dósafjúk: a word invented by Már Haraldsson in the Gnúpverja county; used by locals. The word translates directly as can or tindrift. Opposite to 'snjófjúk' (see further below), 'dósafjúk' is not related to snow weather but is rather a way to mark that it has gotten windy enough for cans and buckets to start rolling around in the farmyard

Fárviðri: hurricane, tempest

Fjúk: driving snow, drifting snow

Garri: blast, gale

Garður: storm, sudden commencement, squall, blast or gale.

Hann rekur á garða: ongoing cold storm from one direction.

Gengur á: used to describe the 'ongoing' of weather, most often in connection with wind combined with hail or snow.

Gengur upp: a wind is accumulating from a certain direction

Gerir úr vestrinu: a wind is appearing from the west

Gjóla: fresh or cool breeze. A playful kind of wind. Can also be called 'vindgjóla' meaning wind-gjóla

Gjóstur: blast

Gjögt: rattle

Gnauð: wind noise, can also refer to howl

Gnauða: howl, hiss

Gola: breeze

Geispa golunni: 'geispa' means yawn and to yawn 'gola' means to kick the bucket

Grágolandi: not found in dictionaries but used by people to describe a certain type of ocean moved by the wind. A compound of 'grár' (grey) and the word 'gola', transformed into a verb, 'golandi'. 'Gola' can mean fresh breeze (see above) but also squall. An uninviting ocean due to wind.
Gustur: gust of wind
Hafgola: seaward wind; sea breeze
Hányrtur: a wind coming from the high north
Hliðarvindur: crosswind
Hrikt/a: creak
Hríð: snowstorm
Hrina: wave, series of something
Hryðja: sudden snowstorm
Hryssingur: nip
Hryssingslegur: gruff, rough wind. Can also refer to a person
Hvass: it is windy, it is blowing hard
Hvassviðri: strong wind
Hvellur: bang, clap, crack
Hvessa: get windy, get windier; start to blow
Hviðóttur: gusty
Hvína: whistle, moan
Hvinur: whistling
Hviða: gust of wind, incidentally 'kviða' means epic poem
Kaldi: (fresh) breeze
Kári: a man's name but also a word for windy weather, or storm
Kóf: snowdrift
Kul: breeze
Landnorðrið: wind direction from northeast
Landsunnan: wind direction from southeast
Logn: calm
    Dauðalogn: dead calm
    Blankalogn: dead calm
    Blæjalogn: dead calm
    Stafalogn: dead calm
    Stillilogn: dead calm
Meðvindur: favourable wind
Meðbyr: favourable wind
Molla: muggy weather, stifling heat
Mó: word for drought, dryness, in relation to hay
Mótvindur: headwind
Næðingur: chilly wind
Rífur í: tears at
Rok: storm. 'Rok' is, however, a common word and often used by people to describe windy weather in general. Thus, although translated by using the word storm, it should be noted that 'rok' is different from 'stormur' (see below), which is also translated as storm. 'Stormur' is more often in common language a met term, used to denote storm from the ocean or storm from the highland.
Hávaðarok: loud storm, meaning raging storm
Hífandi rok: pulling storm
Nístingsrok: piercing storm
Ofsarok: violent storm
Sandrok: sandstorm
Roka: squall, blast, gale
Rokrassgat: windy place. 'Rassgat' in Icelandic means: arsehole. It can also be used for a site that is far away and isolated.
Rosi: related to an Icelandic word, which means violent, tremendous, fantastic. 'Rosi' in the weather sense refers to rainy and windy weather.
Skafrenningur: drifting snow
Skella á: set in
Snjóstormur: snow storm
Staðvindur: trade wind
Staðvindasamur: adjective referring to trade wind or wind that stays on
Standa á: last, continue, go on
Stinningskaldi: strong wind.
    According to the Iceland met site 'stinningskaldi' is a wind force 6

Stilla: calm
   Næturstilla: calm of the night
   Vetrarstillur: winter calm
Stólparok: great storm
Stólpaþurrkur: great dry weather, beneficial for drying hay
Stormur: storm, strong gale
Strekkingur: strong wind
Strengur: blast of wind. It can, however, refer to wind in relation, or running along something, in a persistent way. Such as a 'strengur' that runs along a mountain side or along buildings
Stórhríð: heavy snowstorm
Stæður: as in 'það er varla stætt úti', that is, it is blowing so hard you can hardly stand
Sunnanblær: southern breeze
Svalur: cool
Sveipur: squall, gust of wind
Sverfa: abrade, file
Sviptivindur: gust
Syngur: sings
Útnorður: a wind coming from the northwest
Útræna: a wind coming from the northeast
Útsynningur / Útsunnan: a wind coming from the southwest. It is accompanied by 'hryðjur' that comes and goes
Þeyr: translated in a dictionary as thaw or thawy weather. It is, however, used in daily language to refer to wind that is mild and thus thaws
Þræsingur: rough wind
Þæfingur: snowy road conditions, caused by wind
Þytur: whistling of the wind
Þytur í laufi: wind in the willows
Vindasamt: windy
Vindur: wind
Væla: wail
Ýfa: ruffle, ripple
Ýl: howling
Ýla: howl, whine
Þjóta: whistles
   Hann þaut upp: he flared up
   Láta eitthvað eins og vind um eyru þjóta: turn a deaf ear
Öskra: scream
Öskrandi vindur: screaming wind
Öskrandi stórhríð: screaming great snowstorm

And a mild epilogue

I think that my favourite word is *blær*, although I use *rok* a lot.
I also like *byr*, to have *byr* in your sails. (Ingólfur Björn)

Logn, I think everyone loves that phenomenon.
Then there is *blær* and *andvari*. (Hjörleifur)

Gjóla is a fun word, *vindgjóla* has even something of a friendly feel, then there are *blær* and *þytur*,
but *logn* is the most beautiful. (Árný Inga)

Blær and *andvari*. There is this poem about the Westman islands where I grew up, *Hún rís úr sumarsænum í silkimjúkum blænum* (She rises out of the sea, in the gentle and silk like breeze). (Helena)

Andvari, *logn* and *blíða*. *Blíða* is first and foremost a feeling, all is well and it is like the touch of your mother's hand petting your hair. Mom's palm. (Halla)

The most beautiful words are linked to slow wind, such as *andvari*.
And then I would choose *stafalogn* in terms of calm. (Kristín)

I think *þeyr* is a very beautiful word, as phenomenon it is like *gola* but it is not a cold one, it has warmth in it. The word as sound is also beautiful in itself.
Blær is a very gentle word.

When there is *bliður blær í bænum*
(tender and gentle breeze at the farm)
then all is well. (Stefán)

The author would like to thank Árný Inga Pálsdóttir, Halla Guðmundsdóttir, Helena Hilmarsdóttir, Hjörleifur Pálsson, Ingólfur Björn Sigurðsson, Katrín Hallmarsdóttir, Kristín Guðmundsdóttir and Stefán Guðmundsson for the conversations and for trusting her with their generous sharing and contribution. Gratitude also to Andy Brydon and Curated Place (UK) for commissioning and producing 'To Cairn / Að Vörðu', which included a hike up to Tom's Cairn and connecting with Pete Stollery and other generous voices of Aberdeenshire. Lastly, gratitude to all entities, *gola* included.

Reference
Ingold, Tim. 'Earth, Sky, Wind, and Weather'. *The Journal of the Royal Anthropological Institute*, vol. 13, Jan. 2007, pp. 19–38.

Vah vah
Korhan Erel (Turkish)

This phrase consists of the repetition, or in grammatical terms, the reduplication of the word 'vah'. Vah is a word without a meaning of its own and is an onomatopoeia and also an exclamation (or interjection).

Vah is a word taken from Arabic and is used to express pity or sympathy. An example of its use would be: You receive some bad news about someone you know, such as illness, accident, loss of loved ones, and so on . . . this is what you would say 'Vah vah, so bad that this has happened to her/him/them'. . . . In order to exaggerate your emotions, you can repeat the word more than twice, like 'vah vah vah vah', with the tone of each word going down in pitch. 'Ah' can replace vah. There is actually an idiomatic verb 'ahlamak vahlamak', which means to utter these two words in the face of a sad/tragic/unfortunate event. 'Ahlamak vahlamak fayda etmez' means 'saying ah and vah does no good (to the situation at hand)'.

'Tüh' is another word that has a similar use. In some cases, it can replace vah, but it can also be used without reduplication. It also means 'shame' or is uttered after a missed opportunity, bad news, unluck, and so on. Just like vah, tüh is also an onomatopoeia and an interjection.

Vårløsning (Norwegian)
Paul H. Amble

It goes Whoop. Whoop. Whoop Whoop! At first you don't realize what that sound surrounding you implies. But then you focus your hearing, and you get it. Spring is here! There is no way back. The point of no return has been reached. Even as the sun sets, the inevitable passing of time is audible, and you know it means that life is returning and a new cycle is born.

During the pandemic it is this same point in time that we long for. The tipping point. When will we be vaccinated so that life can reboot? When will we be able to think clearly about an infectious disease that we will have to cope with and keep shielding ourselves against? This will not be the last outbreak of a disease of this kind, but never mind. We want to put it behind us and look forward. Just like it is inevitable that winter will return. But for now!

This is *Kairos*, or time as you experience it. The sun warms you, even though snow is still around. You know the temperature is above freezing and you can expect it to stay that way. Maybe the Snowdrops (*Galanthus nivalis*) have decided to show up, close to your house in the sunny corner. Tits keep on singing in trees. Rejoice.

Our word consists of two different words; *vår* and *løsning*. The first part has two quite different meanings. It can mean spring, as in this case, but it also means 'our' (first person plural pronoun). This can bring some niceties into a sentence; *Det er vår vår!* (This is our spring!). The second part is a contraction of *forløsning*, in the meaning 'to give birth'. This shortening has led to the word

Figure 60 Vårløsning, © Paul H. Amble.

having a double meaning again, since *løsning* also has the meaning of 'solution'. This is the fun part of dealing with words.

The miracle of life can be summed up in the new-born's cry. How eagerly awaited. How miraculous. No one knows what this life will bring. Is it a future president? Is it the mother of a large noisy family of four? Or will it be devastated by meaningless terror or war? All of these options lie within that tiny sound.

They say that the story about the Eskimos having over fifty words for snow is an exaggeration. But in any language, we know, there are of course numerous words describing time, season and the weather shifting. All of them closely connected to geography and locality. How can I explain to someone, who does not know what we call winter, how it feels to hear it disappear? We have a word for it, but the sentiment is not easily translatable.

In his wonderful and poetic book *Landmarks* (2015), Robert Macfarlane takes us on a hunt for words to describe and denote aspects of terrain, weather and nature. What a lovely bunch of words, and good storytelling to go with them. Just consider the onomatopoetic qualities of what the Cornish call *Mordros*, the sound of the sea. You can feel the swell. Or at least I can.

Audible *Vårløsning* happens every year, to some extent. Consider having to wait seventeen years for a sound you know will come. Like waiting for periodical cicadas (*Magicicada*) in the eastern United States. This year, while we are waiting to find our bearings, they return. Like magic. Scientists and musicians alike are steaming to the right areas to catch the sound of this strange phenomenon. What do they sound like, and who managed to sort out the regularity of such a timespan?

In 1896, the Norwegian composer Christian August Sinding wrote a famous piano piece, called *Vårbrus*, probably his most famous work. The title is a synonym to Vårløsning and obviously tries to convey the new season springing to life. It is probably better known internationally as *Frühlingsrauschen* or Rustle/Rustlings of spring.

A rustle is a soft, muffled crackling sound like that made by the movement of dry leaves or paper. Compare with Flemish *rijsselen* and Dutch *ritselen*. The sound of spring is more of a wet one and can be found in the Norwegian word *risle* resembling the words from the lower countries; the sound water makes running over pebbles in a small brook. Whereas our word for the dry sound, more closely associated with Autumn, is *rasle*...

In one of his poems *In der Certosa* Rainer Maria Rilke uses the word *Umrauscht*. George C. Schoolfield writes about the use of this word in a note to his book *Young Rilke and His Time* (2009): Rilke's *'umrauscht'* is a noteworthy choice of word because of its layers of meaning, not only its implication of enchanting natural phenomena, as in Wagner's 'Waldersrauschen' (Forest Rustlings) and Sinding's over-played 'Frühlingsrauschen' (Rustlings of Spring), but its suggestion of intoxication, 'Rausch', drunkenness, intoxication. So, this is what I feel. (It is funny in a way, because the last part of the title, *brus,* is a common denominator in Norwegian for a soft drink.)

Meanwhile,
Whoop.
Whoop.
Whoop Whoop Whoop!

Literal translations; Rustle of Spring, Spring thaw, Spring breaking, Birth of Spring

Vómvos (Βόμβος) (Greek)
Dimitrios Bormpoudakis

- **Bees and drones, and bombs**

The Greek word βόμβος, like so many words describing sounds, is onomatopoetic. Pronounced *vómvos*, in Modern Greek it means:

1. Hollow and continuous sound; buzzing: the sound of an airplane engine, the sound of bees.
2. The ringing in the ears.

In this entry I will make the case that *vómvoi* are the defining sound of the present, either through their proliferation or through their gradual disappearance. I will begin with a consideration of the etymological origin of the word and its various meanings, and how from Ancient Greek it passed into Latin to form the root of *bomb*. Then I will discuss how the absence or presence of particular *vómvoi* defines the present. First, I will juxtapose two types of buzzes: the accelerated extinction of (the buzzing of) bees and the coming insect apocalypse, with the accelerated proliferation of (the buzzing of) drones-as-unmanned aerial vehicles (UAVs) for military and other uses. Second, I will discuss how for some scientists, the *vómvos*-derived onomatopoetic *bomb*, in its thermonuclear incarnation, signals the beginning of the epoch of anthropos, the Anthropocene. In a brief conclusion, I will bring it all together to make the case that *vómvoi* are indeed the sound of the present, and tease out some minor implications of this thesis for sonic geographies.

vyhrávať (Slovak)
Daniel Salontay

vyhrávať – verb
Musical meaning – to play music and/or musical instrument joyfully

Base of the word is 'hrať' (to play), 'hrávať' means to play over a longer period of time and 'vyhrávať' with the prefix 'vy' suggests a high level of involvement and enjoyment by doing that

Secondary meaning – to win (a game, lottery or a dispute)

vytrúbiť – verb

Musical meaning – from the verb 'trúbiť', which means 'to play/blow a horn'

Base of the word is 'trúbiť' (to blow a horn, trúba means horn); the prefix 'vy' extends the original meaning of 'trúbiť' to giving something 'out' and 'completely' secondary meaning – to tell/give away a secret

trúba – noun
Musical meaning – horn

Secondary meaning – in colloquial speech – a person who is crazy or silly, calling someone 'trúba' is a very forgiving way of saying that: 'I love you but you are such a <trúba>'

There is another word which is somewhat beyond the scope of the request but I like it very much:

zvukomalebný – adjective
It consists of two words: 'zvuk' (sound) and 'malba' (painting).

This is the only word in the Slovak language that directly describes the phenomenon of synesthesia.

Regarding a musical piece as 'zvukomalebný' is a very high mark, closest to the meaning of the word picturesque, but in the musical context, that is, providing a strong visual experience.

缘份 (yúan fèn) (Chinese)
Lane Shi Otayonii

There are four stresses to every single Chinese word, '缘分''s pronunciation has the second and fourth stress, which makes it sound like a **circle closing up**.

When I was going to an art exhibition with a group of friends, we all stood in front of a painting, most of us thought that it was a painting that is blend and dull. However, one of us thought that painting was apocalyptic and that he had a life-changing experience. To me that friend has '缘 分' with that painting. '缘分', pronounced 'yúan fèn', has this layer of 'serendipity' meaning to it, however not quite fulfilled. It is a word with the history of

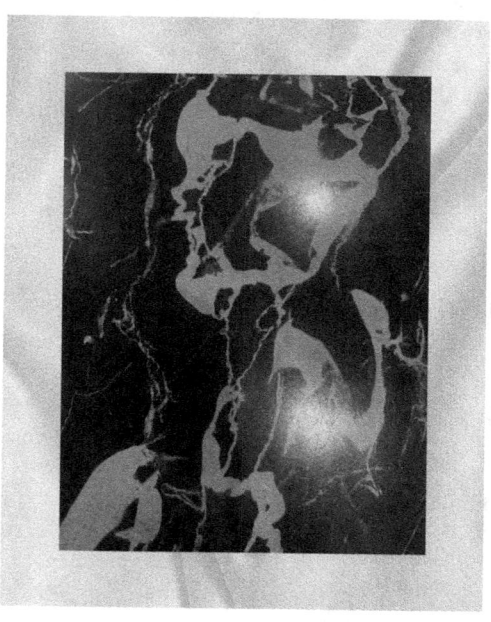

Figure 61 yúan fèn, © Lane Shi Otayonii.

mythological saga passing along the way of 5000+ years of Chinese culture: your present life is a merit of your past life, and your future life would be elevated or demeaned based on your deliberation and behaviour in this life. Therefore, '缘分' caters this sensation of past and future. In the case of a friend who had a compelling experience in a painting, the meaning of '缘分' interprets that friend's contemplation before coming to the exhibition, along with his life events, had a potential link to that painting whether it is literal or metaphorical.

Zaghrouta (زغروتة) (Arabic Dialect)
Selwa Abd (Bergsonist)

The high-pitched vocal sound known as 'Zaghrouta' (زغروتة) in Arabic and 'Ululation' in English is commonly used in North African and Middle Eastern weddings to express happiness and excitement. Typically performed by women, a similar sound is also made by men under the name 'عتابة'. The sound is produced by moving the tongue back and forth, creating a sustained noise. What's particularly interesting about this sound is the accompanying gesture used by the performer, who often places their hand near their mouth as if calling out to someone in the distance. I first heard this sound when I was four years old and attended a Moroccan wedding, although I didn't appreciate its significance until I grew older and came to enjoy the richness and variety of sounds at such events. In addition to weddings, Zaghrouta can also be heard in other contexts such as birth celebrations and funerals. It's remarkable how this one sound can be used to convey such different emotions and meanings, much like the unchanging tone of a notification sound that takes on different significance depending on the context.

zeitkratzer (new word creation in German)
Reinhold Friedl

zeitkratzer has been harvesting in many musical fields since its foundation in 1997: in new music, experimental music, radical rock music, noise music, improvised music, folk music, drone, baroque music. . . . zeitkratzer can be recognised by its sound, that becomes identity-forming, or to put it simple: recognisable. Despite zeitkratzer's unique musical diversity: nine musicians, a sound engineer, a lighting designer and over fifty published records, concerts from Japan to Mexico, one sound.

Condensed in the name of the group: sound, noise, onometopoesy, *zeitkratzer*. Grammatically, 'zeitkratzer' is a compound word composed of two nouns: 'zeit' and 'kratzer'. 'Zeit' is the German term for 'time'; the 'ei' – in the middle of 'Zeit' – is a beautiful diphthong. This leads to a welcome sound quality when people try to pronounce 'time': Almost anyone who doesn't know German will pronounce it in another way. Exactly that was a main criterion for choosing the name: a name almost impossible to pronounce correctly for non-native speakers. Sound diversity, noisy richness. An act of resistance against standardized ensemble names like Ensemble Modern, Ensemble Recherche, Ensemble another-Latin-term, . . . and an aid to memorizing the name sonically: an unpronounceable word, peppered with noise, scratching in the throat. The second noun in the compound word points in this direction: 'kratzer' kratzt: unquestionably an onomatopoeic quality: 'kratzen' does not only *mean* 'to scratch', it scratches in the throat. The word does what it describes.

The term 'zeitkratzer' evokes what the group is and does: a programme of sensual sound quality and musical diversity. Sound is the criterion, not social or aesthetic boundaries, sound as a revolutionary force that opens up countless new listening worlds, just as the

Figure 62 Zeitkratzer, © Verena Grimm.

pronunciation of *zeitkratzer* opens up an incredible sonic wealth if you mispronounce it. But it always sounds!

zompig [zɔmpəx] (Dutch)
Ingeborg Entrop

'Zompig' is a Dutch word, used as an adjective or adverb, and could probably be best translated to 'soggy' in English. It is used to describe waterlogged environments, such as marshes, bogs or mudflats. From a reader's perspective, the written word appears to be a fixed label, an arbitrarily chosen descriptive designation of a place that happens to be saturated with water. However, that conventional existence completely alters as soon as we step into action. If we perform it like a score of a musical piece, or better yet, of a dance, then the word fully becomes alive and even reveals a glimpse of its possible origin.

The action required to unravel the secrets behind 'zompig' is actually twofold. First, we have to pronounce it, as Dutch speakers do. Using the International Phonetic Alphabet its vocalization can be written down as [zɔmpəx]. It is clearly audible that this pronunciation breaks down into two parts. In the first syllable the [ɔ] dominates; in the second it is a sharp [x] that echoes in your ears after the word has been spoken. Both of these sounds take place or are produced in the deepest parts of one's throat. Hence, I tend to associate the word not so much with water as such but more with caves or caverns and pits or quarries, that is, with either naturally formed or intentionally dug out sites where water easily accumulates, resulting in places that are both earthy and watery alike. Examples of earthy and yet watery places formed by nature are marshes, bogs, tidal mudflats, estuaries or river banks.

One obvious difference between the two sounds [ɔ] and [x] is the way these sounds are formed by the speaking body. The first, a vowel, is pronounced without any stricture in the vocal tract; the latter, a consonant, is pronounced with a (partial) closure of the tract. The use of both an open and closed tract produces a binary tension between the syllables of the spoken word. Therefore, I also associate the word with more or less opposed concepts, such as in and out, compliance and reluctance, with opportunism and remorse even.

zompig [zɔmpəx] (Dutch)

Figure 63 Zompig, © Ingeborg Entrop.

The dynamics within [zɔmpəx] in fact presage the second task we must undertake to fully value the charms of 'zompig': we have to move our body. When being pronounced, the word appears to mimic the sound of someone or something that is walking with great difficulty in or through a waterlogged environment. Such an observation is of course only possible if we have had such an experience ourselves in the first place. Indeed, for me [zɔmpəx] builds onto my childhood memories of playing in the fields after heavy rain and of walking on muddy tracks in damp forests. Moving on foot through or in watery surroundings is, therefore, the second prerequisite to activate 'zompig'.

The word would probably not even have existed without our capacity of walking in combination with a landscape full of water and peat or clay. Its apparent onomatopoeic roots, enabled by that combination of our mobility on foot and specific features of the environment, show that landforms and language are often closely connected. Most if not all landscapes bear traces of human interventions or are, as in the Netherlands, even fully man-made. Since language is in essence a man-made system as well, any entanglement between constructions such as landscape and language due to a proximate and long-term co-evolution might not come as a surprise.

A pristine bog. A booted foot takes a step.

[zɔm]

The peat mosses slowly suck the boot into their upper layers,

a guttural [ɔ] denoting the deepening downward movement,

until the boot stops halfway its shaft on a slightly more solid layer.

A hesitation.

[pəx]

The boot struggles to free itself from the grip of the reluctant mosses.

Tension builds up, then its release, marked by a sharp [x].

Up to the next step.

The Netherlands is typically earthy and watery alike. Most of the country has been reclaimed from marshes and mires. Centuries ago monks and farmers started to drain the wetlands by digging ditches and channels. Dikes were erected to protect the land from stormy seas as well as to gain new grounds. I was born on such reclaimed land, below sea level and behind multiple protective dikes along the broad and braided rivers that flow from east to west dividing the country in a north and south. Today I live in the northern part, more or less at sea level, in a region where in former times the sea met the raised bogs that covered large parts of the hinterland. Permanent inhabitation of these bogs began in late medieval times. In those days local people started to cultivate the bogs to acquire new farm lands. In the centuries that followed, most of the remaining bogs were excavated until there was almost no peat left. The same lands are still being exploited today through natural gas extraction, resulting in severe subsidence and earthquakes. After all, when the shallow resources have gone, one has to dig deeper for prosperity.

Most sounds in a contemporary Dutch landscape are originating from human activity. One day, when I walked around in the area I live, and listened to the regular beat of my shoes on the tarmac road and the distant drone of traffic noises, I wondered which sounds the first people who cultivated these lands would have heard. In those early days there were no roads, let alone private property that limited the possibility of roaming around. How would 'zompig' have sounded back then? This question made me look for a place that resembles the medieval version of the landscape I currently live in, that is, a landscape similar to the one around the time when first people started to inhabit the bogs. I found that place in Estonia, in Soomaa National Park, where pristine raised bogs still exist and are protected from further damage and decay. I visited those bogs several times, once every season, to listen to the landscape, to its keynotes, signals and soundmarks of predominantly geo- and biophonic origin, but above all, to my own footsteps on the soft, unstable peat mosses, on hummocks and into hollows, as well as on the flood plains and in the forests along the small rivers that run between the bog domes. In Soomaa I heard many variations of 'zompig', with respect to melody and rhythm, but all beyond any possible description. Most extreme versions arose during the regularly recurring periods of major floodings –referred to as the fifth season– that inundate the lower-situated plains and forests as well as most roads and paths in Soomaa. The only means of transport that enables one to travel around and to keep one's feet dry during these periods is the canoe, an invention that dates back to at least 8000 BC and with which we managed to outsmart any 'zompig' with capital 'Z'.

If landscape and language do co-evolve, then the efforts throughout the ages to keep the Netherlands as dry as possible might have made the language less soggy as well. Did we indeed loose the words to indicate the many variations of 'zompig' due to the loss of typical earthy-watery places?

Admittedly, such places still exist in the Netherlands. There are still some remnants of that huge raised bog area, which outlived the peat excavations in former days, such as the Bargerveen Nature Reserve. Or think of the Waddensea, where the tides alternatingly deposit and wash away large mudflats. All of these areas are sufficiently 'zompig' to keep the word alive. Worrying is, however, that these examples are either part of a UNESCO Global

Geopark or a UNESCO World Heritage Site. Of course, appreciation by the international community helps to maintain and protect these precarious landscapes from further decline, but the fact that these areas are in apparent need for such international recognition is tragic in itself, even more so, because these areas actually include most of the least damaged nature in the Netherlands.

Is 'zompig' endangered? Not if we take action, if we perform it over and over again, in the Bargerveen Nature Reserve, on the mudflats of the Waddensea, wherever. A UNESCO status helps to keep not only the landscape alive but also its sounds, its words and its language. Moreover, when landscape and language are co-evolving, then 'zompig' may actually have a prosperous future ahead. Long-term use of carbon-rich energy sources have led to climate change, causing an increasing sea level, heavy rains and more frequent floods. Water is an increasingly urgent issue to deal with in many parts of the world. Innovative solutions for flood control and water management continue to be developed and make more and more use of natural processes. New wetlands are made on purpose, perhaps new marshes may arise naturally and even raised bogs might re-emerge in due time. So 'zompig' could actually be more vibrant in the near future than ever before.

Notes

1. Michael Weiss, Sarah Kiefer, and Silke Kipper, 'Buzzwords in Females' Ears? The Use of Buzz Songs in the Communication of Nightingales (*Lus- cinia megarhynchos*)', *PLoS One* 7, no. 9 (2012): e45057.
2. https://en.wikipedia.org/wiki/Low-frequency_oscillation
3. https://www.theguardian.com/education/2014/nov/17/animal-noises-in-different-languages
4. I am grateful to Johannes Binotto for pointing this word out to me!
5. John Carrington Sellars, *Chemistianity*. Birkenhead: Self-published, 1873.
6. Daniel Wilson, 'Goception in the Mess: Byways in the History of Noise's Ongoing Transmutation into Music', in *Joris Van de Moortel: A Dubious Pilgrimage*. Brussels: Galerie Nathalie Obadia/Hopper and Fuchs, 2019.
7. Ibid.
8. https://en.wikipedia.org/wiki/Consecutive_fifths
9. Indeed, the circuits of this type of electronic games, which were arranged on a card, are now inserted in a small plastic ball, which prevents its manipulation by hackers adept of circuit bending.
10. We could argue that this goes for any music, and not only for the one which is expressly codified through written notation; this, however, would deserve a separate and much longer discussion.
11. In German, *Nuschler* relates to a male mumbler, whereas *Nuschlerin*, connotes the female mumbler. As is common, I have for the remainder of this essay used the inclusive form *Nuschler*in* to designate both genders, the * furthermore designates a diversity of non-binary genders.
12. Translation from the original is mine.
13. Find audio examples of horse sighs and snorts here: https://petkeen.com/common-horse-sounds Accessed: 31 July 2022.
14. See YouTube video: https://www.youtube.com/watch?v=vbbjN9oP7Ik, particularly from min. 2:56 onwards. Accessed: 31 July 2022.
15. Søren Kierkegaard, 'PMH Et lille Indlæg, Fortsættelse', *Søren Kierkegaards Skrifter* 15 + K15 (2012): 66. 'That an author should decide to write thus may seem puzzling, but it is explainable. While the literature of our time shows that practically nothing is accomplished [. . .], one can *hardly hear oneself* (or, be *heard because of*) the promises, trumpets, subscription calls, toasts, exhortations, assurances, compliments, etc.' (translated by Jacob Eriksen, italics added)
16. https://soundcloud.com/david-nadeau-421485242/what-you-sing-comes-to-life-archeology-of-hope-i-ii-iii
17. https://theepchallenge.bandcamp.com/track/the-egg-hatches-at-dawn-david-nadeau

18 https://camembertelectrique.bandcamp.com/album/davidurgic-neadors-playing-david-nadeaus-compositions
19 https://ia800909.us.archive.org/35/items/GenerativeLoopsCompositionsProject/David_Nadeau_Mixing_Console.html
20 In the following, the word *Rauschen* will be integrated into the text using normal lettering.
21 S. Voegelin, *Listening to Noise and Silence: Toward a Philosophy of Sound Art*. London: Continuum International Publishing, 2010, p. 176.
22 https://curdt.home.hdm-stuttgart.de/PDF/Neumann.pdf
23 R. M. Schafer, *The Soundscape: Our Sonic Environment and the Tuning of the World*. Rochester: Destiny Books, 1994, p. 51. (Original work published in 1977)
24 See under http://woerterbuchnetz.de/cgi-bin/WBNetz/wbgui_py?sigle=DWB&mode=Vernetzung&hitlist=&patternlist=&lemid=GR01643#XGR01643
25 See under https://lsf.uni-hildesheim.de/qisserver/rds?state=verpublish&status=init&vmfile=no&moduleCall=webInfo&publishConfFile=webInfo&publishSubDir=veranstaltung&publishid=70676
26 Schafer, *The Soundscape*, p. 182.
27 A. Niebisch, *Ticken vs. Rauschen: Geräusche bei Poe und Kafka*, 2008.
See under http://publikationen.ub.uni-frankfurt.de/frontdoor/index/index/year/2017/docId/43317
28 Jacques Derrida, *l'écriture et la différence*. Paris: Editions du Seuil, 1967.
29 Alison Jones, and Kuni Jenkins, 'Indigenous Discourse and "the Material": A Post-interpretivist Argument', *International Review of Qualitative Research* 1, no. 2 (2008): 125–44, p. 126.
30 Ibid., p. 127.
31 Chris Atton, *Alternative Internet*. Edinburgh: Edinburgh University Press, 2004; Phil England, 'Dan Wilson: Broadcast Buccaneer'. *The Wire #263*, January 2006.
32 Daniel Wilson, *Dropping Out*. Bishop's Stortford: Self-published, 2006.
33 Ibid.; Daniel Wilson, 'Dumpster Diving and Post-Electronic Soundmaking'. *Leonardo Music Journal* 24 (2014).
34 Counsel (1994).
35 There have been at least five English translations of *Truyện Kiều* in the last half-century. One of the awarded translations, by Timothy Allen (2009), translated that verse as follows:
Her eyes are dark and troubled as November seas.
Spring flowers envy her grave beauty and the mountain ash shivers with jealousy
36 Thompson (1965); Phạm (2001, 2003).
37 *Việt Cộng* (literally "Vietnamese Communist") was the word people in the south of Vietnam called the people in the north those who were part of The Communist guerrilla movement in Vietnam, which fought the South Vietnamese government forces 1954–75 with the support of the North Vietnamese army and opposed the South Vietnam and US forces in the Vietnam War.
38 I am a Vietnamese zither-đàn tranh player. I was born into a theatre family and was raised with traditional Vietnamese music from an early age in Hà Nội. Since 2012 I moved to Sweden to carry out my doctoral project *The Choreography of Gender in Traditional Vietnamese music* at the Malmö Academy of Music.
39 I am a founding member of *The Six Tones* (VN/SE), a group which has developed into a platform for intercultural collaboration across South East Asia, Europe and the United States, since 2006. The name of the group, emanating from

a piece by Henrik Frisk, relates to the fact that the Vietnamese is a tonal language using six tones or intonations.
40 The first word in the Vietnamese translation is *Rượu vang* (wine). This composition is developed from the composer William Brooks' project *After Yeats*, in which Brooks provides an instruction outlining a collaboration between a performer and a composer (who mustn't share the same mother tounge).
41 Frisk and Nguyễn (2019).
42 *Quê/Homelands* was an ecological sound art project, which I carried out with members of the Landscape Quartet in 2013. It was set in the little village of Ngang Nội, where I spent all my summers with my aunts and uncles. The project explored sites with which a performer had deep personal connections, by creating interactions between natural elements and traditional instruments, like here, when my instrument, the đàn tranh, was played by the wind and the rice in the field.
43 In 2016, I wrote a joint article with Stefan Östersjö, 'The Sounds of Hanoi and the After-image of the Homeland' (Östersjö and Nguyễn, 2016). This text revisits *Arrival Cities: Hanoi* and *Quê/Homelands Bắc Ninh*, two music and sound art projects in which we, the two authors, took part as artists and performers. The projects originated in Hà Nội and in the natural landscape around the village of Ngang Nội, about an hour's drive north of the city. By juxtaposing the two projects we hoped to be able to trace some of these afterimages of the countryside in the sounds of the city, but also, to suggest a political perspective on these soundscapes (a perspective which is beyond the scope of the present publication).
44 *Ah Biz Ödlek Aydınlar*, Published July 1995, Adam Yayınları, https://www.goodreads.com/book/show/18190556-ah-biz-dlek-ayd-nlar.
45 Johann G. von Herder, '*Abhandlung über den Ursprung der Sprache*'. In *Johann Gottfried Herder: Werke in Zwei Bänden*, edited by Karl-Gustav Gerold, 733–830. München: Carl Hanser Verlag, 1953.
46 Read 't'.
47 Theoretical physicist Karen Barad would call this 'the touch of entangled beings (be)coming together-apart'. In 'On Touching: The Human That Therefore I am', Power of Material/Politics of Materiality, (eds) Susanne Witzgall, Kerstin Stakemeier, 153–64.
48 'Deep Listening is a form of meditation. Attention is directed to the interplay of sounds and silences of the sound silence continuum. Sound is not limited musical or speaking sounds, but is inclusive of all perceptible vibrations (sonic formations). The relationship of all perceptible sounds is important. The practice is intended to expand consciousness to the whole space-time continuum of sound and silences' (Oliveros, 2005, p. xxiv) P. Oliveros, *Deep Listening: A Composer's Sound Practice*. Lincoln: iUniverse, 2005.
49 As part of the Norton Lecture Series, 2021, https://www.youtube.com/watch?v=6LuKgGn5e2g
50 *Tiberis/Tifernus* may be a pre-Indo-European substrate word related to Aegean *tifos* 'still water'. Yet another etymology is from *dubri-, water, considered by Alessio as Sicel, whence the form Θύβρις later Tiberis. This root *dubri- is widespread in Western Europe e.g. Dover, Portus Dubris. https://en.wikipedia.org/wiki/Tiber
51 https://www.simple-knitting.com/tinking.html

www.ingramcontent.com/pod-product-compliance
Lightning Source LLC
Chambersburg PA
CBHW052050300426
44117CB00012B/2059